MEMOIR OF A MODERN MYSTIC

COMING HOME:

A Surrender to Love

Athena Melchizedek

Table of Contents

Dedicated to my sister, June

and

All who are Coming Home.

Acknowledgments

My life to date has been so rich and so full of wonderful and wondrous beings that I am humbled as I begin the recall the many who have helped me on my way. Those who particularly stand out in my memory are mentioned below, and yet there are many others, too numerous to mention but nevertheless a part of my journey. I honor, acknowledge, and bless them all as my mirrors and teachers.

My dearest sister, June, illuminated the way with her practical gift of a book and the enormous gift of her presence in my life.

Beloved friends Sylvia and Ray Flinn, (now transitioned), Amanda Rowe, Julie Marriot, and Carol Tillett saw, listened, and heard me in some of my moments of deepest sorrow and despair.

To Colin Pratt, thank you for your wonderful sense of humor and your ongoing optimism.

To my dear friend Susan Eaves—my deepest gratitude for allowing me to be part of your own journey and for your ongoing encouragement to write.

To all the patriarchs I have worked with, and who mirrored back to me my own unbalanced energy aspects and my complete denial of the feminine within: without you, I would never have rediscovered her.

To my soul brother Frank Medliecott Shipley—our twelve years together and twenty years apart brought me face-to-face with my shadow self, light and dark. Bless you, for then and now. I always treasure our friendship.

To my soul brother Gerard Hutton—through his yoga, I developed a love and knowledge of the physical body moving while simultaneously integrating its higher aspects. Through the harmonic induction of his exquisite vibrational field, I experienced firsthand knowledge of the beauty of the galactic dimensions, the cosmos within, and a glimpse of my own truest Self.

To Barbara Ann Brennan, for demonstrating the healing power of the written word and modeling the true meaning of leadership: one who simply goes first into the unknown, no matter how crazy the impulse seems to the linear mind or to commentators who do not hear the music or see the vision. I honor your great courage and bravery in your surrender to a higher will.

To the Barbara Brennan School of Healing faculty in the United States between the years 2005 and 2012 and Susan Hewitt in Europe for such dedicated mirroring and modeling of presence. Your gifts of love and dedication are only outweighed by your humanity and compassion.

With special gratitude and appreciation to my mentor, supervisor, and outstanding example of dedicated service to the transformation and healing of the human and animal kingdoms, Dr. Catherine Nelson, PhD.

To the BBSH graduating class of 2009 USA and Advanced Studies Brennan Integration Work graduating class of 2012 USA— what a roller-coaster ride that was, in and out of class. I am so blessed to have been with you then and to be with you now in my heart.

Shar Napp, dear soul sister, and school buddy, blessings for all the work we did together over the years. We had such deep sharing and so many good times together.

To my dear friends and work colleagues in Canada, deepest gratitude: Susan Lynne, Doris Poirier, Lidia Mattucci, Marcia Wilson, Lional Andris; Santino, Constantin; Dave Newby; Roger and Jazz Davies; and the various teams and networks at McLuhan & Davies and Think On Your Feet International, Inc.—all of whom played crucial roles along my journey into the deep dive of self-discovery.

To Sifu Matthew Raymond Cohen at Sacred Energy Arts in Santa Monica, California, whose integrated approach to martial, yogic, and healing arts provided me with fully integrated yogic teacher training. My time in California turned out to be an important phase in my personal transformative process.

To Sang Il Jo of Trainer Jo's in Toronto for training my physical body with such care and professionalism and providing me with lifelong knowledge of practices for nutrition and well-being.

To Susan Howson, founder of Magnificent Creations Limitee, Toronto, Canada, whose program Kids Coaching Connection trained me to effectively mentor children and reintroduced me to my own child within.

To the Masters of Seggau, the group with whom I completed my Master of Science degree at Inter–Universitaires Colleg, Graz, in Austria. This led me to research the science required to write my first book, The Quantum Keys: Unlock Your Energetic Intelligence. The process, as well as the research proved to be another treasure chest of gifts.

To Christof Melchizedek, an Indigo lightworker and brother.Thank you for helping me to implement the production of online education and the mirror you and your family provided for me during my stay in Ibiza.

To soul sister Tiara Kumara, deep gratitude for our Peruvian Amazon and Himalayan adventures together.

To soul brother and sister Toby and Ivonne Delaflor. I trust you have both found your true path forward.

To soul brother Akasha Sananda, Indigo lightworker always in my heart.

Gabriel Melchizedek, Seraph Amber Minton, Asherah Miriam Rose, thank you for your connection and friendship and for being part of my life. It has been my honor to be part of your own journeys.

Sadhguru for the reflection of my own inner guru.

Gratitude and appreciation for the great masters of the written word transmissions that profoundly changed my life: Fu Xi- I Ching, Lao Tsu -Tao Te Ching, White Eagle – Spiritual Unfoldment, Djwahl Kuhl and The Ageless Wisdom Blue Books - Alice Bailey, Omraam Mikhael Aivanhov- You Are Gods, Dr Barbara Ann Brennan – Seeds of the Spirit, Richard Rudd -The Gene Keys, Neale Donald Walsch- Conversations with God, Dr David Hawkins- I, Reality and Subjectivity, Ken Carey – The Starseed Transmissions, Ashayana Deane- Voyagers 1&2, Lisa Renee- Ascension Glossary and Energetic Synthesis, Sri Nisgardatta Maharaj- I AM THAT.

Gratitude for the Angelic Realms and the devas of the animal, plant, and mineral kingdoms—you have played such an enormous part in enabling me to open my heart and mind fully to all life, with the greatest love and appreciation.

And finally, to the great spiritual masters and guardian source aspects of this being who have supported my process of Self Realization. I have been aware of the presence and guidance of Yeshua in my life since the age of twelve. St Germain, Bodhisattvas

Kuan Yin, and Avalokiteshvaraya, and Dr David Hawkins MD, PhD in later years and the full Christ Consciousness field since 2012.

Special thanks to Sri Nisgardatta Maharaj and Thich Nhat Hahn and their most Divine Transmissions of Love and Compassion to this Soul.

Through these connections and presence, I experience the magnificence of Source being in this moment of now and live in awe and thanksgiving as the creation continues to unfold through me.

About the Author

Athena is a pioneer for advanced consciousness on the planet.

Her balanced embodiment of the feminine and masculine energy and consciousness principles underpins all her work and her own extraordinary transformational journey is the key to the successful outcomes enjoyed by her clients.

Athena specializes in Group Mentoring and Group Energy Management for heart-centered Visionary Pioneers and Starseeds, empowering them to discover and transmute the root fractals of all unconscious behavioral patterns that limit the life experience, as well as creative possibilities and the experience of the full I AM Presence.

Her experience over the past 20 years has confirmed the massive acceleration that occurs for all when we do this work together and that individual process is highly amplified when synergized and supported by group energy.

She holds Degrees in Advanced Psycho-Energetics, Energy Healing Science, and Remote Energy Transmission from BBSH, plus an MSc in Psychosocial and Integrative Health Science for those who require credentials. But owns the mirror of her life experience has been by far her greatest teacher.

She published her first book, *THE QUANTUM KEYS – Unlock Your Energetic Intelligence*, in 2017. The book describes a pathway to Self-Realization and the synergy of modern science and ancient wisdom that characterizes all of her work.

Her activities as a Mentor and Transformation Guide are enhanced by her devotion to yogic science and mysticism.

Up to now, her work has been concentrated on online education and remote energy transmission to enable worldwide participation. However, she is preparing to offer more live workshop events and retreats in the near future.

Introduction

Athena is a mystic, mentor, and thoroughly modern alchemist. You are invited to bear witness to her transformative journey of self-healing and Self- Realization in this authentic memoir that describes her initial embodiment as an innocent spiritual ingenue engulfed by abuse, betrayal, illness, death, and tragedy in early life.

Originally propelled by curiosity and then necessity, her eventual site of action became the world of corporate life as she went on to become a highly successful woman of business, shapeshifting to join a toxic masculine hierarchy until burning out and breaking down.

Her story chronicles the life of a woman who came to pioneer change on this planet with a soul contract that included the monumental challenge of internal programs of suffering built into her DNA through the genetic and ancestral lineages that reflected the external corrupt, collective systems that no longer serve humanity.

This profound sharing reflects how we have all kept ourselves in enslavement to distorted influences that have ruled this planet for eons and how we all, often unknowingly, keep these dynamics in place and recycle down the ages until someone in the lineage makes the choice to break the cycle.

The reader will be taken on an incredible voyage with Athena, who began her life as yet another 'identity' and who quickly learned she could comprehend very little of her existence here on planet earth. Deep within her soul was a place that longed to know the purpose of all the darkness. A question being asked by many at this very moment.

Join her in her quest for the answers to life's seemingly impossible challenges and the revelations that begin to flood her awareness as she accesses remembrance of her ancestral ties to the Essenes: Roman Catholicism, Freemasonry, Druid, and Celtic histories down the ages; her Chinese heritage; and her Indigenous Native American lives on two continents.

Explore with her the astral lands of cult and new age spirituality: a history that reaches back to the times of Lemuria and Atlantis; her remarkable galactic heritage as a starseed and a Melchizedek; and an expansion of consciousness that incorporates Christic, Buddhic; and Hindu masters. Learn of her formal training to rediscover her healership and higher sense perception spanning ten earth years and follow her life training: a timeless journey that encompasses four planets, five continents, forty-two countries, and millions of years.

If you are courageous enough, come with her into the depths of darkness that beckoned to be investigated, acknowledged, accepted, and brought back into the light by her own forgiveness, compassion, and love. Come now with her, and perhaps you will remember pieces of yourself in places you had no idea existed. There is no by-passing on this voyage.

Welcome to this wild ride. No one could accuse this being of not giving life her fullest attention and taking on every challenge offered by her soul. The most wondrous element of this story is it is, by no means, over. True to her name, Athena is fully on purpose as a wisdom keeper and the supporter of heroes and heroines, those souls who have taken on the promptings by spirit to explore every part of themselves and rediscover the supreme light awaiting their arrival back to truth, raising all and the planet in their process of transcendence to reclaim the Divine Angelic Blueprint. This is a monumental tale of redemption. It is the story of the spirit of this epochal time on planet earth and demonstrates how we can navigate the treacherous waters of chaos and uncertainty, banish fear, and overcome all programming to bring forth peace, harmony, and balance within ourselves so we may evolve our species and our world into the new golden age.

Accept the challenge and join with her now in this transmission of grace and gratitude. Now is the time for the return of the Divine Mother principle and the restoration of the Divine Father principle, both inherent within all genders, for the well-being of all sentient life on this earth. Everything and everyone are interconnected, interdependent, and interrelated. This always was, always is, and always will be. Join her now as she shares through the medium of her own personal story her journey to traverse the multi-dimensions of the temporal hologram that springs from the quantum field, the Source of all life and the mind of the prime creator from which emerges the gods and goddesses we truly are.

IMPORTANT NOTE

The book is written from the observer's awareness, an open third-eye perspective that sees with absolute clarity. All that is shared here is no longer in the unconscious mind of Athena but has now been integrated and transcended. To speak from the I perspective would only re-imprint all erroneous thoughts and beliefs that have long been transmuted and transformed. This is a highly significant message and a reminder of the powerful I AM Presence within all.

Athena Melchizedek

PART 1

DESCENT INTO THE EARTH
ENERGY GRIDS

The Early Years

Suddenly, she found herself within her mother's womb with no memory of how she arrived there. She could see the form of the child and sensed this tiny body would be her home for a little while. The child was born in 1951 in Liverpool, just six years after the ending of the second world war. She was christened Joan Ellen.

Her father, Kenneth, had only been twenty when he was sent off to war. He was a bombardier in the army and ended up spending three years as a prisoner of war in Poland. Grace, her mother, was only fifteen when the war began and looked after her two sisters and her father for its duration. One could only imagine it would have been such a difficult and frightful time for them both to experience something so fearful as a world war when they were so young with all of life ahead of them. Undoubtedly, it would have a profound effect on both their lives.

Grace was a devoted Roman Catholic at the time of the birth of her first child. She was a very beautiful young woman, the eldest of the three sisters, and hailed from an impoverished background that was bound up in religious guilt and fear of sin. This was the traditional burden of the teachings of the Roman Catholic Church in those days. Joan's maternal grandfather, Aloysius, was a simple gardener, and just like his father before him, he loved all nature and animals. Old photographs reveal he had bred Spaniels and Pomeranian puppies at one stage of his life. She never knew Grace's own mother, Ellen, who had passed away long before she came along. However, interestingly and not by chance, she would carry both of her grandmothers' names for much of her life.

Almost diametrically opposed to Grace's early life was the upbringing of her father, Kenneth, who was the youngest boy in a family of four children that included two sisters and one brother. His own mother, Mary, was a psychic but had also passed away long before Joan was born, and Thomas, her grandfather, had remarried by the time she had reached the earth. Her father's family was much more well-to-do, but alas were dispersed across the world to Canada and Australia. His eldest sister, Florence, lived in London. The men of the family were all engineers of some description, as well as Freemasons and Spiritualists. Her father was a telecommunications design engineer, and his competence in this field proved to be of great significance to this incoming soul in her later life. This side of her family seemed closed and secretive and when the young Joan was taken to visit with her grandfather, she noticed that Grace never, ever came with them. The reason why was never mentioned to the children; it merely was the way it was. However, what was hidden in the relational field of this family was a great chasm of separation between the two sides never to be crossed.

Grace and Ken had met and married very shortly after the war had finished, and were very deeply in love, but each represented enormously conflicting social and religious structures. Thus, even though the war was over, this still meant both their children were born into very divergent ancestral energies that were masked and unconscious for a long time. It should also be noted the overall consciousness of the earth and humankind was considerably lower in 1951 than currently in 2024. The earth and her population had been through two world wars in close succession.

Incredible as it might seem, Joan's earliest memory of pre-birth within her mother's womb began her conditioning for life on planet earth. She can remember being cozy and safe within the amniotic fluid, as well as the memory of her mother's great fear about the birthing process and a sense of lack of any additional family support for her mother around this important time. Grace desperately wanted both her children, but her fear of the process itself factored very heavily, particularly during this impending first birth.

This ability to sense what was happening in her environment and beyond was the first experience of the child's intuitive knowing and empathy as she took in information from the surrounding energy fields of her existence. These gifts would not be truly recognized or even understood until much later in her life. However, this first memory of fear, experienced through this early connection to her mother, suggested to her that earth may not be such a safe or great place to be.

The next important landmark event for the newly birthed consciousness occurred when she was taken home from the hospital and was unable to sleep. She has a very clear and distinct memory of being held in her father's arms and reaching up to play with his long ear lobes. She was staring up at him, smiling into his eyes, and could feel his heart and the almost overwhelming sense of his love and the safety and protection he offered her. There was such a sweetness and harmonious impression upon the child in his arms. She became aware of a very beautiful and special connection to this being, who was her father, as early as a babe in his embrace. Her soul had recognized and connected deeply with him.

For five years, she had a happy and unremarkable childhood playing with her cousins, the progeny of Grace's two sisters, and also the little boy David, from her flat block, who became her best friend. She loved him, too. There is little memory of her mother from this time, other than she knew she was very loved from a distance. She could feel within her mother how very much she was wanted and loved, but at the same time, there was also a presentiment of some kind of absence there. The connection was not the same as with her father. Even in these early days, something was amiss. It seemed there was a predisposition to depression and anxiety in her mother, and most of the baby's soothing came from her father.

This baby Joan was a huge bundle of life and demanded much attention from a mother who, although she truly loved her child, somehow could not respond adequately in those first few months. Later, Joan's guidance would reveal Grace's post-natal depression. A depression that would characterize much of her mother's life.

She has a vivid memory of sitting in a pram, dressed in a knitted blue hat and coat, and screaming and screaming until almost choking because Grace had left her outside a grocery shop. She was afraid to be left alone; she did not feel safe alone on this earth after picking up Grace's fear in utero. She thought her mother had gone away and deserted her, and she was terrified and helpless. The child was also already unknowingly connecting to the abandonment wounds of both her mother and father, who had both lost their mothers very early in their lives. This would build unconsciously in the baby's psyche as normal life started to resume for the two young parents.

One of the quirks of her early childhood was her visits to the cinema with each parent. They never ever took her together. Her mother would take her to see musicals, which she loved, and her father would take her to see westerns. She was always happy to be with him but not really very interested in cowboys fighting one another. Obviously, her parents had different tastes, but later, as her life unfolded, she would often wonder to herself if her father had wanted a little boy and perhaps she had been a big disappointment to him. Her very vivid memory of herself in her pram, all dressed in blue, might later give some credence to this unconfirmed belief. These visits to the cinema, however, instilled in her a great love of film and its ability to connect to deep places within her, and, like many of her generation, she became an avid fan of all this storytelling art could and would encompass in her life.

By the time she had reached five years, her life was dramatically changed again by a new addition to their family unit. She went to stay with one of her aunts and cousins while Grace gave birth to her sister, June, in a private nursing home. This occasion was her first time away from both her parents, and she could feel an anxiety in them both about this impending birth, particularly her father. She associated this feeling in herself with being disconnected from them and her home and felt very afraid and very uncomfortable with the whole set up. She felt very vulnerable and was hyper-sensitive to any unexpected shock in the form of pranks played by her cousins. Although they meant her no real harm and were just being playful, all she wanted was to go home.

Despite all the anxiety surrounding this birth, all went well, and very soon, she was back home with a new baby sister, June. She was completely enthralled with this new little bundle of joyful life. She loved to play with her and would spend time all the time allowed, pushing her in an enormous navy - blue pram around the public gardens outside their apartment block. She barely reached the handlebar but was determined to do this. It was such great fun.

As the new child grew and demanded more and more of Grace and Kenneth's attention, life changed quite considerably for her elder sister. Joan was still just a little girl, and she felt very alone.

For five idyllic years, she had been the sole focus of her parents' attention. But this all had changed quickly and without warning, when her sister had arrived. She used to crawl underneath her bed and try to hide away from her aloneness, but it always followed her. There were even times when she felt some resentment towards her little sister because she could not make the feeling go away. This was expressed as anger and unkindness on more than one occasion. More than anything, she missed her mother.

Life in Suburbia

A new adventure began two years later when the family moved out of their flat into a new house with a lovely big garden. It seemed a much nicer place than they had come from. She liked their new home. There were lots of trees and gardens and, better still, lots of children in this new area with lots of friends to play with. Joan soon forgot about any resentment towards her little sister and felt happy and safe once more.

Sadly, her euphoria was not to last, as shortly after moving into their new home, her dying grandfather Aloysius moved in with the family along with his terminal cancer. Darkness descended upon her world once again. He would sit in his rocking chair and just rock, day in and day out. She had very little connection or relationship with this man. Understandably, he could not be bothered with little children; he was far too ill, and his presence cast a big shadow over the whole family, particularly her mother.

Joan was not even sure if he was a very nice man. She had never enjoyed going to visit him with her mother when they lived in the flat. He lived in a very poor part of the city. His home was dark and dreary, and he was not interested in her at all. She could not connect with him in any meaningful way. He was closed to her and there was something bleak and dismal in these visits. Grace was the only one who ever visited him. She was the eldest daughter, and everything seemed to fall to her. Grace had a lot of responsibility for her own family. The sisters had lost their mother, Ellen, when they were all very young and Grace had effectively become the mother figure for her two younger siblings. Perhaps this had prevented her full experience of her own children, for even in adulthood she continued the responsibility for mothering them, whether consciously or not.

Grandfather Aloysius died quite soon after coming to stay, and the darkness in the house eventually lifted, but his death left a profound sadness and desolation within her mother.

Joan's relationship with Thomas, her paternal grandfather, was only marginally better. He was also very ill. She only ever saw him in a wheelchair, and she sensed he really did not want to be bothered with little girls either. At least there was a garden where she could play when she went to visit! He always bribed her with sweeties to go and play outside so he could talk with her father privately. Just as with Grace, the burden of care for his father fell to her own father. His other family members had either left the country or lived too far away to be helpful.

These two bright, young beings each had a lot of additional family responsibilities at the start of their married life when they were trying to build their own family unit. They never shirked that responsibility. The young Joan was a witness to their care and attention until the end of both her grandfathers' lives and also an ongoing pull for Grace's energy from her sisters. In particular, her youngest sister, Alice, had contracted tuberculosis when young and had to have a large part of one lung removed. Her devastating operation had left this beautiful young woman with very poor ongoing health, several years in a sanitorium, and Grace in a permanent state of anxiety.

Despite the illness and death of their only surviving parents, Grace and Ken did the best they could to make a happy family environment for their two growing girls. They were dedicated and caring parents, and Ken worked diligently to make a nice family home while Grace stayed at home to look after both her children until June began school when she was five.

Eventually, she returned to part-time work as a shorthand typist. She had excellent credentials, was conscientious at her work, and had no trouble finding a good position.

Every day, she walked at least two miles and back to drop off both her girls at the nearest Catholic primary school. This rule was part of Grace and Ken's agreement. In order to be able to marry, their children had to be brought up Catholic. This was what was demanded by the Catholic Church. It may seem incredulous now, but their union was called a 'mixed marriage' and, at that time in our history, carried its own stigma. Perhaps because of this secret knowledge, Grace was anxious and guarded with her neighbors and reluctant to make friends. Ken, on the other hand, was much more easy-going but also had few friends. They kept themselves to themselves, and any interactions with neighbors were usually a result of the children's playmates, who, needless to say, were only concerned with playing and having fun.

Grace found solace in her church and prayer. She was the organizer of the finances and the disciplinarian of the family. She was very determined to be a good mother, and she was. Ken was very sensitive to her needs and would do anything to keep her happy. He devoted himself to her. He worked hard to keep money flowing for them and handed everything over to Grace so they could make a comfortable home and provide lovely, fun-filled holidays for their young, growing family. Eventually, Grace's part-time work provided little luxuries in the form of a lovely puppy, a fluffy miniature poodle called Mitzi. They became a happy little family unit and had many exciting outings to the profusion of beaches in the south west of England during their school holidays. These were fun-filled and carefree times. The sun always seemed to be shining, the sky always seemed to be blue and southern England was dressed in her very best natural overcoat of greens and abundant flora and fauna. The sand and sea beckoned them.

From her babyhood Joan had developed a strong and powerful connection with her father. She wanted to know why he didn't come to church with them. It was a reasonable question.

His answer was to sit her on his knee and enthrall her with stories of mediums and the spiritualist seances he attended. He spoke to her of seeing energy and plasma bodies and told her stories of his experiences at the Spiritualist Church. He also spoke to her of healing and a famous spiritual healer who was doing incredible work in the UK at this time. This was her first introduction to the world of what was then termed the supernatural. She loved all his stories and could never wait for the next one.

He spoke to her of astral flying, coming out of his body and being able to fly through the air just like an airplane. He described all he could see: a landscape of hills and trees and houses and lakes and even the sea, all flashing by beneath his gaze below. All that he shared with her made total sense. For her, it was remembering rather than learning. Because she could do this too and often, she would find herself on the ceiling of her bedroom looking down at herself in bed asleep. All perfectly natural for her and her father, but the subject could never be brought up in the presence of her mother. It was their secret.

Church, Sex, and Music Magic

S he would continue her informal spiritual education with her father and her formal 'religious' education at a Catholic primary school affiliated with a group of Benedictine Monks.

Here she followed the normal practices of taking First Holy Communion and then Confirmation, where she took her paternal grandmother's name, Mary, not really understanding what it was all about. Yet she seemed to be able to understand all her father shared with her because she could at least experience the gentleness and peace that seemed to emanate from him whenever she was near him.

Her only real visceral experience with the teachings of Roman Catholicism came from the beautiful mural that adorned the altar at their local church of St Anthony. This painting of Jesus at the Last Supper with his arms outstretched to his disciples absolutely mesmerized her. She always felt that he was including her in this gesture of an invitation to join him. She literally felt it as such, an invitation. She loved the image and what it invoked within her. She could never take her eyes off this beautiful image all the way through every Mass she attended. She would think to herself how much she would love to meet and be with this being. It reminded her of how she felt when she was with her father. Although she had no words to describe this feeling then, it was the unmistakable essence and energy of a soul that she could experience as a real feeling in her body.

Joan was an avid reader and whatever literature was available from the local library, she would devour. She was very lucky to have access to a beautiful library located in a large country house in the park close to her new home, and she would walk weekly to browse for hours, searching for good books to read. Sometimes, she would take her little sister, who was still very shy but loved to be included. Joan would often read four or five books a week and particularly loved ghost stories. Of course, if the Church ever got wind of this there would have been pandemonium, but they never did.

And so, her life went on. She had friends, she rode her bicycle, she played, she climbed trees she read, she sang in the school choir. She loved her sister very much and had forgotten any reason she had to be mean to her. She looked after her and played with her. They would take trips together to the Penny Shop near the park and pick as many sweets as they could with their pocket money. It was an idyllic and happy time of growing and learning. The only stain on this beautiful picture was the stern, authoritarian school headmistress, who was taken to task several times for caning Grace's eldest child for 'sins' not even remembered now.

Grace was like a tiger mother. She would fight for and defend her children to the last. Sometimes, this created feelings of discomfort for the growing girl. Not only was she being punished over-severely, but she also had to deal with the fallout in the playground. She was actually embarrassed by any undue attention because she knew it might affect her friendships and reputation at school. The seeds of wanting to fit in within a particular social structure were already being sown. The headmistress's entire family all went to the same school and the children had become friends. Grace was somehow convinced that Joan was being punished unduly because she was from a "mixed marriage." She was very sensitive to this issue. She may have even seen it as an attack on her mothering abilities. Unsurprisingly, because in those days, both sides seemed to lack tolerance, and this was very unsettling for the growing children.

Despite her battles with the headmistress, she sailed through her eleven-plus examination, and the time came for her to leave her sister and move on to high school. She was accepted for her first choice, La Sagesse, a convent grammar school run by a group of nuns whose order hailed from France, founded by St Louis Marie De Monfort and described as the Daughters of Wisdom. And indeed, these teachers did turn out to be the daughters of wisdom. This was not a criminally abusive, hypocritical congregation of loveless women. It was a loving and nurturing place and a very special time for Joan. The nuns were kind and friendly, and she found she had an aptitude for study that they enabled and encouraged. There were no violent punishments or castigations here. She loved learning and particularly loved the arts: English Language, English Literature, Latin, French, and History. The school had some secular teachers also. She got on well with them all, nuns and secular alike, and thrived in this environment and came top of her class every single year, bar one when she was second.

These attainments seemed to please both her parents very much. She quickly learned that she received favorable attention and congratulations from them both when she did well. This was not only an incentive to do well but also to be the best. She learned quickly that striving for recognition and reward went hand in hand. One can see how the best of parental intentions can easily create a conditioned paradigm.

On a personal level, there were three major developments around this time of her success. She had her fist menstruation at twelve years old with no real explanation of what this was all about. This was severely painful for her and would continue to be for the remainder of her life until menopause. Her body was coming into puberty, and the hormonal changes also affected her moods, and she became very shy and self-conscious. She was handed a pamphlet from her mother for her to read about the mechanics of sex, which was published by the church. Grace seemed embarrassed and reluctant to spend a lot of time helping her understand this subject. This reaction instigated a perception that all this was not quite right or acceptable behavior, as there seemed to be a projected air of guilt and wrongdoing around the whole situation. Remember, the young girl was 'sensitive' and could pick up unexpressed feelings very quickly.

The brochure from the church was sterile in its approach. The huge downside of being in a convent school during this time in history was this particular subject was never, ever presented or discussed. It was considered the parental duty rather than any responsibility of the school process. There was never any education on this subject or any information about the social implications of sexual activity. It was almost a taboo subject for a child in those days. There was certainly never any talk or explanation of sex being a pleasurable experience, and therefore, this held no real interest for the child. Her introduction to the topic was clinical, matter-of-fact, short, and with a nuance of guilt and disapproval.

However, this resulted in a change in the friendships Joan had with boys, which, up to this time, had been fun and inclusive. She became even more self-conscious of her body and inexplicably shy and embarrassed by her own body's development. Her reactions to the opposite sex from here on in became clumsy, reserved, and even fearful. These reactions were heightened when she realized that her relationship with her father was also changing.

He seemed to distance himself now. No longer would they enjoy the long chats they had when she was a child. There was most definitely a chilling in their relationship, which saddened her immensely. She could no longer feel the beautiful essence of love emanating from her father and did not understand why. It was just like a light bulb had been switched off inside him or maybe it was inside her the light had been switched off. She was in the midst of great change within her physical body chemistry. Whatever the reason, he seemed reserved and kept his distance now with no explanation. Emotionally, she was at a loss to understand and felt she could not approach her mother with this dilemma.

Joan ramped up her effort to please her father by bringing home excellent reports from school, but her sadness and feeling of loss was inconsolable. His main concern was making sure Grace was always happy, and anything either of the two girls might do or say to cause any upset was severely admonished. Still only twelve years old, often she would gaze out of her bedroom window, look up to the stars and call to go home. This is where she intuitively considered home, amongst the stars, and often, she would cry silently to herself, wishing she could go back. There were the deepest feelings of grief bubbling up inside her that had to be kept away from the eyes of her parents. She had no idea what this was all about and felt it could not be shared with either of them. Everything seemed to have changed. She blamed herself. She did not understand what was happening or why life was changing in this way. She did not really understand anything about her body and hormonal change at this age. Why would she? No one had ever told her it was normal or even what she might expect.

After school sometimes she would take herself off on her bicycle and cycle to the park by the seafront. She could be alone here with her thoughts and feelings, away from everyone.

She had always loved to be out in nature. She felt closer to what she perceived as God and the picture of Jesus at St Anthony's that she loved so much. She climbed to the top of the highest hill in the park, and suddenly, a voice began to speak to her. There was no one else there. She was completely alone. It was strong and kind but also authoritative, and it did not originate from anywhere outside her. It seemed to be inside her. It said:

"Your real work on this planet will begin after you are sixty years old. Up until that time you will have many challenges and many hardships to face. This will be your training cycle."

It did not speak to her of her mother or her father or why things had changed. She received no reply to her most pressing questions. Nevertheless, she would discover, nearly fifty years later, that the voice within her had told her the truth.

Puberty was a difficult time for the growing girl. She continued to excel in her studies but became almost reclusive and was happy to be alone with her books.

Around the age of 13, she fell over on her roller skates and sliced one of her front teeth in two. This caused a really intense reaction from Grace, who seemed to think it was the end of the world for her eldest daughter. The dentist had told her mother that the girl would need to wait until her teeth stopped growing before he could do anything to fill the awful gap it left at the front of her big smile. Her mother seemed inconsolable and Joan thought this was because it had made her ugly in some way. She had no real awareness or vanity until then about her appearance. But this event brought her attention to her looks and how they were now damaged. All she knew was it seemed to upset her mother a lot. It was easy for the growing girl to believe there was something wrong with how she looked, and perhaps there was something really wrong with her.

As she grew and began to develop the body of a young woman, her relationship with her parents seemed to grow more and more divisive. Her father was always criticizing her looks, particularly her hair and her mother was totally 'in charge 'of the clothes she wore outside school. She had very little true space to find who she was growing into. Her remedy was to introvert even more into her own world of books and ideas and to play records on her Dansette record player. She was a shy and self-conscious teenager and had a habit of blushing deeply, which embarrassed and sometimes horrified her. When it happened, she felt like the whole world was looking in at her innermost secrets, and she felt very ashamed as she could not control this response of her body. She was beginning to think there was something really radically wrong with everything about her.

She had a wide taste in music and often buried herself deep in its sounds. She found this soothing and later exhilarating as her musical experiences expanded.

An uncle gifted her Tchaikovsky's Nutcracker Suite, and this began her love of the classics. Grace helped her develop and widen this appreciation by buying her a comprehensive vinyl classical collection. However, she was equally entranced by the cultural pop phenomena that was birthing on the Liverpool pop music scene in the 1960s and thus developed a wide taste from the Beatles to Beethoven from an early age.

Once the music had entered the teenage girl's life, her perceived parental suppressions and disapprovals resulted in a small but secretive rebellion of regularly visiting the popular local Motown Café called the Rumblin' Tum in the city center with her 'bestie' schoolfriend. Marilyn was, needless to say, not approved of by her parents, but together, they would drink lemonade and dance the time away with the locals until exhaustion.

So here it was, the first awakenings of life within her new body. She found it loved to move and sway. She loved the music and how freeing it was. She loved how music seemed to change her emotional responses. Sometimes, she felt really good, joyful, and exuberant. Other times, her response was melancholic and deeply sad, but nevertheless, it was a time to learn and experience. None of this went down well with her parents.

Grace seemed to want her to stay a child forever. And by now, her father ignored her mostly, except if she ever upset Grace in any way. His whole life was concentrated, as it had really always been, on keeping Grace happy. The older her girls grew, the more anxious and paranoid her mother became which caused a lack of harmony generally in the household and in particular in Ken's world.

They had all stopped going to church because Grace had a falling out with one of the priests at St Anthony's. This didn't bother Joan at all, for she had long realized that what the priests preached and who they were was very different. She was not impressed with the inauthenticity and hypocrisy she perceived present there in both the clergy and the congregation. When she was sad and didn't know what to do, she would walk to the church so she could be with the mural of Jesus, but the church was always locked. She could never get in when she really needed to. The only thing she would really miss about church was that beautiful mural of Jesus behind the altar.

The young girl was now becoming more aware of how she looked as well as how she felt and realized she needed some independent income to buy her own clothes even while she was still studying intensively. This dilemma was solved by a Saturday job in one of the big chain stores in the town center. Here began her introduction to cigarettes and alcohol. Every Saturday, after work, she would visit the local pub behind the store for a lager and a smoke with Marge, a new friend from the store. She was now seventeen, and on the one occasion she came home a little bit tipsy, Grace clobbered her all the way up the stairs with a stiletto shoe.

On hearing of her demise the next day, her father chased her with the vacuum connector piping for upsetting her mother. She was terrified and had to hide from him behind the wardrobe in her bedroom in order to prevent another physical assault. These incidents were a great source of distress for her, as it was the first time either parent had ever hit her. Both were quite severe attacks in different ways and shocked and terrified her at the same time. There was a lot of anger within them both that Joan could not comprehend. She was absolutely traumatized and deeply wounded by what she considered to be unfair and abusive actions from both parents. It left a lasting impression and confirmed there was something radically 'wrong' with her. Worse still, she felt deeply alienated from them both.

By now, she had reached the upper levels of high school, where students were prepared for university. Of course, her parents and also her teachers expected her to go to university without question as she was an almost model student. However, for the hesitant student it was not so clear cut. She really did not know what she wanted. All she knew was more study didn't really register as a deep longing or desire. She realized very early on that what she studied was always someone else's opinion, someone else's writing, someone else's thoughts. Even though she was shy and often awkward, she perceived at some level she needed to be independent and quietly thirsted for her own experience of life.

Homelife had become a quiet routine after the two attacks. Her parents still kept themselves to themselves so there was little social interaction there. June had begun her own secondary education at another highly acclaimed Catholic convent school, Belle Rive, and the sisters naturally drifted apart at this time. Their five years difference in age seemed to heighten the developmental difference between them during this growing period in their lives. If the truth be known, it was still Joan's deepest desire to get out into the world and experience life. She felt stifled at home. In her mind, the time had come for her to stop going away with her parents and June on holiday, to stop studying and start experiencing life.

Unlike many of her school friends, she had never even had a boyfriend.

The Vale of Shadows

The cloud of secrecy that surrounded the whole subject of sexual relations for the developing young woman had definitely created some curiosity within her. Several of her schoolfriends had boyfriends and seemed to be very grown up and in touch with this side of their nature. It is fair to say Joan's self- consciousness and shyness around men had been induced to some degree by her steadily waning relationship with her father, who basically now only seemed interested in her grades. And was exacerbated by her overprotective and controlling mother, who did not encourage any possible friendships with boys but rather discouraged them.

Joan wanted to find out what all the fuss was about and felt she was old enough now to experiment a little. It was her last year at grammar school, A-level exams were completed and her parents wanted to take the two girls to Poole for their annual break. Joan decided she would not join them this time. She wanted to celebrate the end of all the hard work of the last school term with her school friends. She knew that soon the class would disband and that she may never see some of them again as they set out on a new course for their lives. This might be the last opportunity they had to be together. The girls had chosen the best disco club in town for the venue. People flocked to it from all over the North West of England. She had saved her Saturday job money and bought herself a beautiful new dress and shoes especially for the occasion.

To her surprise her parents had given their blessing. She was allowed to stay at home alone while they traveled south. She immediately confirmed her plans with her schoolfriends to join them for an evening of fun and frolics in the city.

It was a hot, steamy summer. The girls were excited, and there were copious amounts of alcohol being guzzled by most of them, including Joan. She loved disco music and loved to dance and was not short of partners. Soon, she found herself dancing with a tall, handsome, tanned young man. Her night was complete. He was attracted to her as she was to him and he offered to take her home. This seemed a wonderful option, otherwise it would have meant a taxi. She had already said goodbye to most of her friends, and the others had already arranged lifts home. Naively, she agreed, not even thinking to ask where he lived. She was just so pleased it had been such an enjoyable evening for them all, and she was happy to be riding home in a snazzy sports car with this handsome beau. She had told him her parents were away and when they reached her home, he asked her if he could stay over as he lived far away in Southport.

She lost her virginity that night in her own bed with this almost complete stranger. No pill, no condom, no nothing. It was a clinical occurrence with no affection, foreplay, or real lovemaking of any kind. He did not even kiss her. It was an almost mechanical action, devoid of any feeling or sensitivity, with some physical pain, followed by a deep disappointment and incredulity on her part. She felt numb and violated. She had, unknowingly, set the whole thing up and had to take full responsibility for this gross and unseemly incident. What in God's name had she been thinking? Yet worse was to come.

He left very quickly in the morning. This was just as well because her parents, prompted by Grace's discomfort at leaving her alone in the house, had decided to come home. Everyone was in a bad mood. Her father was seething as he was driving and going nowhere. June was fed up as she had been looking forward to the summer break and Grace was in one of her famous moods of melancholy and kicking herself for agreeing to go in the first place. Maybe they had sensed something was amiss. Very likely, given Ken's psychic abilities and his closeness to Grace. It was something that only occurred to Joan much later when both of them had passed.

She felt sick. She managed to get him out of the bedroom, down the stairs, and out of the house without anyone seeing him. He left with a promise to call her, which, needless to say, never happened. But the whole incident had left her feeling truly dreadful. Her stomach was churning, and she was shaking from head to toe with nervousness and real fear that her parents might discover the tryst.

She was still trying to come to terms with the appalling insensitivity of the event itself while, at the same time, trying to keep the secret. Even though she was innocent, she knew she had invited the experience and had consented, yet she still felt at some level she had been violated. She felt a huge sense of shame and that she had taken advantage of her parents' trust. The deception that had followed made her feel ill. Joan never really knew if they had seen or heard anything. If they knew, they never spoke of it, ever. But overall, it was not a good day in the family's history.

A few days later, when the atmosphere in the home was getting back to a semblance of normality, Joan found herself once again alone at home. Emotionally, she was a mess. But absolutely nothing could have prepared her for what was to come. A visit to the bathroom became a horror story as she removed her panties to reveal her genitals crawling with insect-like living parasites. More commonly known as pubic lice or crabs.

She cried out in fear and loathing. She screamed in shame and terror from the impact of what she saw and felt on her body. After the screaming and crying subsided, she calmly went downstairs, boiled a kettle, and promptly doused her genitals with near-boiling water.

She was inconsolable and felt filthy, fouled, impure. It left an indelible mark on her sexuality and womanhood. She hated that boy from Southport. To this day, although she can see him very clearly in her mind's eye, she cannot remember his name. Most of all, she hated herself for her curiosity and compliance.

Time passed, and the drama quickly became a distant, distasteful memory. She was now more concerned about her future. She had briefly flirted with the idea of applying to university to do American Studies and gone through the motions, but in the end, this was not what her soul was calling her to do at this time, even though her choice of study would have meaningful significance at a later time in her life. To the chagrin of both her parents and all of her teachers, she made the decision that felt far more life-affirming for her, and that was to explore life in a different way. The fall-out from this decision caused her huge personal sadness as overnight, it seemed she lost all the relationships she had built with her teachers over the past seven years. She had been a shining star and an ace student. Everyone had high hopes for her, which she had squashed by turning down the chance of further education. But she knew instinctively that this what not the type of education she needed, and she was adamant.

Perhaps it was because she had been so isolated and sheltered in her upbringing and the influence of her Saturday job that gave her the sense and feel of what it might be like to have an independent income that she could call her own. This had certainly helped provide her with some little freedom at the time, and she felt this was the right way to go.

She had no idea what she wanted to do or be and certainly no idea of who she even was.

When the opportunity arose to apply for a position at the head office of the store where she had been a Saturday girl, she excitedly grabbed it with both hands. She felt very sure and intuited, quite correctly, that this would open up the world for her. It did.

It was only years later she realized her acceptance of the position had been influenced by her father's connection to another Freemason in the office she had applied to. She joined one of the largest clothing retailers in the UK at that time as a full- time employee at the age of eighteen.

By now her relationship with her parents, almost at rock bottom, was alleviated somewhat by the fact they had another more pressing issue of concern to confront. Grace's younger sister Alice had always been in poor health since her teenage years due to the ravages of tuberculosis. Grace had been very close to her as the youngest of the sisters and had always been the mother figure for her since Ellen, their mother, had passed. Alice was rushed to hospital unexpectedly just soon after Joan started work. She passed in the summer of the following year at the age of forty-three.

This was most definitely a defining moment for the family. Grace was inconsolable and started to drink quite heavily following the death of her youngest sibling. Her relationship with Ken, who had always been amazingly supportive of Grace through all her family issues, seemed to be at an all-time low, and no one really could comprehend what was happening. He had confided in Joan much later that in the earlier years of their marriage, he had wanted to emigrate to Canada with his young family to join his brother but Grace had refused.

Poor June, who was in the throes of adolescence at this highly emotional and irrational time, had become even more introverted than usual. Joan, who had been so looking forward to a new and exciting life of exploring the world, was once again thrown into an emotional maelstrom of exploring the effects of illness and death upon her and her family.

She had loved her aunt Alice and had fond memories of spending time with her two aunts and her cousins on special away days all together when they were growing up. These were happier times when the three sisters were thriving. And now she was suddenly gone from their lives. Not for the first time, she wondered what exactly was life truly all about? Illness and death had loomed large in her experience of it so far.

The effect this great loss had on Grace was the beginning of the end of their cohesive family unit. Grace continued to drink and shut herself off from the entire family. Ken worked and sat to watch the TV alone every night. Something was very wrong. Joan felt the collapse of this familial unit very deeply, and although she put on a brave face, she was very afraid. It was as if the whole structure of her world had changed, and she could not get back into balance with it. The realization that her mother and father might no longer love one another anymore rocked her to the core. Her parents were her stability and anchor to this world. And now, this was truly in jeopardy.

During this deep period of family grieving for her aunt Alice, one day, she found her dressing table mirror face down in the middle of her bedroom floor. The mirror was large and heavy, and there was no accounting for how it could have made its way to the center of her room. It was not broken. Who had placed it there? She checked with June, and her parents, and no one could offer any explanation. She carefully picked it up and placed it back in its proper place.

The very next day, it appeared again in exactly the same position in the middle of the floor. Joan sat on her bed bewildered. She sensed another presence in the room and then could smell perfume. She knew it was Alice, and this was confirmed when Alice's voice asked her not to be afraid, telling her all was well and pleading with her to be gentle with Grace and help her as much as possible through her terrible sadness. She never came again, and the dressing table mirror remained firmly against the wall.

The following years were indeed a sad and strange mixture in terms of homelife. Joan's memories of her mother at this time were of a grieving and lonely woman who closed herself off from her family and used alcohol to deaden her pain. At a time when life was stirring within her daughters, and the adventure and excitement of its exploration beckoned, Grace was spiraling down into darkness, and this caused great conflict within Joan. There was little she could do to change what was happening within her mother's psyche, and for this, she felt guilty. She also felt guilty about wanting to follow the very natural impulse of her youth that wished to expand and experience.

Grace's depression steadily worsened as, indeed, did her relationship with her husband, who see-sawed between sullen acceptance and bouts of releasing pent-up anger and frustration. There were occasions when he took his anger out on his daughters as if they were to blame. Joan and her father had terrible arguments that caused her to wonder if he had ever really wanted children at all or if the presence of her and her sister was merely to satisfy an early longing within their mother. There were unsettling rows, juxtaposed with long periods of silence between her parents about something unknown and that the girls would not find out about until long after both parents were gone. It was not a happy, welcoming home any longer.

First Job and a New Romance

It was a pleasant relief for Joan to have another place to go to every day, and she really made the most of what she saw as the freedom it brought her.

She was a smart girl and fitted into the buying office of the large corporation very well. She was keen to learn, and they were keen to train her. She quickly found her place and settled into her working life with equal speed. She really enjoyed the friends she made, their joyful camaraderie, and the sense of achievement she took from her work. She loved the merchandise and the vibrancy of working in a large and growing concern. These were the days when everything was done with a pencil and paper and adding machine. Seriously, no computers. Perhaps hard to imagine, but nevertheless so.

There was so much to learn about the business, and everyone was so willing to help her. She had a great time, made wonderful and lifelong friends, and earned her own income. It may have been low, as she was just a junior, but she saw it as a pathway to freedom.

Here she had met Sylvia, a zany, wacky, artist with high energy and with whom she worked all through her time in corporate retail. She was an Aquarian with a rebellious spirit and true to her star sign, a changer of the status quo. Both she and her artist husband Ray turned out to be her greatest cheerleaders, supporters, and friends until her early death at age fifty-three.

This was her first experience of being with a group of relatively happy people since the very early days of her childhood. And she loved it! When work finished most of the single folks in the group would take a stroll next door to the Spiral Staircase at least one night a week, on quiz night, to continue the fun and laughter. Her social life had also begun.

The choice to join the workforce and not go to university was the beginning of a highly successful business career that ultimately spanned nearly fifty years. Joan trained on the job, and she blossomed. Eventually after promotion to buyer at age twenty-four, she got to travel all over the UK initially, getting to know her own country in a much deeper and extensive way. In due course, she would travel to France and Italy, the hub of the knitwear fashion industry, many times, which was also a wonderful experience for her. She particularly loved Italy. There was a familiarity about it for her. She made wonderful new friends in each of the countries she visited and worked in and truly thrived.

While relations on the home front were still deteriorating, a year after beginning her new job, she was sent to London overnight to attend a staff training program. It was her first time in the capital, and co-incidentally she found another employee of the company was staying there also. He was a trainee quantity surveyor from the building department who had been sent to do some work in one of the big London stores. He made a beeline for her, and she was intrigued. She had never even given another thought to a relationship with anyone after the shame of her first attempt in that direction. She was an attractive young woman with a good figure and knew how to present herself well. But she was very naïve and still found it impossible to think of herself as attractive. Inside, she had felt like used goods, dirty, and deep down thought that no -one would ever desire to be with her if they knew the real truth. She kept trying to bury the memory and really had no desire to bring it all to the surface again by going into another relationship. Friendship maybe. Sex no.

However, this young surveyor was determined and turned out to be very persistent. She was very flattered and even grateful for his attention. It was the beginning of a relationship that would span a total of seven years. When they got back home, they began to see one another regularly. It was so easy as they worked in the same building and they were able to meet nearly every day. She was still living at home, and he also lived with his parents on the other side of the River Mersey in Birkenhead.

In the early years, they would just meet for drinks and car sex. She did not realize at that time she deserved and was worth so much better than that. Over time, they would take week ends away in the UK and, in the summer, took several holidays abroad together. He was studying for exams to become fully licensed and she was continuing to develop her blossoming career that involved more and more travel. But she was beginning to feel uneasy about the set -up. Something was wrong. She knew it but didn't know what.

She always felt there was something he was not telling her. She still was a highly intuitive being, even if not consciously aware or socially savvy. Finally, he broke the news that he was getting married! She was grief-stricken. Once again, she felt dirty and used. She cried all the way home and for many days afterward. He had told her he was marrying for money, and if she could provide three thousand pounds for a mortgage deposit, he would marry her!

Her parents had finally put their heads above the parapet of their own dysfunctionality and began to notice something was wrong. Her twenty-first birthday came and went as she drowned in a sea of tears. She locked herself away. She did not dare tell them. He did marry the other girl and she had to somehow reconcile to the loss as well as deal with the rejection and betrayal.

Needless to say, what little self-esteem was present within her had reached rock bottom once again. The only good thing in her life was her work, and she pursued this with a vengeance. Here she was, someone not a no-one. This was her lifeline, and she seized this with both hands. Since her early years, she was able to feel very deep pain and sadness in herself and others. She was an intuitive empath. But in intimate relationships with men, it was as if her entire inner guidance system just shut down. As she dealt with the blows of her own bad choices, she literally buried her feelings into the dark recesses of her body and mind and went out to greet each working day with vigor. It was a miracle she was able to keep it all together, but she had a strength beyond her own knowing, and somehow, she forged ahead. She had made really good and steady friendships with several of her colleagues and had the respect of the suppliers she worked with as well as the folks in her office. She received a good salary, and they gave her a company car. The company sent her all over the world: Mauritius, Seychelles, Hong Kong, USA. This was the 1970s and almost unheard of for a young woman in business then. Although she was still very young, here, at least, she felt she was valued. Through her work, she received validation. Her friends, who were all by now in coupledom, loved and supported her. However, she was always the odd one out because she had never sought marriage or children. In truth, she desired neither. She wanted independence.

Throughout this time, she was having very lucid dreams of being chased by men, persecuted, and burned as a witch. She could see and feel herself very clearly burning. Her dreams were like horror stories. She started to have an aversion to the name Joan. She had been fascinated by Joan of Arc as part of her eclectic childhood reading but wasn't too impressed with her demise and often wondered why her parents could not have found a better name for her. She also had dreams of being dismembered alive around this time. Emotionally, she was very unstable as she had no way to process her dreaming or the self-loathing she was suppressing. When the rogue lover turned up to rekindle their affair as the marriage began breaking down, she foolishly took him back.

But something had changed within her. She now seemed obsessed with him but loathed him at the same time. She loathed herself even more for allowing herself to be used in this way. She was strong in so many ways, but not this. She felt like she was in hell. It was what most would define as a very toxic relationship. There was a darkness within it. She could never really relax. It was a miracle she could keep her career going, but she managed to by compartmentalizing her emotions and simply put on a mask of sophistication with clothes and make up and an attitude of defiance to anything that would have been considered a normal loving relationship. It seemed as if this part of her life was engulfed in darkness.

By now, he had moved offices but continued to contact her at her office. He constantly pressed her to meet with him, and she was complicit in continuing this unhealthy relationship. She knew something was really off but went ahead anyway, with the same desperate feeling that no -one else would ever desire her if they knew the real her and her background. It went on for a couple more years like this. Maybe it suited her that she was complicit in the toxicity. It was a dark time. Although she never lost her trust in a benevolent God, spiritually, it was a bleak era, and God was the last thing on her mind. She felt completely engulfed in darkness, and her strong willpower seemed ineffectual in this setup. It was almost like she was possessed by some demonic force. It finally ended as it was always going to. There was a heated argument about evidence she found in his car of another woman. He was back to his old ways. He ripped the gold cross and chain she had always worn from her neck, told her she should go marry a parson, and then he beat her black and blue and almost scarred her face for life. He certainly scarred her psyche.

Before he had used words and deceitful actions, never a fist, but now she realized there was a deep hatred of women within him. Finally, the darkness she could recognize because this hatred of herself that lay deep within her was being mirrored externally through him.

Of course, she had no idea or understanding of this psycho-energetic play until many years later. She somehow got away from him and managed to get home. This time, she could no longer hide. Grace brought her in and laid her down and for the first time since she was a baby, put her arms around her and held her close to her heart. Both of them cried and cried and cried. Her father noticeably did nor said anything.

She took some time off work to let the bruises subside and went back when she could cover them with make-up. This was her only therapy and the best way she had to deal with what had happened and what it had evoked within her.

That same week, she received a phone call from his secretary to say she was on anti- depressants and begged Joan to please give him up because they were having an affair and all the deceit was making her ill! She calmly rose from her desk, went down to the car park, jumped in her car, and waited outside the building where they both worked. They came out together and started to walk towards the train station. She got out of her car and, with a rolled-up newspaper, proceeded to beat him in full public view, in the presence of his secretary, while exhorting him to never, ever contact her again. She warned him the police would be summoned if he tried to make any further connection. It was the absolute end for her. He called again the next day. Her father answered the phone and, for the first time in the entire relationship, supported her and gave him a full dressing down. His perversity seemingly had no bounds as he tried to connect with her once again the following day.

This time calmly, with no anger, but with absolute and total resolve, she told him it was finished, and she never wished to see or be with him ever again. As she replaced the phone, she literally saw black smoke coming out of her own body as she released the darkness that had been somehow trapped within her. She went to the kitchen and told Grace what she had done and what she had seen. Her mother somehow knew and understood, and they hugged one another. It was some kind of an exorcism as the entity left her system, and it was over. Several weeks later, she received a card from him asking if they could be friends. She never did reply.

A Cosmic Kick in the Right Direction

By now she was twenty-four and had enough money saved to put a deposit down for a maisonette property on a new building estate several miles away from her parents' home. Her mother had not wanted her to leave, but she knew it was long overdue. She felt her father was glad to see her go. June was busy with her own life and her own romances. During this time the girls had not been particularly close. Both had been outward-focused on their respective worlds and away from the restrictions of family life. Grace had wanted them to stay children forever. But, of course, they could not. She felt as if a whole new chapter was about to begin and was so excited about her new residence. It was only small and had a small front and back garden, but it was perfect in every way for her needs at the time. She thoroughly enjoyed making it her own with her considerable book and record collections. Yes, it was vinyl in those days. Sylvia and Ray, her beloved friends from the office, helped her get things set up, and soon she was throwing a housewarming party. Finally, she was properly independent in every sense.

During this time, whilst away on a business trip to France, she was introduced to a friend of one of her work colleagues. He was a handsome, dashing, dark-haired man with the most beautiful, soulful eyes she had ever seen. She was instantly attracted to him, and they spent what became, for her, an unforgettable romantic interlude together in Paris.

Sadly, the euphoria of these joyful times was very short-lived. Very soon after her move away from the family home, Grace became seriously ill, and another descent into darkness began for this beleaguered family. Joan was in Amsterdam on business at the time. It was the spring of 1977 and the daffodils and tulips were out everywhere.

She flew back in a panic and drove, with a high level of anxiety, to the hospital where Grace had been taken for prognosis. It was not good, and she recalls how ashen and bereft her father was at the breaking of this grotesque news. She had terminal bowel cancer. At that moment, she could feel his heartbreak. June was silent and withdrawn, burying her feelings deep inside. No, this could not be. This would not be. This was the reaction Joan had as she also allowed the shock wave to come in but stopped it and pushed it away from her heart deep, deep, deep into the beyond. She did what she did best for the years of this gross illness. She stopped all feelings and started taking action, any action that would take her thoughts away from the tide of sorrow that she could not bear. She drove the three of them home that night and then took herself back to her new little place. She poured herself a large drink and carried on until oblivion came.

Grace was in and out of hospital for the next four years. My God, she was such a fighter.

Joan never believed she would die, and perhaps Grace didn't either. Grace was a warrior. She had coped with so much illness and death in her own family. She knew how to do this. Life had to continue somehow, and both her daughters tried to keep going as well as they could. Her father did his best to carry on. She had remembered him speaking of a well- known spiritual healer called Harry Edwards based in the south; however, when she tried to contact him, she was informed he had just passed over. However, fortunately, through a work contact, she found another renowned healer in the North West. They were few and far between in those early days of alternative medicine, and her father and sister accompanied her on an exploratory visit to see if he could help Grace.

The visit with the healer re-introduced Joan to her psychic abilities and her ability to receive and channel energy. She had a profound interlude with this being where she levitated out of her physical body and into her energy body with full consciousness. She found she could also levitate in his presence. He did not even touch her but simply stood in front of her a few feet away. In another session as he stood beside her and as he placed his hands on her body, she became aware of an aspect of her own energy body that was an electric blue light surrounding and interpenetrating her entire physical body. On his mantel, there was an intriguing painting of a Native American Chief called White Eagle that mesmerized her with its familiarity, and during yet another session with him, she met, saw, and heard her own Chinese guide. The healer had placed her on a mattress in the center of a large hall with many people lying on the floor around her. He seemed very interested in her own abilities as she began to work with her guide and all the beings around her. She seemed to be channeling healing energy to all of them. This was not even a conscious intention on her part; it just started to happen through her presence there. They had visited with the healer to ask if he would come to visit Grace in the hospital, but he was more interested in studying her than helping Grace, and he finally declined. Joan hoped that what had occurred during these several visits might somehow be able to assist in the healing of her mother. Her father also held on to this hope. Meanwhile, Grace continued with chemotherapy treatment, lost her hair, and lost her teeth. It was such a struggle to watch this suffering. But Grace got a wig and the dentist made her smile beautiful again. She would not give up.

Joan's life was on hold as she spent as much time as she could with her family, and the times that Grace was out of hospital, life nearly felt normal again. However, calamity struck the family once more, two years into what they perceived as the fight against cancer. Due to downsizing, Ken was let go early from the telecommunications company that had employed him for the last forty years. He had been only five years away from his retirement. They gave him a payoff, but he never spoke of it. It was Grace who broke the news to her daughters.

Ken was a broken man. Humiliated by the loss of his work, betrayed by the company to which he had devoted his life, and emotionally torn apart by fear and anxiety over Grace's health and impending death. He had lived and worked to make her happy, and now everything he loved was either lost or in a shambles.

Grace spoke with Joan and asked her to have compassion for her father but also asked her to make sure she looked after her sister when she was gone. It was as if Grace had a foreboding of what would unfold after her death. Her mother had no need to even ask, for there was no question that she would help and support her sister if and when that time came. She loved June and would always be ready to help her sister, if it was necessary, without any request from her mother. It is only in hindsight she truly understood why her mother had made this request of her. Perhaps her mother had received a premonition. She also noticed how Grace had treated her in this situation, almost as if she was relying on her to take over the mother's role in the family when she was gone, just as she had done for her own family. In effect, she asking her to be strong, put aside her own feelings, and look after the family. At least, this was how Joan had received the request.

She finally had to come to terms with the fact that her mother was going to die. The cancer had spread. Her whole body was riddled with tumors, and by now, she looked like E.T. Grace would not let her daughter wash the large open sores that had appeared under both her arms. The guilt at not being able to either help or heal her mother to live was intensified as Grace went into hospital for the last time in early March 1981.

This time, she had asked for compassionate leave and was with her mother daily at the hospital. She prayed to God to help her mother live. She bent the metal on her mother's bed rail with energy expelled from her third eye as she rested her head in supplication. She would place her hands on her mother's tumors, and they would disappear only to return the next day. She thought she was going mad. She placed photographs of the healer on the diseased areas of her mother's body. Nothing worked.

The three of them took turns to be with her so that she would never awaken from her morphine-induced oblivion and find herself alone. The last words that Grace ever uttered to her distraught elder daughter, as she lay on her mother's bed beside her frail body, was she hoped Joan would find a nice, good man and settle down. This, it seems, was all Grace had ever wanted for her, and it was her dying wish.

The one thing Joan had never been able to provide. Her shame and guilt over the pain her dysfunctional relationships with men had caused her mother would haunt her for many years after Grace's death. This also deepened within her each time she recalled her choices for independence that had caused her mother so much pain.

She could hardly bear to look at her mother who was by now almost unrecognizable.

She made one promise to herself in these moments of sheer despair: she would never, ever allow her own body to become diseased in this way. Grace's terrible demise shocked her to the core and caused her to deeply consider what could possibly be the purpose of all this tragic suffering for Grace, her family, and herself. She could not believe that any human being should have to suffer so much physically, mentally, and spiritually. It catapulted her into a profound search for the meaning in all that had transpired in her own short life to date and why it should be crowned by the terrible suffering of her mother, whom she had witnessed slowly die in grotesque physical decomposition and agonizing pain over the past four years.

The moment of realization of her own helplessness and complete inability to halt her mother's downward spiral into death brought with it an inconsolable anguish and trauma that would stay with her for many years as she watched this gruesome event play out in front of her. It had caused her to vow never to allow an illness such as this to take root in her own body, combined with a burning desire to know why such terrible events followed this family even unto death. There was so much she needed to know and understand that no one could even begin to explain.

Only June was actually in the room when Grace passed. Joan was glad she had this time to be with her alone in her silent praying. As she walked back into the room, she saw the same dark smoke arising from the diseased body of her mother that she had expelled from her own system the day she terminated her abusive and demeaning relationship. Unknown to the numbed and grieving threesome, Grace's passing marked the beginning of the deconstruction and virtual destruction of this small family unit.

Her mother's death had been such a long, drawn-out process, and her decline had been so gruesome that now the end had come, none of them could find words for one another. Her father was almost collapsing with fatigue and grief; her sister, as always, kept everything inside, and Joan moved into her perennial defense against feeling anything and sprang into action. She took them all home to her parent's house and then drove home alone to her own little place of refuge. She took a large tumbler of whisky. She felt sure she could feel her mother in the corner of her small lounge at ceiling level, she was distressed she could not bring solace for her daughter. Joan was sobbing profusely and uncontrollably. Her sorrow and pain sat within her being like a coiled serpent that was slowly unwinding itself. It felt as if it was upwelling from a bottomless pit and would devour her eventually. She finished the bottle and fell asleep on the sofa.

The funeral came and went. The burial came and went. Her father, her sister, and she were like automatons. She had only one conversation with her father during the whole process and one more on the day of her mother's funeral with his sister, who had come to stay with her. She felt like she was in a nightmare. As her mother's coffin was lowered into its grave, a primal scream arose from a place so deep within her that it shocked her to the very core of her being. There is no recollection of her ever speaking to anyone about any of this. It just happened, and the consequences for her were still to unravel.

That same year, in an effort to help themselves reconcile to their new existence without Grace, they accepted an invitation to visit Ken's brother Tom, who was now living in San Antonio, Texas, after emigrating to Toronto, Canada, as a young man. It still all felt surreal. Like it was all happening to someone else. Neither of the two sisters had ever met their uncle or his family. It seemed like something that might help their father, and they went along for his sake, but in the end, it did not really help any of them. They were strangers who had never been in their life. His brother's wealth and largesse seemed to only rub salt in the gaping black hole of despair that had opened for Ken when he was let go from his work. How could they have thought this would support any of them? It didn't.

New Horizons and New Challenges

Time passed, and with it, slowly, their lives evolved. Joan was offered a new position in the garment import trade. This was an opportunity for a fresh life in a different location and after the horrendous stress and strain of the past years, she had developed a somewhat 'carpe diem' attitude to life. Grace was only fifty -seven when she passed, and she had been ill for much longer than any of them had truly recognized at the time. Her downward spiral after her own sister's death was tragic and had really constituted a ten-year cycle, four of which she had been terminally ill. Much of Joan's young life had been concerned with abuse, illness, and death. She had done her best and she somehow needed to let it go now. She sold her place in Liverpool and went to stay with her friend in Southport until she had some clarity. This proved to be a highly significant event in her life, as through this connection, a new life cycle would begin.

Ken had managed to gain employment as a security guard at the large museum in central Liverpool, and this at least gave him an excuse to get up and leave the house every day. He was only a few years away from retirement. His pride may have been hurt but this opportunity brought him into contact with other human beings and, under the circumstances, could be viewed as a blessing. June stayed at the family home and had followed her sister into the garment business. None of them had ever really processed their grief with one another. They did not know how.

A year later the still grieving elder daughter was now living in the beautiful valley of Ripponden in West Yorkshire. Her new home overlooked rich and verdant forests and rolling hills, a magical and enchanting landscape that she could look upon out of every window in a quirky building that had once been a village shop. She loved this place. She found some kind of peace and solace there. Her garden was the entire valley. Here, nature literally seemed to wrap her in its arms, and here she truly began her love affair with this earth as she allowed it to envelop her and her grief.

She had taken a new position away from her hometown after Grace's death. Her job was demanding but also exciting and fulfilling and distracted her from her sorrow for much of the time. She threw herself into it wholeheartedly. Her regular runs were to Hong Kong, Taiwan, South Korea and Thailand. It would only become apparent to her much later why she would be drawn to these countries. She would also occasionally visit the Philippines, Malaysia, and Indonesia, and prior to each buying season, there were visits to France, Italy and the USA. She stayed in the best hotels and had expense account living for much of the year while traveling. She was earning good money and had a company, BMW. A new vista had opened for her with new places and new people to explore. The friends she had made in the garment industry in the UK stayed with her, and they had many good times together even though they no longer worked together. She had even asked her father if he would like to come and live with her. She thought it might help them both heal their grief and improve their own relationship. She had enough room and she was away a lot and was willing to give it a try. He declined. This new life had come rolling in in the space of a year. She had found a lively new group of friends in Yorkshire that diverted her from her pain as she tried to build a new life for herself.

Her father's refusal of her offer became clearer when, a few months later, she received a call from her sister to say their father had told her to leave the family home as he was selling and moving to live with a twenty-one-year-old woman and her three children he had met at the spiritualist church. He was sixty-three at this time. Both of the sisters went into shock.

June was particularly traumatized as she was still living in the family home, and only a year had passed since their mother's death. Neither of them could believe what was about to unfold. The sale was already underway June had nowhere to live and not enough money to buy anything. He disposed of all Grace's clothes, jewelry, papers, everything. They had nothing of their mother. Devastation once again hit both the sisters as they struggled to come to terms with events. June came to stay with her sister when the sale went through and he left their family home and told neither of them where he was going or how they might get in touch with him. It was another ending.

Emotionally, for both sisters, it was all too soon after Grace's death to process. June had literally been kicked out of the family home by her father without discussion and with no place to live, and both were once again in panic mode over events that seemed totally out of control. It felt like no sooner was one tragedy over than another began. It was like a never-ending story of disaster and darkness with no room for joy or happiness. Joan was now really concerned for her sister's health and well-being as the disintegrating relationship with their father had taken its dreadful toll. As usual, she went into her typical response of shutting down all feelings and into a hyperactive mode of trying to 'fix' everything as best she could for her younger sibling. It was all she knew how to do. It seemed her inbuilt response to the tragedy was to attempt to re-create equilibrium somehow. Also, she was not unaware of the deep pain within her sister, who had, by now, almost completely shut down.

She eventually set about helping her sister buy a small one-bedroom maisonette on a housing estate just on the outskirts of Liverpool. It was not the best place in the county, but not the worst. At least for now, she was safe and had somewhere to live, and so once again, the storm had passed. The devastation it caused, however, had not.

Joan would lie in her bed in the attic of her old, rambling Yorkshire house and realize that she was on her own now with no safety net of a family and could only remember Grace's last wish to always look out for her sister's wellbeing. She drank herself to sleep most nights.

She had formed a couple of really solid friendships with two women who happened to live in her hilltop village of Millbank. They were also friends with Carol, her friend from Southport who had originally introduced them all to one another and who had now also moved back to her home in Yorkshire. Just like her, they were strong and caring women but broken by life in their own ways and had allowed themselves to be abused and betrayed. She found a close-knit social scene in the valley that centered mainly around pub life and private parties, and there were several folks from the garment industry that she already knew, as well as others whom she was introduced to who became solid friends for many years. The distraction of alcohol, partying, and shared wounds bound them all together, and they stayed close friends until she left Yorkshire.

Time rolled by. Work really became the only thing in life that could be relied upon. It provided resources, and the pressure of responsibility for others in and out of the work environment became the norm for the emotionally exhausted older sister. When the opportunity arose within her company, she was able to arrange an interview for her sister who turned out to be a natural for the position. She joined the company and, very shortly afterwards, her sister's department with responsibility for her own section. Although this tested them both and changed their relationship somewhat, it actually proved to be a wonderful experience of growth and expansion for June. Joan had specifically asked that her sister be placed in a separate department from her own so there could be no charges of nepotism. However, due to company re-organization eventually June would be under her leadership.

This became a big test for them both. A test incidentally they both passed with flying colours. June developed and flourished. She made wonderful relationships with all her clients. She proved her own worth and value. Of course, this made the hire completely honorable, and no matter what the gossip said, none could fault the decision, no matter how hard some tried.

June was able to move nearer to her work place and rented accommodation nearby in Hale, Cheshire. As for her part, Joan really had to ensure there was no favoritism or special treatment. This became a test of her own integrity. To some extent, there had to be a distancing between them, and she felt deeply the loss of their old relationship. June was the only close family she had left.

During this period, Joan's on-off relationship with the beautiful man who had seduced her in Paris was not a source of any great support or even much joy. It seems he was either working abroad or conveniently involved with another woman. He only turned up occasionally, and this was the most she would allow herself in terms of emotional attachment to a member of the opposite sex. It perfectly matched her feelings of loss and abandonment that had been consistently building since the early days of the broken relationship with her father and echoed the same pattern of always being placed last. It was all she could conceive of at this time of her life and had been compounded by the latest developments.

Several months later, her sister called to say their father had turned up on her doorstep, saying he had nowhere to live. June had only one bedroom, and even if she had two, it was doubtful she would have taken him in. The family saga resumed as Joan drove to pick him up and take him to her home in Yorkshire as she had originally offered.

He stayed for around twelve months. He had no transport, no money now except a state pension, and would barely speak. He smoked continuously, and the very elements of the remoteness and privacy of the place in nature that had made it a sanctuary for Joan became a cross for him to bear. She did her best but could not hide her pain and resentment when he would not engage with her in any form of communication that could make sense of his actions. He was not willing to discuss anything and it was obvious to her that he wasn't there out of love or care for her or her sister but merely out of expedience. When he did speak, it was to criticize her. The way she acted, the way she looked. She had put some weight on and he criticised this. When she did try to engage in any kind of meaningful conversation, he just said to her, "You'll always be alright, Joan." Not in a supportive way nor reassuring way, but with a flavor of self-pity and almost a sense of jealousy, maybe even envy. She felt caught between a rock and a hard place. Life became like a gunpowder keg, ready to explode at any minute. After some time, she realized she needed a break and agreed to take a ski holiday with her old work pals. She was glad to get away from the home that was now a prison for them both.

On her return, she found correspondence between her father and the woman he had been living with. He had taken her and her family on holiday abroad. He had taken Joan's car over to Liverpool and had been visiting with her whilst she was away. When confronted with all this, he became very angry and began to shout at the top of his voice the words that she would never forget....

"Don't you realize I don't care about you or your sister? " with a twisted look on a face she could not even recognize.

This was the man whom she had full memory of holding her so gently as a baby. This was the man she had unconditionally and spontaneously loved so very much as a child without even knowing why. Her heartbreak was now unbearable. She calmly told him to pack his things, called a cab, took all the cash from her purse, and told the cab driver to take him wherever he wished to go. Unbeknown to her, this was the last time she would ever speak with him. She shut down the break in her heart.

The aftermath of this event was tumultuous in every way. Over the next four years of her life, she began a downward slide into alcoholism and workaholism. She did not know how to process her feelings in any other way. She felt alone and abandoned by what she perceived as this second gross betrayal by her father.

When she gave in to the need for a little comfort from another human being and allowed her old paramour, back from his travels working in Saudi Arabia, to visit with her in Yorkshire, she immediately fell pregnant. She was aware of the very moment she conceived. She felt it as an energetic charge within her body that had nothing to do with orgasm. When she took the pregnancy test, it was positive, as she knew it would be, and she agonized for weeks before deciding what she should do. The choice she took to terminate her pregnancy took her into the realms of hell, literally.

This was against all her beliefs, against all her knowing of life, against all her instincts, and yet she was so alone with no family support and could not see any kind of future for her unborn child. She could barely support herself emotionally after the traumas of the recent years. She felt it was not the time to bring a new life into her world. How would they live if she could not work? These were different times. Working from home was not an option for her, and the concept of a nanny was not even on her radar. She was so ashamed. There was no one who could help her. She went alone to the private abortion clinic in Manchester without telling a soul.

The darkness that opened up in her psyche for her whilst under anesthetic felt and looked like she imagined hell to be. The screams arising from within from her entire body were from somewhere dark and distant, not from this dimension. This whole event had triggered some kind of other trauma on a completely different level.

She was still screaming as she came round and had to be sedated. She went home alone and collapsed into a coma-like trance. Many endings took place at that time.

It took her six months before she could share her decision with her sister and a couple of her close friends. Deep within, she felt a constant self-loathing that she could never truly share.

Life went on, and she continued her downward spiral. It seemed to take more and more alcohol before oblivion finally set in. Her father came into her thoughts a lot. Even when she took herself away to remote places, his memory would be brought in by a favorite tune of his wafting across the airwaves in the most unexpected places. It almost seemed like he was trying to contact her. Perhaps it was so.

Memories of her early childhood and her early relationship with him softened her view of the whole sordid mess that was their later life relationship, or rather lack of it. Sometime after he had gone, she had found a bunch of photographs and a few papers in a brown paper bag underneath his bed. She wasn't sure if these had been left there on purpose or by accident, but she was able to trace him to an address in Liverpool. She finally plucked up the courage to drive to Liverpool to try to see him again. She was successful, she did find him back living with the young woman and her three children. He was just sitting there in a chair in his dressing gown, but he did not want to see or engage with her, let alone talk.

The only positive that came out of her impetuous visit was a better understanding of why he was so besotted with this young woman. She looked exactly how Grace did when she was young. She ran out of the small apartment as fast as she could, shaking and in floods of tears. There was nothing more she could do.

Soon after this failed mission to reunite with her father, she discovered, through her sister, that he was in hospital after suffering a heart attack. She could not bring herself to visit with him in case of another rejection. But what she did do was send a large bouquet of beautiful white flowers to the hospital with a note that said. "I am here. If you wish to talk, please call me." The call never came.

Breakdown

Joan felt she needed a move away from the property that held so many sad memories. She had considered a move away from Yorkshire altogether but ultimately settled for a change of environment and house. She found a beautiful cottage in the Ripponden Valley with a lovely garden and scope for improvement, and although she didn't know this at the time, it would form a foundation for a new life that would enable her to live in a very different way. The sale of her hilltop house at Millbank and the purchase of her new cottage went through very quickly.

The only real constant in her life had been her work, but now, even this was changing.

She had risen to the level of Director within the very successful import company she worked for. This was the early days for the garment business in the UK, which still used importers to help source large amounts of cheap goods for the lower end of the market chain stores. At this stage of her life, she did not ever consider the larger implications of the morality of her chosen career.

By a remarkable quirk of fate, the responsibility of the entire buying office of their largest account had just been placed in the hands of a previous employee who had been fired by their own current chairman some years back. As soon as the Buying Director took over his new role, he cancelled the importer's account immediately, and as a result of this devastatingly ruthless action, the company lost more than fifty percent of its business. In order to stay in business this caused her employer to look for a new business partner who could immediately replace this turnover and its profits, and so very quickly, a suitable candidate was found, and a company merger took place.

As is common in these situations it resulted in a restructure of the business and its employees. And yes, Joan and her department were 'restructured' without any real consultation or consideration.

One of her most poignant memories of this awful time was being forced to let go of a young administrative assistant called Angela, a beautiful soul who had been so very grateful to be 'saved from the slaughter' in an earlier reconfiguration of this company's employees.

She had some learning disabilities, but Joan had been able to find her work that she could complete to the standard required and she had been so delighted to be kept on and worked diligently in her new role.

Joan called her into her office and explained what happened and why she must let her go.

The young woman came to her side of the desk, put her arms around her and thanked her profusely for having had faith in her and allowing her to stay in her department when others had been asking for her dismissal. This event affected Joan very deeply. After the deed was done, she simply closed down her office and wept profusely. It slowly dawned on her at this juncture that this was no longer a viable place for her to be. To be forced to take this kind of action because of someone else's poor decision. It quite suddenly dawned on her there was no real independence in working for others. It was all about their money, their power, their ego, their mistakes, and her compliance. The bigger realization began to unfold through her tears that her mistake was continuing to be there at all and that she herself was moving out.

Her move out coincided with the passing of her father. It all began on a business trip to the Far East when she received another message from her sister saying that the personnel department had received a message their father had passed. She was numb and frozen within.

She decided not to fly back for the funeral as she had not heard back from him, and her sister was not going to attend either. However, his spirit did visit her in her hotel room in Hong Kong, and he embraced her while she was still in a drunken stupor. To this day, she has no idea where he was buried or who buried him. But could only assume it was the people with whom he had spent his last years.

Her own rejection of her father at this point pushed her into a breakdown. She was already in a very fragile state emotionally after the trauma of her mother's devastating death that had still not been fully accepted and grieved, swiftly followed by the loss of the child that she had considered she had 'murdered' by termination. The actual death of her father could not be integrated in any way that made sense to her psyche.

She eventually flew back to the UK and, within weeks, walked out of her office for the final time without any explanation or goodbye to anyone. She was sick of the late nights, the childish competition between departments, advances from sexual predator colleagues and their chauvinism and total lack of care for anything but the money, profit, who had the biggest and best car, and decisions made by seeming incompetents who supposedly ran the show.

One late night as she was picking up the latest telex messages from Hong Kong, something inside her just snapped. She packed her briefcase, jumped in her BMW, drove to Yorkshire, and gate-crashed a friend's party in the beautiful place in nature that had been her only true place of nurture since the death of her mother. She knew she would never go back and was fully aware she was stepping out into the unknown as the distinctive strains of Labi Siffre's voice could be overheard assuring her there was 'something inside so strong.'

When she finally did reach her home the following day, she switched off the phone and stayed in bed for weeks. She was afraid and could no longer think. She was in despair and knelt beside her bed in supplication for relief. Again, she heard the voice that had spoken to her all those years ago at the top of the hill when she was only twelve years old. It said clearly, "I am with you always, even until the end of time."

Finally, she went to a local GP who, when she told him her sad story, offered her a blessing that she could hardly believe. She had eighteen months of her three-year contract to complete. He offered to sign her off for the entire term. This means she would be paid for the entire contract even if she did not go back. This provided her with the negotiation power to leave her company with some money rather than be forced to work out her contract. It truly felt like something was protecting and helping her broken being.

June had never seen her sister as vulnerable before. She had to carry on working for the company for some years before she too left, but wanted to help as much as she was able.

She gifted her own adored pet cat, Ollie, to her sister's keeping. Caring for this animal not only helped Joan get back on her feet but also opened her heart to the animal kingdom. Actually, it began the opening of her heart that had shut out so many feelings in order to operate in the dark world in which she lived. Joan never forgot this simple act of kindness that resulted in such a profound opening of love for her.

She vowed to herself after this never to work for anyone again. Her eyes had been opened. She could finally see. She could see that she had used work as an emotional prop without ever really considering the abuses that this company and its structure embodied. She had enjoyed the travel and the expense account living, her fancy car, and the home it afforded her, but ultimately, it was all about power and money, and she was merely a pawn in their game. She had been used and willingly consented to be so.

The BMW was returned. She bought the smallest Ford available at the time and set up her own sales consultancy in a small space at the back of her house beside the WC. She was free. The money from her contract gave her a breathing space.

Her first business venture with an ex-colleague and his partner to export and import goods from Zimbabwe was another nail-biting ride into unknown territory. She went to Africa and helped the designated factory to design merchandise for the lower end of the UK retail market. She was to be paid commissions on the sales. Her partners were supposed to look after the quality control and ensure all goods met the contracted standard. This did not happen, and they shipped the goods anyway. It turned out to be a money laundering scheme and involved her opening the letters of credit, so all the risk was hers, and for a time, there was a possibility she could lose her home to pay the letter of credit if it all fell through. She managed to re-negotiate with the buyers, who finally accepted the goods, and the whole debacle ended with her slamming the door on the partner's corruption and deceit.

It was another learning experience, and once again, she was protected from any real danger of loss despite being threatened with being knee-capped. The only good thing about the whole venture was she got to experience the energy of Africa, visit the impressive Victoria Falls, and really take in the essence of this great continent and its wildlife at the Hwange National Park and Nature Reserve, where she was blessed to stay for a few days. Amidst all this wreckage of her previous life, the universe had her back.

PART 2

THE GREAT COSMIC EMBRACE

Return to Spirit

A s she overcame more and more of her fear for the future and placed right action as her north star once again, this created an opening for her guidance to activate.

The illness of her mother had introduced her to her Chinese guide and re-introduced her to some of her own inherent gifts. It seemed this watchful eye on her progress took the form of leading her to what would become a twenty -year relationship with the texts of the I Ching and the Tao Te Ching. These two books had literally become a private course of study since her mother's passing. These ancient books she would study and become imbued with their energy and refer to when needing to make decisions. This was like having access to a very wise sage and a way to begin to connect to her own inner wisdom. However, just like all spiritual information, the guidance required lots of practice to decipher. At this stage, she was a beginner, having been immersed in the darkness and density of the earth realm, and there was so much inner work required of her yet. One can only choose a course of action based on their own level of awareness and so there is still a propensity to choose a less wise path of action. The books do not predict the future; they simply point to choices and possible paths of action. However, they allow for personal interpretation and meditation on the texts and encourage one to look within for one's own authentic truth. Any decisions and actions are always determined by one's own personal perspective and choices and how conscious these are. She was still most definitely not aware at this stage that all wisdom comes truly from within, but they were a tool that pointed her in the right direction and helped her to start the reconstruction of her life. And she most gratefully accepted the support.

Both texts are based on the Taoist concept of Wu -Wei that holds everything in the Universe is generated from the Yin-Yang polarity and the flow between the two. And so it is that the philosophy of the I Ching welcomes change, movement, transformation, momentum, and regeneration. Her true spiritual education began.

She started to refer to the books constantly. In many ways, the loss of her family and her rejection of the regulated church, plus her wide travel in the energy fields of the East and her experience with the healer of meeting, seeing, and hearing her first guide had brought her to an openness and willingness to explore more. One cannot refute their own lived experience. It was unsurprising she had been supported by a Chinese guide initially for, as she was to learn much later, she could speak Mandarin when in an altered state and had experienced several 'past' lives in China. This would be confirmed much later by a Chinese healer she would meet in 2018 and a very clear download she received during an indigenous ceremony,

For now, it may have seemed to her that she did not have a lot of support in the physical world. However, when one really analyses this story, one can see how beautifully protected she was at every major turning point. She was being guided and protected by the spiritual world, even if not fully consciously aware of any of this at the time.

The erratic lover from Paris somehow found her again. They had several mutual friends, and one, in particular, he could always contact for an updated address. He had called her several times before actually engaging in conversation. She always recognized his voice even when he would not identify himself.

The sound of his voice always had a profound effect on her system. She was in a different place now and wanted to see him. He came for dinner, and they chatted as though nothing had ever happened. She could not bring herself to tell him about the child or her desolation. They had never really even been a couple. It had all been so casual on both sides and yet she had really cared for him deeply if the truth was known. As much as she could care for anyone at this stage of her life. She just could not admit this to herself because of the living rejection he represented for all the years she had known him. She let him go again for the final time. But not without regret. She wept as she always did when he left her. He had been the only man she had ever truly cared for throughout all those years of pain and sadness, death and betrayal and destruction. He was enmeshed somehow in all of it.

He made himself so unavailable, and yet she allowed him in each time he contacted her, no matter how long the gap. She knew somehow that she had known him before, in another time and another place but with no recognition of where or when. He had told her several times he felt she was like a magnet. She did not have enough remembrance of the mechanics of creation and manifestation at this stage of her life to know that it was her thoughts about him that would bring him back to her time and time again.

After some time passed, she wanted to come clean and tell him the truth, so she drove to Southport one wet and windy night to the restaurant that belonged to his best friend, in the hope he would provide her with an address. This man had been her work colleague in Liverpool who had introduced them in the first place.

She spilled out the truth to him, and then, more shockingly, he revealed to her the very same situation had occurred to the woman with whom her errant lover now lived. She had also lost a child in a similar fashion. On hearing this sad truth, Joan decided not to pursue her mission to re-discover her lost love.

There was something about him that was mercurial and magical and she was undoubtedly attracted to him in a way that was inexplicable to her. Was this merely the wanting of something she could not have? The competition, the need to be chosen above another in order to feel enough, the need to be put first to feel loved. Was this really love at all? She had recreated her familiar pattern with all the men in her life, including her father, and that was, as a woman, being placed second or even last but never first in their considerations. At this stage, she could not see this pattern. She would only find out what it was all truly about much, much later ….

Dawning of a New Day

S he had moved to Yorkshire because she had friends there. Her friend, Carol in Southport, was originally from Yorkshire and was another chance meeting at a fashion show for work. Carol became a close friend for the next ten years and would play a big part in her unfolding destiny. She had stayed with her in Southport for a short time after selling her place in Liverpool and before moving into her new home in Yorkshire. Carol had introduced her to a whole new social scene that included a contact that would be crucial for the outplay of the next ten years of her life.

Through this contact she was introduced to an American company director who was looking for a sales agent to represent their company in UK and Europe. It was a perfect situation for her. She instinctively felt the contact who had introduced them was reliable and trustworthy. He knew her situation and he also knew she was reliable and trustworthy. She had built a very good reputation in the industry throughout her career.

She could easily do the job and could also remain self-employed which suited both parties. She was attracted to the set up because it was a reputable company with a good ethic, not too large, and they viewed the people that worked for and with their company as one big family. Oh, there it was, the magic of belonging to a family again! This was the deciding factor for the woman who had lost her own birth family.

They paid her commission only, but there was a reasonable turnover already established in the territory so she was not starting from scratch. It seemed like a miraculous godsend. She felt as if she could breathe fully again. She had just turned forty. The only catch was they insisted on her exclusivity. She agreed. Although this may not have seemed like good business sense from her point of view, ten years later it was to prove an invaluable asset to negotiations that would occur. Again, unknowingly, she was being guided and protected.

Very shortly after this another very good friend, Mandy, had invited her for a summer break to Marbella, Spain. You may notice throughout this story, how many good friends and connections have been there just at the right time to support this wild and chaotic journey.

On the beach at Cabopino, on mainland Spain, she would meet the man who would be her partner for the next twelve years. He was gentle and kind and so different from the men she had met during her insane corporate business life. It was this that attracted her. She had really had enough of the posturing, ego play, chauvinism, and deceptive antics of the men she had met in the world of international business.

She did not need the wealth of a man in order to live. She had always had her own work and her own independence and wanted to keep it that way. And for the first time in her life, she had an opportunity that gave her time to build a proper relationship without working crazy hours or spending weeks on end living abroad. It was like a dream coming true.

And so, for the first time in her life, she stepped outside her front door, stopped, and looked at the spring flowers growing in her garden. She bent down and looked into a pure white columbine. It seemed to speak to her of beauty and love. Something happened in her heart. She could feel it opening as she breathed in the full beauty of the single flower. A new day was dawning.

Joan and her new partner Frank spent two further years in Yorkshire getting to know each other. He was a keen sportsman and an ex-footballer who had played League Football in the UK. Now he had his own plumbing business in the historic city of Bath. He had been married twice before and had a son from his first marriage. They bought a lovely Black Labrador, Josh, followed quickly by another Sammy, before leaving Yorkshire to live in Bath permanently. Joan was doing well and at the start of expanding the base of her new business in Europe and the UK. She was enjoying this immensely and began brushing up on her French. It was a new challenge without being draining of all her energy and time. This meant she could give them her best self, and she did. She had amassed many skills during her career in retail, but above all, she truly loved and respected her clients, enjoyed creating trusting relationships with those she served, and was grateful for the values and professionalism that the company she represented held. This made her own work so much easier and gave her space for life. It felt really good to have her independence and yet be part of a great team also. She had finally found herself in a situation that felt healthy and life-affirming. There were many good and abundant years.

She had built good equity in her properties over the years and was able to put down a substantial deposit on a new property in Bath. Although they both would live there, the property was in her name as she paid the mortgage from her commissions. Frank had no cash to put into their home but did a considerable amount of work on its refurbishment, and together, they built a beautiful and comfortable shelter for themselves and their animals.

Although very astute in her business life, she was still very naïve in her personal relationships with men. Her past history had been one of abuse. Her beloved father had betrayed her, and she had no real understanding of a balanced power dynamic between men and women at an experiential level. She had never considered marriage important as she knew she would never conceive another child and, at that time, saw this as the only reason to marry. She was fulfilled with her work, her animals, and her new partner. They had a vision that bound them, and that was the renovation of the property and garden. It became fulfilling for them both to have a project they would work on together and the funds to create beauty from the tired old building and its unkempt garden.

Frank seemed very happy to be back in his home city of Bath and Joan was charmed by the historical Roman Spa city with all its splendid architecture and historical nuance. They both loved their animals, and both loved music. She saw the relationship as an opportunity to create the extended family that she lacked. They lavishly entertained his son and his various girlfriends, his sister, her husband, and their children, and his own father and new partner. Frank's own mother had passed at the same age as her own. She spared no expense and truly wanted to share her new found happiness and good fortune with them all.

She also had the blessing of making a lovely new friend, Susan, who had also recently moved to Bath to be with her own new partner, who happened to be a friend of Frank. They found they had much in common and, as 'outsiders,' quickly formed a lasting friendship which continues to this day. Life was good.

Athena Melchizedek

A Call from The Past

They had been in Bath only two years when she received a very strange phone call. The phone in her office began to ring quite early in the morning. She let it ring for some reason instead of answering, and the caller left a message.

When she checked the message, it sounded strange, as if someone who was drunk was speaking. She could not understand what was being said. It sounded like gobbledegook. It sounded as though the caller was in real trouble of some kind. She knew she had to decipher the call. Something deep inside her prompted her to keep playing the message over and over. She played it around thirty times. Somehow, she knew she had to decipher this message. Slowly, the words formed: "I can't keep bloody going. I 've got to talk. Dad."

It was her father. She recognized his voice and his accent. The short Liverpudlian pronunciation of the letter 'a' in the word Dad confirmed to her it was him.

She was dazed and didn't know what to think, do, or say. Perhaps he had not died when she thought. She was told that he had passed 8 Nov 1989, but she never had any proof of this, and neither did her sister. All they had was a telephone call to their place of work. It was now March 1995.

Her first thought was that he was alive and roaming the streets, trying to find her home. He obviously had found her new phone number. But how? They had been estranged for so many years, and she had moved several times. This thought brought her to tears as she could not bear the picture of his life that this conjured. How could she find him? She was beside herself. All she wanted to do was find him and help him. The past was the past.

The first thing she needed to know was if he was alive. She contacted the records dept and received a copy of the Death Certificate that confirmed he had passed 8 Nov 1989 through myocardial infarction.

Now, she was in even more turmoil. And then she remembered her last missive to him through the flowers she sent to the hospital. She was there, and if he ever wanted to talk, to call her. Here it was. Here and now, he was calling her. He had been a telecommunications design engineer. He knew how to manipulate this energy and it was obvious he had not, could not, pass on out of this earthbound level of the astral plane.

For the next weeks, her father's spirit filled her home. At night, the image of him as a young boy would appear on the net curtains in her bedroom. She recognized it from the photos he had left hidden under the bed on which he slept when he came to live with her in Yorkshire. Overnight, while they were sleeping, suddenly, the CD player switched itself on automatically, and Annie Lennox began singing:

"No more I love you's,

Language is leaving me in silence

No more I love you's,

Changes are shifting outside the world.

I used to have demons in my room at night ... desire... despair"

Her father was trying to speak to her from another dimension!!!

Even Frank instinctively concurred when he heard the voice on the tape; it was not from this world.

She knew she had to do something, but what?

The internet was only launched to the public two years prior. She did not even know of its existence at this time. To find anyone, she still had to use the local phone directory. She was looking for a healer initially but was guided to contact a local Light Centre, having no idea what this was. She found one that was conveniently located just two miles away! When she spoke to the owner of the establishment and described what was happening and asked if he could help her, he invited her to come to meet with him.

Joan felt she should involve her sister somehow in whatever was going to be revealed, and so June drove down the next day from Cheshire, and together they went to the Light Centre.

Neither of them had attended his funeral nor even knew where he was buried.

After a small ceremony of preparation, the healer told them both to close their eyes and bring their father into their thoughts. When the spirit of their father appeared to him, he told them both to visualize someone who had passed that was familiar to their father and to see that person in the light. He asked both of them to ask their father to move towards that light. Of course, they both immediately brought in their mother and asked their father to move towards her and the light.

As he began to leave, Joan could feel a very powerful pull at the very highest part of her heart. She would later find out it was the high heart just beneath the clavicle. It was as though cords or tentacles of some kind were being wrenched out of the top of her chest. She would later discover this was the location of the high heart or oversoul portal that was being disconnected. This aspect of her father could not fully pass on into a new incarnation because of their unfinished business. She was crying as he disconnected, and even though there was still so much work for them both to do to resolve the issues between them, at this point, she could only wish him love. And did so with her whole heart. Even after all that had passed between them, she could not bear to think of him in a terrible place without help. At the final part of the release, she saw a very clear vision of her maternal grandmother, who had passed long before she was born and whom she only recognized from an ancient photograph, also left under his bed after his stay, smiling and playing piano in celebration and she knew the passing over was fully completed.

Despite their estrangement, she had helped her father to pass from beyond the astral earth to a realm of light. She had such a mixture of emotions as she thanked the healer, and they left the building.

It was so strange because, after this, she could never find this building or the healer again.

She would often drive down this very busy road many times during the time she lived in Bath, but it was as though the building had never existed. It had just disappeared.

She knew there was much more to do with her father, but this was another confirmation for her that there was life after physical life. This was his gift to her, and as time went by and she continued her journey, she would see how it had all been planned and was all meant to happen the way it did.

Her father came from a long line of psychics and mediums. He was an engineer and designer of telephone exchanges all his life. He had used this method to awaken her to a possibility. In so doing, he was teaching her 'from the grave.'

A few days later, she was sitting at the desk of her home office. A framed photo she kept on the shelf of her mother and father during better times suddenly fell onto her desk face down. At that moment, the phone rang and kept ringing, and she had a vision of her mother and father reuniting, hovering above her and smiling at her. As soon as the vision disappeared, the phone stopped ringing. It was 24 March 1995, her father's birthday anniversary.

The profoundness of what had happened was not lost on her, and from this moment on, she began to read anything and everything she could about healing, spirituality, energy, and consciousness. She amassed an incredible library as she was guided to book after book on various subjects and authors. It seemed quite a planned education but not by her, rather by whomever or whatever was guiding her. That very same year her sister bought her Hands of Light by Dr Barbara Ann Brennan. Once she read this, she knew that one day she would study with this teacher. She did not know how or when but was sure it would happen.

While she remained in Bath, death was still no stranger. Death came visiting again to claim her best and oldest friend, Sylvia, from the Liverpool days. Just like her mother, she was too young to die at only fifty-three. Joan was in Italy at the time and knew she could not make it back in time to be with her. However, that night, she was at her friend's bedside, holding her as she passed. It seems she was able to bi-locate with just an intention. At the funeral, they told her the details, but she already knew because she was there. Once more she was being shown how to help another pass into a new dimension. The same happened with Frank's sister, she was guided to be there at the end even though they were really not that close.

Similar for the next- door neighbour and her friend's mother. She was present for them all.

Perhaps people thought her hard-hearted because she did not weep at any of these passings except that of her father. But even at this stage, she knew there was no need. She was being shown by all of them that this was not the end but a new beginning for them all. Her father's visits had confirmed for her that life continues, albeit in a different form, and as she would learn later, it was possible to meet many soul contacts from different time periods in their new different forms. This period was her first lesson in multi dimensionality and also her ability to be in more than one location at a time.

Perhaps this would explain why, wherever she went, people were always telling her they had seen her before somewhere. Perhaps this was really true?

Death had become something different for her, and her father had shown her the continuity of all life.

The Great Cosmic Slap

Physical life also continued, and the cracks in the relationship between her and Frank started to show. Frank began to slowly change once he got back to his home landscape. He was more comfortable within himself and more confident. She detected a shift in his relation to her. He was pleasant, charming, and kind. And now he was back in his own familiar home ground; he was a little less attentive as there were more distractions.

In her mind, it didn't matter who had the money as everything was freely shared, but as time went by it became obviously taken for granted and caused many problems between them.

She grew more and more successful and became a very high earner, whereas his work trajectory moved in the opposite direction. He gave up plumbing and started a taxi service, and the chasm between them widened. There was very little gratitude or appreciation; rather, the abundance seemed taken even more for granted, and this placed the relationship on a very slippery slope downwards. She had never even considered this could be a problem at the outset. To her, abundance was to be shared, and she had not given this possibility even a second thought.

They had a beautiful home in a beautiful place and a wonderful lifestyle. They wanted for nothing, went on expensive holidays, had a car each and one for the dogs, and yet it became increasingly obvious that neither of them were truly happy. They really had little in common now the project of restoring their home was finished. She was a deep and intense thinker about life and its meaning, widely read, and a seeker of truth. He was a charmer, a sportsman, a gambler, a chancer. He had a good heart but very low self- esteem and even lower motivation and became dependent on her generosity of spirit. However, she also had a very low self-esteem that had been buried and camouflaged by a successful career.

They were on course for a breakdown. As the relationship began to disintegrate Joan became more and more angry at the lack of any real loving attention and affection. The less she received, the more needy she became. It was a vicious cycle. In the meantime, Frank slowly slipped into depression punctuated by panic attacks. He had a nervous and anxious temperament and finally started medication. This brought the true dynamic of their co-dependence to the forefront. He basically became a child who was needy and was looking for a mother. As it turned out, eventually, Joan realized after much inner work he was a father replacement for her and could never fulfill that gaping hole her father had left within her, reflecting her own neediness. They both needed one another to replace what had been lost rather than loving one another from a place of fullness within. This is something she would learn much more about in the future: how our individual wounds and conditioning and the imprinting these leave on the psyche will always show up in our most intimate relationships. She herself was becoming less and less stable and more and more under pressure to try to keep things going.

Momentum for change was building. And then, out of the blue she received a Fed Ex letter from the USA to say her partners of ten years no longer required her service. As she read the letter, she could feel her entire body drain of energy. She felt as if she had been hit with a baseball bat; it was always the stomach that she felt these "shocks " to her energy system. She could no longer speak. She can remember clearly, as she tried to take in the contents of the letter, she became aware of the presence of a very tall, silvery, plasma-like , luminescent being standing to the left side of her, watching over and supporting her as she received this huge life-changing "cosmic slap. "

The aftershock was exacerbated by her recent actions to help her sister acquire a new mortgage to establish a new home for herself and the new building extension that was underway on her own property. This all seemed like extremely bad timing. But more than any of this, she could not understand why this had happened when she was at the peak of her career and in her best earning year ever.

It brought up so many feelings of betrayal and sadness and an inability to really comprehend the why. After the shock subsided, she felt another deep loss of 'family,' but even more insidious, it seemed at the time, was the complete loss of her own identity. She no longer knew who she was. She had identified deeply with her work as a way to make sense of her being here at all. This cut to the very core of her being as her sense of self /ego began to dismantle. She had been so thrilled to join this group of beings she had thought were decent and had believed them when they told her they saw her as part of their family. After all the trials and tragedies of the early years, she had only ever been able to identify herself and her meaning and purpose through her work, and now this was gone.

Here it was again, another repeating pattern: the betrayal and loss of a family. This, more than anything, hurt her beyond measure. Yes, the financial situation was grim and they were proposing to cut her off without paying her commissions earned in the past year. She was paid when the goods were actually delivered, and so in effect, always was working for payment the following year. This would have been her best performance year yet.

The day after the letter was delivered, they called her, and she was instructed not to speak with any of her clients. These were people she had made strong relationships with and served well on their behalf for over ten years.

She was completely devastated at the cold- blooded way all this was conducted, and it took her three months before she could gather some kind of composure and her wits and go to a lawyer. She had never had any legal dealings though out her entire life and was once again very afraid of the unknown. However, she was determined to fight this unfairness and loss of livelihood.

As it turned out, her initial agreement to work on their behalf exclusively worked in her favor. The fact that as she was based in Europe, on behalf of the USA and under European law at the time, meant she could sue the New York-based company for two /three million dollars, as a sole agent having represented this company in the European union for over ten years as the law stood then. At this time, the UK was part of the EU.

She had no wish to be in litigation for a couple of years, which was the estimated time it could have taken to resolve. Neither did she wish to have anything she had not earned in good faith. As soon as they realized they had underestimated her and their legal standing they buckled and paid her every penny she was due in commission and her other contractual pension benefits due. The CEO's son, who was being prepared for his father's role and who must have been consulted on the entire action and perhaps even instigated it, called her to thank her for her 'ladylike' handling of this gross situation. Yet she wasn't fooled. And was pretty sure the entire team was breathing a long sigh of relief she had not gone for their jugular as they realized the law, in this case, was on her side.

However, it was a bittersweet victory. Nothing could take away the pain of this betrayal. She had really loved working with them and the many clients with whom she had established such wonderful relationships. For her this was always that which brought the greatest joy. Creating and being in a win-win business. She did remember thinking to herself on one occasion it was all too good to be true and that maybe she didn't deserve all her good fortune. It would seem, on reflection, that this was a huge lesson in the power of her own negative thoughts to create a devastating outcome.

At this point she did not remember how she was manifesting her own life or how physical reality all truly worked. There was so much for her to still realize and recall. The thought that she didn't deserve her good fortune had created the entire life breakdown. Her belief she was unworthy of good fortune and perhaps was really a 'bad person' had been building as a potent negative thoughtform since the beginning of her life. She had no knowledge at this stage that this was all part of her soul plan.

This was, of course, also a pivotal moment in her relationship with Frank. It went steadily downhill from this moment on. Although her debts were high, the tasteful extension of her property had meant she could let it out as a bed and breakfast after a short interim period of taking a job with a company nearby whose CEO happened to have been her friend in the earliest days of her career. This was her way out. She stayed for eighteen months and gratefully took their wages. Again, she made some great friends with the staff, but the European family that owned the company itself was a dinosaur and full of cronyism. She knew this could not be a permanent position for her. She had vowed never to work for another company again, and certainly not one with their ethos. Frank helped with some of the refurbishment of the home, and when it was all finished, she gave up the job, and they opened up for business.

This was another complete shock to the system to have one's private dwelling opened up to the public while actually living in it. It was very hard for them both, but the mortgage had to be paid. She earned just enough to keep the payments going and pay the bills and knew it could only be temporary. At this point, Frank began seeing his ex-wife again.

Those two had a relationship a little like the one she had had with her own ex -lover. There was a soul magnetism that kept them looping around the same circuit. The difference being once Joan committed to another relationship, she held it sacred and was fully committed and fully faithful to it no matter how tragic or toxic it became until there was no other recourse but for it to end.

The work was hard because there was no real break away from it. She did it all herself and she gave all of herself to ensure her guests had a beautiful experience. Her home and garden had become truly a place of beauty with a lovely view and a convenient location. Eventually, she took on Rosa, a dear young Spanish university student, to help her with the cleaning. But she knew she had to sell because there was no way for her to increase the business to allow for a more sensible life. She had no more space. However, she was thanking God that she had the courage to go ahead with the extension that literally saved the whole show. This in itself was another example of Divine Intervention.

The builder she engaged to do the extension appeared out of nowhere. He was in a tricky place financially and needed cash only to do this work. She had to take out a loan to pay him, and he could have absconded at any time with the money. Instead, he provided her with two builders, Mark and Tom, who built her a most beautiful "extra house " attached to the original, who changed the designs as they went along to make it even more beautiful and probably increased its value by around thirty percent more than the original design, all for the same price. They were charming and a delight to have around; her animals loved them, and they turned what was a sad and tragic experience into a beautiful creation that not only saved her in the short term but also provided the funds for the next most important stage of her life. Once more, she was blessed by life itself.

Her BnB business boomed even when tourism in Britain itself was at an all-time low due to Mad Cow Disease, and she eventually sold the property to a cash buyer for a good profit.

She was truly blessed and supported through all this mayhem.

Time passed, and she learned that Barbara Brennan (Hands of Light and Light Emerging author) was coming to London to host a three-day workshop. She knew she had to go. Unbeknown to her at the time, she was about to begin the next most amazing learning cycle of her life.

The workshop was buzzing with excitement and anticipation. Brennan herself was mesmerizing, and what she was sharing seemed so familiar to Joan's battle-worn soul. Brennan taught and demonstrated her very own 'hands of light' and her pioneering research into what she called the Human Energy Field that she had the ability to actually see. It was a pivotal point in her life, and Joan was absolutely certain that one day she would go to the USA to study with this incredible being.

It seemed after the workshop, the deconstruction of her current life rapidly ensued confirmed by one of the strange displays of kinetic energy she had been used to as a child.

While she was sitting for dinner together with Frank, the day after her return from the workshop, a large old antique painting of the child Jesus with Mary, Joseph, and the child's maternal grandmother, St Anne, on the wall of their dining room just came crashing down from the wall in a straight line. It was a heavy-weight antique frame with a glass cover, yet there was no breakage of anything nor physical damage to anyone. But both were shaken, and Joan knew it was literally a wake -up call from the being who had promised to be with her always.

Soon after this, Frank left their home and their partnership, never to return.

They had been together for twelve years. The parting was desperately hard, sad, and unpleasant at the time for them both, but deep down, they both knew it had to be. Although the relationship had been very dysfunctional in many instances, they did have some unforgettable times together, but both were broken in their different ways. One who was always giving and one who was always taking. Totally unbalanced and distorted energy dynamics all rooted in their own deepest wounds unknown to either of them during their time together. Their partnership had to end, but ultimately, through forgiveness, compassion, and love that entered this relational field when she could fully address her own wounds and understand Frank's wounds from what she learned at healing school, their relationship miraculously reconfigured into an acceptance and friendship that would last until this day.

For now, she was in a full dark night of the soul as the work through which she had known her identity was gone. The home which she had taken such joy in building was now on the market and the partnership she had expected to be lifelong was over. She felt as if her heart was again breaking and her whole reality was breaking down. Indeed, it was, as she was about to begin the most incredible journey of self-exploration and remembrance. And, of course, yes, her heart was breaking, but only further and further open.

Soul Alignment and Effortless Manifestation

The house took six months to sell. All she could do was work as hard as she could, look after her animals, pray, and sleep.

When the time came, it was sold to a cash buyer and whilst the sale was going through, her next home just appeared on the front of the local newspaper's property insertion the very same week just before Christmas. More than anything she was worried for her animals and how she could care for them without her huge garden.

And so it was that her next home would be a most beautiful country cottage on a large private country estate on the outskirts of Bath for rental. It was located in a favorite beauty spot that she had brought her dogs to many times. She remembered thinking at the time how much she would love to live there each time she visited. The gardens were so beautiful; they were opened in the summer to the public and the whole estate nestled in a valley with a crystalline river running through it and rolling hills on either side protecting all. It was so beautiful it took her breath away. Perfect space for her dogs and cat. Perfect for her. It all happened like clockwork. The owner, who had said no dogs, melted when she met Josh and Sammy and saw how well-behaved they were. Those boys knew exactly what was going on.

They were all moved in by mid-January 2005. She had left her Bath home of twelve years without a backward glance. It had held so much joy and yet also so much sorrow. And yet, now she felt so very blessed. Because, of course she was always, in always, as she was yet to learn.

After some little time at Iford, the decision was made, and she enrolled and was accepted as a student with Dr Barbara Ann Brennan. There was so much soul retrieval work for her to do, and of course, this was the basis of the next six years of study that would take place at the Brennan School of Healing, USA. Although they had recently opened a school in Europe, which would have been an easier option, providence had other opportunities in store for Joan, and her guidance prompted her to attend the mother school in Miami. She would begin her formal studies in October 2005 and had almost a whole year to prepare.

And so, her life immersed in nature at Iford began. She could rest a little and prepare. Her entire body could take another deep breath again.

She walked in the beautiful countryside every day with her dogs. They loved it. She loved it.

Everything seemed different here. Within a week of being there, she had a strange occurrence at the back of her head where the skull meets the spine at what she would later come to know as the Ninth Chakra Point or Mouth of God, also known as the Well of Dreams. There seemed to be some kind of automatic energetic manipulation happening there. She did not feel afraid, just curious. She found the very next day, she had stopped smoking and drinking and wanted to eat only very healthy foods. She walked daily in the very heart of nature, and nature held this breaking being tenderly in its embrace. Daily, she would be streaming tears as all the pressure and hurt that built up over her lifetime to date slowly started to release. It seemed a never-ending process. She began meditation in earnest. This was the perfect spot for her healing process to begin. It was all happening without any conscious awareness of her own will, for her soul had taken over running the full show. She was guided to exercise her body and started to revisit the gym she had used while living in Bath.

Combe Grove Manor was placed in another breathtakingly beautiful location, nestling in the lushness of the gorgeous Limpley Stoke Valley. All of nature was conspiring to help her, and she realized once more how much she deeply loved this earth that was loving her and holding her and supporting her. The cottage in which she lived was just a delight and a beautiful feature of the country estate and gardens that could be described as a place of rest and retreat, tucked away at the bottom of a tranquil valley with terraced Italianate landscaping and lots of narrow and uneven paths that twist and turn with a river running right alongside. It always felt like she was stepping into a magical and mystical place. She had the genes of a gardener from her mother and her grandfather Aloysius, and she truly appreciated this beautiful place of rest and regeneration.

Kundalini Awakening

Her guidance was to pay attention to her body and take some additional exercise other than dog walking. One day, she was in the gym and a young man walked past and cast her an enigmatic smile. There was something very beautiful about him that she could not fathom. It was not his looks particularly but an essence that draped over her as he passed by. Again, somehow, she recognized the very essence of Unconditional Love that was emanating from this being. She discovered he was one of the Yoga teachers, and of course, she joined his class immediately.

And thus, her soul training began in earnest.

She was very drawn to this Yoga teacher, and they became friends. They corresponded by email. He looked much younger than he actually was. She learned he was a healer and, unbeknown to her at the time, he would play a huge role in the reclamation of her own soul memory. Once again, she could feel the same frequency that she originally felt emanate from her father whilst in his arms after her birth. She was recognising the energetic signature of her soul family.

Her teacher ran three classes per week at the gym, and she attended them all. Very shortly after their first meeting, she experienced a major kundalini awakening where the energy that lies dormant in the root chakra at the base of the spine rises through all the seven body chakras and delivers a major expansion of consciousness where one experiences an overwhelming sense of bliss, love, joy, peace, calm, contentment, oneness, ….

The yoga sessions were opening further her psychic abilities to see energy; her intuition was heightened, and she felt a deep soul connection to this being. She had incredible out-of-body experiences with him. He would visit her etherically and fill her entire mind screen with his healing energy as he placed his hands on hers. During a physical visit to the cottage one evening, he sat in front of her, and she was able to see all his different incarnations, including his extra-terrestrial origin, just pass through her physical eyesight like a film. She saw this at least twice. When she asked him about this, he mentioned Sirius as his possible home planet but was not absolutely sure. He could bi-locate like her. Whenever she was with him, she would receive information of when they had been together in different lives as nuns and priests, as mother and son, she would see other incarnations of her own without his presence also. She was beginning to recall many memories of her own past lives and could clearly see herself in different times in different bodies. It was almost like a kaleidoscope of form, color, and light. It must be said at this juncture that she thought of them as past lives, but in actual fact, she would come to understand they were all happening simultaneously, just in different frequencies or dimensions of light.

And then a most memorable incident occurred when he visited her mind screen at night while she lay in bed. She was wide awake, not dreaming. He appeared; he took her hand, and she left her body and joined him as they transfigured into a roaring blue, violet, and gold flame in space amongst the stars, and they 'stood' joined together in the flame without physical bodies. She heard a voice say, "Take a look at yourself; this is who you really are. " She was looking down at her body and saw only One flame but his and her head. And then they took off into space and circled the planets and the moon and stars. And then suddenly she was on her own, she was astral traveling as One, playing amongst the stars just as she had done as a child, and as her father had spoken of …. This sequence finished suddenly when she looked down, and a human hand came into her view urging her to take hold. She took hold of this hand, and it pulled her down back into her physical body. It was her teacher's hand.

At the physical life level, they were a teacher and a student of Yoga. Yoga means union, and in other dimensions, it certainly was. It means the union of the energy and consciousness with all that is, with God, with Source, whatever you wish to call the un-nameable.

When she told him about these experiences, he knew what she described.

And so, of course, at the physical level, this changed everything for the Yoga student, Joan.

At the physical level, she loved him as the perceived Source of these experiences when, in fact, he was merely a mirror showing her True Self. He did tell her so at the time, but at this stage, she had so much more work to do on her own ego nature to enable an integrated expansion of her consciousness into a fully unified state and a full understanding of his words. This state is the realization that everything that appears as external is really only a projection of the inner landscape that is being projected out by the inner consciousness and registered by the brain through the senses. It is literally all a picture show and transient.

He had acted as a catalyst for her energy system and showed her the potential.

Of course, at the soul level, they had planned to meet at this juncture of her life as she began her new cycle of training for her true work in the world. She had much more to learn and experience before she could truly understand the scope of what had happened. All she knew was that she loved him, and this became very painful for her still-present human ego when he turned up with his new girlfriend, and she suddenly had to let it all go. He also was embarking on a new cycle of his own as he prepared to marry and travel. Here it was again, that same old familiar pattern. At this level, it felt devastating at the time, even though it was a monumental teaching of non-attachment.

Here is what he wrote to her after she described what was happening within her:

"What you are experiencing is pure love from God, love of life, love of yourself. You are experiencing this for the first time in this incarnation. It is awesome and very normal to think you are going crazy. You have chosen to stop spinning everyone else's plates (a phrase she had used to describe her previous life situation and tendency) and focus solely on your own, well done. This is of absolute paramount importance that you do. From here on in, your life is about you. You are the center of your known universe. You are where it began and where it continues through eternity. The only person you will always have is you, so it makes very good sense to get to know yourself in your totality, which means total surrender to the Divine. Total surrender to Love.

Yes, the power of pure love is immense, beyond the comprehension of our mortal minds. Pure love can, however, be felt and experienced in its fullness of abundant magnificence when we simply choose to feel it. In the process of surrendering to yourself, you are at a universal level surrendering to the Divine. What you are experiencing is God's pure love for you and your pure love for yourself. They are, of course, one and the same. As above, so below. *As within, so without.*

As you know, I am simply the catalyst for the process you have chosen to embark upon. Being that this is the first time you are experiencing this in this incarnation, it is very normal to crave more and to hold on to these feelings, this is the human aspect and response.

Your spirit knows that God's love is eternal; it is always there. We feel God's love when we love ourselves; they are inherent within each other. Before you can love outside of yourself, you have to love inside of yourself. It is the pre-requisite of Love. Absolutely everything begins inside. It is the nature of life and energy to expand outwards. That is the flow. It is natural. Remember, wherever your intention goes, your energy flows. It is also very natural to seek an association from which any new experience has derived. It is born from the ego's search for identity. It must identify the source at all costs.

Like studying an enemy, the ego will convince you that anything other than itself is harmful and of no value.

In this instance, it is convincing you that love is an illusion and that you need to give love an identity, that you need to find its source, and that you need this information so you can harness love and cultivate love on the basis it will not always be there.

Your spirit, however, knows the truth, it knows that Love is Eternal, Love is Almighty, Love is your birthright. It is your God-given right to live in Love. To live in trust and trust in love.

This is the test. Trusting in Love and Loving in Trust. Allowing the sensations of love to flow through you at all times, completely allowing the flow with a totality. God wants us to celebrate life, to realize our own Divinity, to honor our own Divinity as the Gods and Goddesses we truly are.

To bring spirit through form and the etheric through substance.

Being in a relationship is natural, to desire to share your truth and life with another is a truly beautiful enactment of Love.

When you are able to live without the desire for a relationship, then you are ready to receive it. Loving oneself on every level completely is required before you can love another.

Relationships are to enhance the truth and beauty of who you are, two whole people living from their truth and being two whole people.

For some, it is perfect that they live their purpose and do their life's work on their own. For some it is perfect that they live their purpose working with others. The only right way is that which exists within your own truth.

Seeking to differentiate between right and wrong is a judgment performed by the ego.

Be centered, balanced, and calm; live in the light and love of your truth. That is Divine. That is Love.

Namaste."

Eighteen years later, she re-reads the words with not only an absolute knowing of their truth but also now with a full embodiment of what is truly described here.

Her encounter with this being was profound and led her straight into deep research of the starseed phenomenon.

Galactic Ancestry

Her experiences with her yoga teacher had brought in the information that perhaps was for them both. She remembered the day he came to Iford to reveal his many aspects and on that very day, she was wearing a sweatshirt that she loved with the inscription I am a Freaky Alien. What was happening here? What truth was wishing to be shared? She was guided to read all the material available at this time about the Star races and humans who remembered their lineage. She began to receive conscious awareness of her own different lineages that are merely different aspects of the One Self. These planetary lineages were revealed as Pleiadian, Sirian, and Arcturian. These are called the sacred galactic heritage and form part of the consciousness remembrance and inner journey of the soul back to its Source.

The term starseed is the modern name for souls who have reached and expanded awareness and remembrance of other dimensions or frequency bands on their path back to Source. They have a specific DNA template that provides this information when activated. We can look to the skies, wherein lies a multitude of planets, stars, solar systems, galaxies, and universes, and know all is part of the creation, and all is life, and all is sentient. This means this is all part of our own consciousness at some level. Some star seeds are advanced spiritual beings from different planets, solar systems, and galaxies that have specifically incarnated on Earth with the intention to help raise the consciousness of humanity and have come to Earth at this time to advance and support the current Ascension process for the earth and all her inhabitants. These are often ancient, evolved souls that hold a multitude of wisdom and experience and have specific abilities and gifts. All carry different activation encryptions and special codes designed to unlock their knowledge and abilities at a pre-determined time in this dimension.

However, it is very important to note they are not immune to the human experience. In order to fulfill their soul contracts, they purposely shapeshift into human form and, therefore, of necessity, come to earth with the same veil of forgetting as all other humans. Therefore, they experience all the trials and tribulations and life challenges, plus their own karma and healing journey, as well as their own unique themes for their own spiritual growth. By doing this, they learn how best to help clear the collective consciousness of the planet and help raise the frequency of both the planet and all humanity.

There are many here now on earth during this cycle of ascension or, shall we say, expansion. Typically, there is a strong feeling of love for the planet and a deep desire to help others.

They are deeply attuned to the human experience by taking this on and are equally aware of the forms that attempt to keep humanity in enslavement. Through the experiences of their own challenges, they learn how they can best help eradicate that which keeps humanity recycling these same old patterns and cycles that do not serve either their growth or the highest good. This is connected to the themes of sovereignty, freedom, and liberation in this current earth cycle.

They are deeply connected to nature and love the earth and all its kingdoms: the rocks, minerals, crystals, plants, animals…as well as its human occupants, and of course, are aware of the other many spiritual dimensions.

It should also be recognized the term starseed can also be used to manipulate the ego and often create a false sense of superiority and specialness if they do not come out of their own forgetting. This will depend on their level of consciousness and if they have been able to do their own inner work to transmute lower-frequency energy, just like all humans are required to. Their purpose is to help the earth and its inhabitants shift from the timeline that is represented by the military, industrial complex of war and enslavement, poverty consciousness through manipulation of the financial systems, and the trauma-based mind control presented under a disguise of love and care to encourage humanity to be involved in the process of its own demise. This is all the distortion of the masculine electric energy and consciousness, which includes the development of the patriarchal, hierarchical structures and systemic misogyny and persecution, including child abuse down through the ages. The starseeds are here to help humanity spiritually evolve out of these old masculine energy distortions and access the new timelines of sovereignty, freedom, and abundance and to bring balance and harmony through the development of the magnetic energy of the Feminine Principle, bringing in Unity Consciousness also known as Christ Consciousness. This has absolutely nothing to do with religion and everything to do with non-duality and non-polarity.

Another note of great importance is the name might imply that all humans do not have a celestial or star origin. However, this is not the truth. Humans are a microcosm of the entirety of existence. Yet most are in spiritual amnesia and disconnected from the higher dimensions of their energy field and the totality of their being, just like Joan was at the beginning of this story. In this story, we are, in fact, tracking her own awakening to her own full remembrance.

Some human beings may have only experienced incarnations on the earth but still have all the information of the cosmos in their template, but it cannot yet be accessed. This remains in what is called junk DNA, which accounts for around ninety to ninety-five percent of the DNA of most humans. Even the star seeds themselves do not access this information immediately, as you can witness from Joan's journey to date. But they have the propensity for a more rapid remembrance because of their DNA coding and particular soul missions.

The starseed has taken human form and its associated DNA imprinting in order that they do not violate the free will of humanity. To be in a different form at this stage of humanity's conscious awareness may possibly violate free will. This is what negative forces try to do.

Joan was only able to see this form in her teacher's field because of her own frequency match and eventual remembrance of her own lineage. Not because she was forced in any way. He was catalyzing her own remembrance. The kundalini experience activated her own inherent DNA coding and why she was accessing more and more of the gifts and experiences this allows for.

For a starseed to incarnate in human form to assist humanity is an act of true love.

They have to step down their own frequency in order to incarnate into these dense dimensions. They often can, and do, incarnate over many lifetimes, playing out different roles in order to understand the earth system so they can learn how to best trigger humans out of their distorted situations. Each has its own abilities, characteristics, and codes and can more positively influence humanity by being part of it.

And yes, they have developed their own karma by being here lifetime after lifetime. The main difference is they eventually have a strong remembrance that is activated according to Divine timing and it is easier for them to break out of the conditioning and deprogram themselves.

They choose a specific lifetime to activate the remembrance when it will most serve humanity. This is why there are many here now in these great times of collective transformation, and many remembrances are being triggered.

There are many different types of starseeds, but their overall mission is to create new pathways for innovation, healing, creativity, understanding, expansion of consciousness, and shift in the earth's overall frequency.

They are here to bring remembrance and realization to humanity of its true purpose of recognizing the I AM within which is no less than God/ Source experiencing itself in the entirety of its creation.

Some are way-showers

Some are healers

Some are seers

Some are visionaries

Some are coders

Some are guides

Some are transformers

Some are alchemists

Some are artists

Some are earth grid workers

Some are networkers

Some are sages

Some are builders

Many have more than one of these gifts to aid humanity's rise in consciousness, frequency, and vibratory levels. Their lineages can be multiple, although usually one is activated and predominant. Through the unfolding of their life journey, they begin to access more and more memory and activate all the dimensions they have experienced. Joan was able to access remembrance of the Pleiades, Sirius, and Arcturus.

Just like humanity, the starseeds themselves can be highly targeted in order to lower their frequency, and some have polarized back into the system they came to free humanity from.

Through the presence of ego, it is possible they can be led to a synthetic path of prophecies and false light. Humility is paramount and they must act as stewards of the race for their own progression and evolution as well as the humans they are here to help.

By their ability to do the inner work of transformation, transcendence, and transfiguration, they are able to hold a high frequency and, through resonance, uplift humanity and the planet.

Their own particular coding will attract those they are meant to help without any outside intervention or marketing. Their own journey is the process by which they help all as they forge new energetic pathways for others to follow.

Please know any attachment to an identity of any kind takes one out of unity consciousness.

Our identification with any part of our manifested form is the beginning of duality and results in polarity. Yes, this is the setup here on earth for us to learn about who we are and what we are not, but we are aiming for the full self-realization that we are all of it, and what we experience is a matter of where we place our attention.

Below is a list of possible characteristics based on Joan's lived experience:

- Strong sense of being different or not 'belonging' on Earth.

- Homesickness and not fitting into the prevailing consciousness

- Empathetic.

- Strong intuition

- Read between the lines and pick up on nuances.

- Strong sense of an 'unfulfilled purpose'.

- Freedom seeker.

- Intelligent and love learning.

- Experienced a deep spiritual awakening.

- Highly sensitive

- Psychic or paranormal abilities.

- Experienced major traumatic life experiences or events early in life

- Feel like an ancient soul with multiple life experiences on Earth.

- Interest in holistic health and natural remedies

- Aversion to harm or violence.

- Babies, children, and animals are drawn to them.

- May know of life on other planets, solar systems, and galaxies.

- Interested in cosmology, astronomy, astrology, and spirituality

- Others are drawn to them naturally for help and support

- Vegetarian, vegan, less common breatharian

- Usually, will feel at odds with their parents and may develop imaginary friends as a child.

- Drawn to crystals and their healing properties.

- Can daydream a lot and be ungrounded.

- May have memories of living on another planet.

- Read about starseeds and are interested in science fiction and science fact

- Often have seen and experienced things science does not explain

- Belief that there's life elsewhere

- Sometimes love extra-terrestrial shows and programs

- Some follow alternative media

- A deep quest for knowledge and understanding of the universe

Specific Missions and Descriptors

Blue Rays came in after the two world wars. A few started after World War 1 in the 1920s, then the bulk 1940's the 1950s after World War 2 and atomic bombings specifically to heal the ancestral and genetic bloodlines and shift the timeline and known now as Baby Boomers.

Indigos A few in the 1960s but most in the 1970s and 1980s - Warrior and Rebel Energy, outspoken, concerned with change, and are paradigm changers. Often associated with ADHD, Autism, ADD- Gen X.

Crystal Children Born to Indigo parents 1990s-2010 usually have a higher vibration, are all about inclusion and love, and are less polarised often ADHD, Autism, psychic gifts, creative. Millennials, Gen Z

Rainbow Children Pure Love, fewer veils, super hi-dimensional consciousness, psychic gifts, gender fluidity, sensitive, empaths, help to heal humanity, service oriented. Gen Alpha

These are general descriptions, and of course, there will be exceptions to every category. It is a guide only. Each new generation comes in at a higher vibrational frequency with less karmic baggage. It is ultra-important that the generation prior, i.e., their parents, have done their inner work so life here becomes easier for the new generations and they are not conditioned by parental distortions. If you are guided to have children, they should be your prime focus, along with your own inner work of remembrance.

Ultimately, we are all here to realize Unity Consciousness and hold that frequency for the earth and all its inhabitants so that through harmonic resonance, all have the opportunity to rise.

Synchronicity, Serendipity, Magic and Miracles

The story from here on in recounts the wild and wonderful adventure that became the path to Self-Realization and embodiment of her own Divinity.

From this moment, it was as if life had stepped into an overdrive mode. Everything just fell into place without her doing anything. She was offered a position in Toronto, Canada, by the man who was the son-in-law of Frank's father's lady friend. Such an incredible set of synchronicities, but nevertheless, this man had visited with them when they had been together as part of Joan's drive to restructure a family. He had been impressed with her, and when he heard of their break up and the loss of her business wondered if she would be interested in helping him run his business communications training company in Toronto.

As she would be required to travel five times per year to Miami for school weeks, this was indeed another perceived blessing that would make her attendance much easier as well as be paid for it. This was not achieved by any conscious manifestation techniques. She had merely signed up to attend the program. She had simply made a conscious decision to follow her heart and her guidance. This was all organized by the soul at the soul level. All that was required for this superb outcome was for the ego, soul, and spirit to be in perfect alignment. She had started school in 2005 and, on the way back from Miami flew to Toronto to visit the offices of the training company and meet the staff.

The first person she met would become a lifelong friend and course facilitator, Susan. She had also studied transpersonal psychotherapy, practiced reiki, and was on her own spiritual path. It was as if, by magic the universe had arranged such a lovely being to welcome her to her new home. The company had arranged a work visa. For the second time, within two years, she was moving home, letting go of things, giving furniture away, and ensuring Frank was fairly dealt with. In return, he volunteered to look after their last living pet, Josh. This was such a blessing to her. Sammy had to be put down before she left. His time had come to leave. Her cat went to a friend. She had cared for them lovingly and conscientiously all their lives. They had good long lives of fourteen and fifteen years, respectively. Josh survived one more year with Frank and then also left.

The animals had contributed so much to her life process. She had loved them ferociously, and they had furnished her with their love and loyalty, beautiful and wild walks in all weathers, and been greatly responsible for her progressive appreciation and love for the natural world. They had softened her heart and helped her through the sadness of another dark night of the soul that, although was challenging and often painful, when she got to school and finally understood what was truly going on, she could only bow down in awe of the Divine Plan that turned out to be her life. Each and every human being, animal and nature itself had played their part in the tapestry of her unfolding. And for this realization, she felt so blessed and could only bow down in awe and thanksgiving.

Life in Toronto and School in the USA

In Jan 2007, life in Canada began in earnest. It was also the year she found another member of her soul family, who had just started running the Children of the Sun Foundation in the USA. She became a member and did the regular monthly group meditations with her and her members until they would actually meet physically six years later when she had finished her studies.

It took a while for her to get used to city life. One of the conditions of working with the new company was that she lived not more than ten minutes away from the office. Given they had offered her a generous package and the ability to travel five times per year for nine days of study including her travel days plus a vacation package, she felt this was a reasonable request.

The work was easy for her, and it provided the space and time for her real passion which was "getting to know herself in totality " via her studies at the Brennan School in Miami.

These did not disappoint. It was an intensive four-year curriculum each year of integrative distance learning modules, healing science, psych-spiritual development, creative arts, general anatomy and physiology, anatomy and physiology of the human energy field, professional practice, integrative care, meditations and in-class psych-spiritual sessions plus a fourth -year project. She had signed up for the degree program, so on top of this, there was around nine additional subjects of general education in Social and Behavioural Sciences, Humanities, Science, Math, Creative Writing, Ethics, Ecology, and more. It was full-on, and she absolutely loved it. She took to the studies like a duck to water. She also had to engage a Personal Process Facilitator recommended by the school to cover the eighteen sessions required for every school year. Her first four years provided her with a BSc in Healing Science.

Nothing could have prepared her for what was to come as now she was going to unpack the first fifty years of this incarnation and much more material from other incarnations than she could have ever believed. The guide who had first made himself known to her twenty years prior, when her mother was dying, came with her and introduced himself as Huang Po, whom she later found out was the Chinese Zen Master and Buddhist Sage during the Tang Dynasty who passed in 850 AD. During her very first class, he came flying across the circle she was sitting to show himself to her. Her formal spiritual education had begun.

Her first year concerned her relationship with herself, her year two relationship with all other life, her year three relationship with the Divine, and year four integration of it all.

She learned all about the human energy field and the consciousness associated with each dimension. She learned about the science of the new physics. And the true nature of holographic reality. Healing was hands-on and she learned new and advancing techniques each year. She learned all about Core Energetics and The Pathwork, the psycho-spiritual path that Brennan herself had followed. The school's teachings were built on these modalities, as well as Brennan's own channeled teachings from her own guide, Heyoan. The name is Kenyan and means 'The Wind Whispering through the Centuries.'

Essentially, it was a path of transformation built upon the new emerging science of quantum physics and the tenet that body, mind, soul, and spirit were not separate. Energy and consciousness were inseparable, and all healing came from within.

The curriculum offered many opportunities to be together in a group form to sing, dance, chant, drum, and meditate. She was free to express and enjoy herself in a myriad of different ways throughout her training.

By far, the psycho-spiritual work was the most intense as she started her own lived process of transformation of her energy and consciousness. This allowed for more and more creative energy to be released, and through attention to the creative arts, this was given an opportunity for full expression. Even though it challenged everything she thought she knew, it was a wondrous and joyous time for the student, Joan.

She had mistakenly thought she was going to be trained to be a healer, still not yet fully realizing this was already inherent within her and her training was a process of emergence. And it was through this education process that she learned of the power of the group to accelerate inner process and outer transformation.

The program was very intense and required deep commitment. Many dropped out as the years progressed. A brave and courageous few made it to the end.

The time will come when, with elation you will greet yourself arriving at your own door, in your own mirror, and each will smile at the other's welcome. Derek Walcott

PART 3: THE DEEP DIVE

Relationship to Self

Each year, the students were asked to set an intention and, at the end of the school year, determine how far it had been accomplished. For her first year, 2005/6, she set an intention to discover more acceptance and love for herself to replace the severe judgment accompanied by the dreadful buried shame and guilt with which she had lived her life to date. Her preparation with her yoga teacher had enabled her to see this was neither useful nor did it serve her or anyone else.

She could feel the great Love in which this wonderful school was held by Brennan and her magnificent faculty and all their own guides as soon as she crossed into the classroom on the first day, and it never left her.

During her first year, she became aware that it was okay to have needs. She had reached an age of over fifty years and had never realized that it was not only acceptable to take care of the self at all levels but absolutely a necessary condition before attempting to help others.

She had been so focused on just trying to survive her challenges in what seemed a brutally cruel world that she had never really considered any of her own natural needs as a full human being. She cried and cried as she realized she had never even considered she had needs. She could not even describe what they were. The early example set by both her mother and father was to always help others and consider it selfish to be concerned about the self. This is what both had modeled and was echoed by the teachings of sin and guilt of the Catholic church. However, she learned quickly this was a false premise, for she could not fill others with an empty cup. This exactly echoed the words of her yoga teacher. One must learn eventually that all needs become redundant because one's own system is most automatically creating everything that will fulfill all the basic human needs. That one's birthright is one of abundance at all levels.

Every time she left to go back to Toronto, she would take more of herself with her and the love that was growing within was there with her in all her transactions during those years of business and living. The company and the folks that she worked with were all affected in some way by the incredible energies that were now emerging through her own energy field. Totally unknown to them, of course, no one ever talked about it, no one ever even asked her. But the company changed, expanded, and thrived while she was there, just as she did.

The work was not for the faint-hearted. It demanded vulnerability, truth, love, acceptance, non-judgment, perseverance, courage, non-attachment, and so much more.

There were schools in the USA, Europe, and Japan in those days. The relationships that were made were of the deepest kind because they were all programmed by each soul to be there and do the work with and for each other so all could transform and bring forth their deepest shadows for reconciliation and integration.

She had learned that one could not do this work alone. It required the guidance of spirit and, therefore, genuine contact with the soul, and it required the mirror that the others in the small class groups and then the larger school group and faculty could provide. It required courage, vulnerability, and compassion. This would all then be transposed to the external world when they departed after each school week, and the work would continue in each of their lives and with their practice clients. At the time she joined, there was an intake of around four hundred students, and two thousand had been already trained. The fees were high and really only for the truly committed, although a few scholarships were available for those who could not pay.

Every piece of learning and experience was guided by the group soul and the Divine Feminine. This occurred through the Goddess energy that would be called forth each school week in meditation. The work was truly phenomenal and she dived as deep as was necessary to find truth for herself and all those she worked with over the years. There were many realizations for her, not the least of which was why she had been guided to the US school and not the European which was closer and potentially more convenient.

Gradually, it was revealed to her she had spent many lifetimes on the continent of North and South America as an Indigenous Native American. During her school time, she had many visions of her life here and the healing that this land required through her own contribution to the healing of her own being now. She was, in fact returning home in a different dimension. During one powerful heart meditation, as she followed the teacher's instruction to jump into the left ventricle of her heart from her breastbone, her heart broke open as a great stream of light pierced the darkness within … as she arose out of the blood of her heart it changed into an ocean from which she emerged to be greeted by an entire tribe of Native Americans in full dress welcoming her and saying to her "you are coming home, "you are coming home." She was in truth coming home to her own beautiful heart.

She learned of what she then thought was the first time she had lost her tribe/family through a vision that showed her as a young male native American wading through a field of blood and the maimed, dead bodies of an entire tribe. She could feel his guilt at being the only survivor. Here, once again was unresolved loss being shown that had resulted in the continued loss of family in this lifetime iteration.

Over her first four years, hundreds of healings took place. Students took turns to practice on one another and were always guided by the spirit with whom to partner for any healing session. They practiced their newly gained healing skills always guided by the great group spirit as well as being in group process with one another daily. There were also larger group process classes for the entire school year and then a final meet-up at the beginning and end of each school week of the entire school where there were ceremonial healings with great Goddess energy that came forth in all the full school meditations.

Her first school year was a tender year of sensing once again that great Love that she had first felt as a babe in arms and that had been so tragically 'lost' in what she could only describe as a 'descent into darkness.' This loss indeed could be seen as a metaphor for all humanity as they perceive themselves as separate from their Source. By the end of this year, her relationship with herself was beginning to be transformed. This was mirrored in her own external appearance softened as she began to find the aspects of the feminine energy that had been squashed by fear and lack of self-love. It introduced her to the different realms of her egoic mind and the difference between emotion (reaction) and feeling (response). The first three layers of her energy field had truly started to be cleaned up. Her awareness expanded further as she began to see herself mirrored in others: the good, the bad, and the ugly. She wrote the following poem at her first school year end.

Athena Melchizedek

Remembrance

To be the Sacred Self

To see the sacred Self

To feel the Sacred Self

To taste the Sacred Self

To hear the Sacred Self

To breathe the Sacred Self

To bring each shattered fragment of the self back to the whole

This is the purpose of our lives

To know this self in all its pain and doubt and fear

In its sorrow, deep

In its loneliness and despair

In its abandonment and shame

In its betrayal and grief

In its anger and humiliation

Athena Melchizedek

In its rejection and helplessness

This is the work we chose

These wounds we brought to earth to heal

The child's essence which could not grow

But froze in time

Bound in darkness, behind dark walls of illusion

Separate, alone, terrified

But still, the core light shines, this wounding

T'is but a gift to urge us on

To awaken us from our dreaming

And so, we begin the journey home

Piercing layer upon layer of dark, deep pain

To find t'is but a phantom, a ghost, not real

And in the depths, we find the light again

Shining brightly, fiercely

Exploding, pulsing, healing

Athena Melchizedek

Radiating outwards, above us, below us, around us, in us

This is our destiny

And at once, we remember who we are

We recognize this Sacred Self

As love, as joy, as peace

A being radiant, of wondrous light

Returning home to the Self Divine

All wisdom, truth, and beauty

Knowing for others, we will light the way

This is why we came

Relationship to Other

Her second year was much more dramatic and even deeper in its reach. Energetically, this was a trip into the astral dimension via time capsule healings. Her intention was to allow herself to be and feel vulnerable enough to drop any habitual masks and defenses and be truly seen. The psych-spiritual development concentrated on the importance of the relationship to others and all life and the fourth dimension accessed through the heart. It is only through the mirror of the other can we deeply know the hidden parts of the self and why duality and polarity are useful in the healing process. Healing is essentially bringing back into unity those parts of the psyche that have separated within our own consciousness and projected out as an experience.

One of the very first astral healings, where it was her turn to 'be' the client, resulted in the removal of a huge thick dagger, about fourteen inches long, being removed from the front of her heart in the astral dimension. She could see and feel it, the healer could see it, the teacher could see it. It was happening. When it was removed, she could feel the relief in her field and the release of the pain in her body, which had held it in place in her body since ancient times, long prior to this incarnation.

Another healing involved the release of thousands of small daggers that had pierced her back and been plunged into her shoulders. As the light came in to release them, they all raised together from her back as the transmutation dissolved them. This represented the many backstabbing or betrayals she had encountered over centuries, both as a woman and a man.

She watched the various persecutions she had undergone for being considered a witch and death by fire, drowning, and strangulation. Also, she saw she had had her throat cut several ways and times. She had been subjected to brutal torture during the Inquisition, which had affected her genitalia and anal passage before the relief of death. The visions came thick and fast, and pain was released at the cellular level in her body. Her knees held a time capsule during her life hood in China and the essence of an attack that was time-coded to be released at a later date when it would bring the necessary opportunity of resolution to the other party concerned.

She was able to see the lover she had let go of and his pain, sorrow, and regret at their ending based on his own woundings and erroneous beliefs about himself and women through his own dysfunctional relationships with his mother and father.

So many of her previous life situations unfolded through the many visions that came pouring in during this time. Each bringing new understanding, healing, and closure.

While she lived in Toronto, she met many people with whom she had an association in a 'past life' and would be given the full scenario, who they were to each other and what role they had played in the particular life-hood which required resolution now in some way. There are so many stories to tell that perhaps might fill a book on its own, but what is presented here is enough to demonstrate how deep and thorough she was determined to go to find truth and reclaim her true self in every dimension.

She was given the whole background to her work with her Yoga teacher in the UK who prepared her for this work.

He had been her son in several lives and her chaplain when she had been an abbess in a European convent. She already knew this before school. They had had many lives in various situations in religious orders together. In other timelines and other relationships, she had betrayed him, and he had betrayed her; all became clear.

In one most extreme case in Roman times she had been forced to betray him, as her eldest son, to save herself and her other younger children. He had been crucified upside down as per St Peter. She carried the guilt of this down the ages. He had shown her the stigmata that appeared on his palms from time to time during one of his classes. Now she had more of an understanding of why he might have been uncomfortable with her in some way and, of course, why she could see the marks on his hands.

She had been a poor mother who had prostituted herself in order to feed her children while their father went to war. She carried this guilt also. She met the father again in Toronto at a dinner party. He was a Romanian now. There was a strange attraction for them both. Her vision later revealed he was a powerful shaman and also the father of her children in the previous scenario. He never returned from the war, and she was alone with children to bring up and feed in times when Christians were being persecuted in Rome. This imprinting had a particular reference to the sexual toxicity she had experienced as a young woman and the kind of relationships she attracted to herself due to shame, guilt, and lack of self-esteem and self-worth. The feeling of evil or badness had never been resolved, and she had carried this forward. Remember also, as a starseed, the soul contract is often one that purposely brings this victim's consciousness forward so it can be transmuted for the whole.

Joan had the triple victim consciousness imprinting of the Roman Catholic Church hierarchy and its misogyny, plus the cruelty administered to those with special gifts perceived as witches through her maternal lineage. Patriarchal and hierarchical Masonic imprints and their misogyny through her paternal lineage and Indigenous and Racist victimization in the Americas through both lineages, as we will witness in later chapters.

She had many connections with life in Italy through another son she met in Toronto.

He was an Italian who became her hairdresser. In other times, he had been a Franciscan monk in Assisi where they had lived. She saw him vividly in the brown robes of his order and the large dark brown beads of the rosary and cross that dangled from the waist of his tunic. She was able to work with him, through their attraction, to help him rebalance his marriage after the death of the couple's baby. His wife had fallen into a deep depression, and their marriage was teetering on the brink of disaster. He was in a lot of pain. She would talk to him about all she was learning at school and what she was doing. As she spoke with him, she could often see a beautiful emerald green iridescent light emanating from his heart and filling his entire energy field. He shared with her some of his own mystical experiences in this life, and one, in particular, stood out as time stood still for him and all creation was reflecting back an incredible light. His own Divine Light.

He was a very loving and caring man and used to provide food for the street beggars on Yonge St and offer them uplifting and kind conversation on his breaks between clients.

Before she left Toronto, he had told her relations with his wife had vastly improved, and she was now pregnant again, and he showed her a photo of the unborn child within her womb. He thanked her and told her he knew in some way she had been instrumental in this conception. She had never shared with him their true connection but now it seemed he was becoming aware of it in some mysterious way.

Around this time, she also remembered her own time as a member of the Poor Clares, the Franciscan nuns who took vows of poverty, chastity, obedience, and enclosure. Her home in Toronto then was based, as usual, only ten minutes from her office, on St Clair Ave East.

Whether formally at school or informally in life generally, it seemed she was a healer of some kind. There was still so much she did not understand, but slowly, so much was being revealed.

Each of the revelations and the release of any associated distorted energy allowed for an increasing capacity for seeing, sensing, hearing, touching, tasting, smelling, and intuiting as her awareness expanded exponentially and brought more information in.

Throughout the psych-spiritual process work insisted on by the school she was learning much about the psychological process and how the mind worked to create our experience of an 'external' reality. The tapestry of her own life to date was rich and her psychic abilities, as they became enhanced by her experiences at school, enabled her to not only see the current life but also all the 'past life' scenarios related to what had happened. She had lived through each of the major psycho-dynamics of humanity and was slowly working to transmute them within her own transforming energy field.

Her poetry for this year denotes her struggle to reconcile the relationship of masculine and feminine energies within.

Athena Melchizedek

Come Dance with Me

And so, I wait with patient heart and trust inspired, knowing what I

see will come to be

But it was not always so

For as I look back across the eons of my lives, a tapestry stretching

to eternity

I see you there beneath it all, hiding in the shadows, dear one

Will you not come and dance with me?

And thus, it began: you were a king, a great man to me, my first

true love

That feeling, innocent, guileless, unseen, unspoken, just there

Pure, lying between us like a sea of soft feathers, comforting,

cradling, safe

I would lie in the arms of your strength, bathe in your devotion

deep, and all was well

'Til into woman turned I and no longer would you dance with me.

And shame came creeping in, slippery, stealthily like a poisonous snake

As her body grew and took the form of goddess shape, with this came the evil one

For surely, she was evil, this being, whose presence could not be countenanced

And with this dark one, a pain so deep, for what had she done but be?

And in this very being, she had betrayed herself and could no longer dance with thee.

And so this changeling drew unto herself a new kind of feeling to replace the old.

For it had been ordained before she came this must take place

And this brought to her side a cruel, destructive creature, all wrath and hate

Who beat her body blue and black, unhinged her mind, soul wandering, lost

Forgotten and abused, but still, she danced and danced and danced with he

And his legacy was great, this dark, remorseless one

For the very fight had made her strong like iron, warrior queen she became

As she rose like a phoenix from the ashes, resolving never to feel again such pain

She fought and strained and stretched the very sinews of her soul

To have no need and no desire to ever, ever dance again

And nothing could she receive; hard and brittle, she became

And into the wilderness she crossed, wandering lonely in her solitude

Hiding away in the shadows, locked in anguish, betrayed

Extinguishing slowly and crying silent tears for her lost life

And so it was she came to ask the gods, 'Shall I never want to

dance again? "

The prayer was heard, and sweetly, gently, the angels came

Awakening her from her sleeping, she stepped out, hesitant and

afraid

Into the arms of the earth which held her as her mother /father had

before

And she saw the love that was there in each flower, in each rock, in

each tree

And one by one, each said to her, come, come now, dance with me.

And then a being beautiful and bright appeared and took her

shaking hand

Together, they journeyed into the skies, across the galaxy, to many

a starry land

They played and flew and laughed and cried with joy, and the two

became Divine Ecstasy

And the being said to her, 'See, see dear one, now see, for I am thee and thee is me. "

And I will dance with thee.

So turn not away from me, beloved one, but stay here a while and see

Be witness to my light, and all that is yet to come

For I am but a reflection of thyself, so stay and dance the dance of life with me

The eternal dance of love Divine, the light that shines in all there be

Come .... dance and dance and dance with me.

Relationship with the Divine

During her third year, the subject of authority and Divine Will was the main topic. They were now working with the upper levels of the energy field. She approached this with her usual determination to be open to truth no matter what the cost.

It concerned her relationship with authority and the ability to surrender her own will fully to spirit and Divine Will. Her intention this year was to fully submit to Divine Will.

It turned out that this would be severely tested by the head of this particular year's study. She had to choose whether to follow her own guidance or obey the school in the form of this teacher. It was the inspiration for her creative project this year that guided her decision to question the school and its directive and to finally stand her ground.

The year was 2008, and she had brought forth a piece of artwork Divinely inspired by the Blue Moon of this auspicious year. The piece was called "Once in A Blue Moon."

A Blue Moon means that the moon appears twice in the sign of Taurus, once on April 20 and then again on May 20. The significance of the moon in Taurus is that it denotes a Buddha Moon when the earth feels the Loving and Unconditional Presence as embodied by Buddha.

Calendar Blue Moons occur when lunar and solar cycles do not match. Usually, each calendar year will contain twelve full lunar cycles plus around eleven days to spare. These spare days accumulate over the years, ultimately resulting in a year with thirteen full moons. Hence the saying "only once in a blue moon.

2008 was such a year, and, more significantly, it occurred during the Wesak festival.

Wesak is named for the legendary convergence of the energies of the Buddha, the Christ, and other Ascended Masters at the hallowed Wesak Valley in the Tibetan Himalayas during the Buddha Full Moon. This convergence is celebrated by various cultures all over the world and by pilgrimage to the original site. This particular year, it is celebrated on both days.

She did not know any of this when she began painting. She just felt compelled to paint something in blue and felt she needed to make the expression of her Surrender to Divine Will.

For her, it turned into an ongoing meditation, not only to honour Divine Will but also other aspects of the Divine, the Divine compassion embodied by the Buddha and the Divine Love embodied by Christ, the convergence of these Divine energies, the unity of east and west, the balance between Yin and Yang, the Enlightenment of our beloved planet as we shift from dualism to holism and thus to unity and peace on earth.

"If your compassion does not include yourself, it is incomplete. Buddha

"Love one another as I have loved you" Jesus Christ

With the painting, she included the following prayer to honor the more balanced expression that was occurring within and to honor the Divine Feminine energy that was emerging through her at this time;

Goddess of Nature and Nurture

Relinquishments

I surrender

Any self- defeating patterns of behaviour

Any family involvements that only serve to suffocate

Any unhealthy expression of Femaleness or Motherhood

Any self- limiting attachments to my roots or home ground

Any negative childhood experiences or maternal influences

Any fears of being open to receive or of the unknown or unfamiliar

Any neurotic emotional reactions or feelings of insecurity or abandonment

I surrender these all to you

Goddess of Nature and nurture

I receive from you

An attunement to nature and to the abundance of the unconscious
realms

An ability to empathize and to meet the needs of myself and others

A rich dream life and imagination. Powers of receptivity

A capacity for giving and receiving care and nurture

A wholesome state of Femaleness and Motherhood

Healthy instincts and a sense of safety and security

A strong feeling of constant support and supply

And all these are also my Gifts to give

They did not ask her to leave.

Integration

Her fourth year brought her first graduation but also many other blessings.

By synchronicity it turned out one of her small class teachers was also her own Personal Process Facilitator for her final year. While she was still in her third year she had watched this particular teacher work with a final year student case. This was a procedure to guide class members in the mechanics of their presentation and what they could expect. She remembered when first encountering the presence of this teacher what a beautiful, serene, and peaceful energy she emanated, and she had hoped to work with her one day. Her dream had manifested.

Her intention for her fourth year was to reach the highest potential possible in human form in this incarnation. This intention has guided her entire life ever since leaving school, as she sensed there was still so much for her to accomplish after she had completed these first years of formal training.

In the fourth and final year, a case study that demonstrated all her skills had to be presented and passed, and a project describing how she could take her skills out into the world had to be completed before she could qualify.

She has already been in some conflict with the school's authority concerning the case she wished to present. The physical wounding of the client for her chosen case was so severe that the school attempted to stop her from working with him as they feared for their reputation, and it seemed they doubted that she had the competence to deal with the complexity of this case. If she moved ahead with this in year four, there was a real possibility she would be asked to leave. She was devastated at this threat of removal, and here again, was the looming possibility of losing her soul family.

It shook her to her core. She had been guided to work with the school. She had been guided to work with this client and the client had been guided to work with her. Despite the school's objections, she felt she must trust that guidance, even if it brought her into direct opposition to them. She actually had to 'fight 'the school for the right to present this case.

She went ahead after an emotional address to her class around the right to have her joy and follow her own guidance. This was not about her ego. It was about whether she could follow her own guidance even in the face of great loss.

Her client had been in a motorbike accident when he was only twenty-one years old. He was now in his early sixties. His entire left side was distorted and broken. He had lost his left arm. He had broken his left hip and leg. His entire pelvis was out of alignment. He had endured a quadruple heart bypass. His back and right shoulder were out of alignment. He was in continual pain and being prescribed by the allopathic medical system very heavy opioids for this. Because of his poor physical condition, he was afraid to leave his home and travel to see his family.He lived alone and in isolation from life itself.

It had taken her some time to realize that every 'client' she worked with was actually showing her something about herself and her own wounds.

Her final case was revealing to her all her own wounds and the distorted consciousness they had engendered. It was, in actual fact, such a gift, and she could no longer ignore the mirror that external reality provided, and she began to experience how that mirror of reality truly works. This client's physical and psychological issues mirrored the entirety of her own life prior to school.

The decimation of the Divine Feminine within her was shown in his broken left side. The loss of his left arm, her inability to receive. The broken pelvis represented distorted thinking and behavior around her sexuality due to the time capsules she had unearthed during her second year that had given rise to this incarnation's dilemmas and the many brutal attacks made on her physical person in the name of 'regulated religion' down the ages.

The distortions in his shoulders and back, the many betrayals, and the 'burden' of this carried through the ages. The physical pain he felt echoed the pain of guilt, unworthiness, self-hatred, and shame she had carried in her unconscious mind, all in shadow. The quadruple bypass of the physical heart, the times her heart had been broken by loss and betrayal and closed down in order to not feel. During various time capsules, she learned she had been stabbed at least four times straight through her heart and once through the high heart.

This had left her with only a distorted masculine energy of constant action ... doing, trying to fix everyone and everything in order to feel safe and secure, a distraction and defense against true feeling. The struggle she had to keep her heart closed and the pain it caused her. She had carried guilt, self-hatred, unworthiness and shame, and many other imprints. And she had carried them into this incarnation specifically so they could be transmuted and transformed at this specific time by forgiveness, compassion, and love.

She knew this client had been sent to her in order for her to see how wounded she truly was. `And she knew his healing would be her own.

By the time they had finished their work together, his physical body had reconfigured to the degree it was possible for him. The physical pain he endured was considerably lessened, and his dependency on pain-relieving narcotic drugs was considerably reduced. He had enough confidence to travel again and see his son and his family in California. He smiled and laughed and regained self-confidence. His life was transformed.

It was only in hindsight could she see that guilt, self-hatred, unworthiness, and shame and their associated masks, defenses, and separative behaviors are the very shadow structures that are being challenged now by the collective at this point in human history.

They translate into war, disease, poverty, victimhood, and enslavement. It is no surprise she embodied it all in order to create a new energetic pathway out through her own empowerment and healing.

As her site of action always been the business environment, how could all this be translated into a meaningful proposal?

Her project for her final year was a piece on Core Communications for Business, and it was based on all she had learned in her four-year training combined with all she had experienced in her work at the communications training company in Canada.

It was an interesting dichotomy that the CEO had a most brilliant mind but personally struggled with authentic heart-centered communication because of a defensive and overcontrolling persona. This was undoubtedly brought about by childhood conditioning and imprinting and the learned responses that shut down a response to feeling in order to keep safe and in control. Just as she had shut her feelings down, this profile matched her own energy signature of the distorted masculine and feminine energetics prior to healing. One of the reasons she had been hired was to help manage relations with the workforce.

The past years have brought into focus the undoubted importance of multi-dimensional communications, particularly for the younger generation, who were already moving to more right-brain dominance and even more so now as the earth moves into its new frequency.

Her work in the company, coupled with her own personal work at school and the urging of her own creative expression, as more of her own core essence was accessed, had resulted in an inspirational vision to create communication tools based on a wholistic and relational approach that could bring more consciousness into the workplace and healing and transformation to the world of business.

The business had always been her sight of the action. In moving into a communications training business while simultaneously studying the physical, auric, haric, and core dimensions of humankind and her own conscious embodied experience of these dimensions brought her an opportunity to build and bring a consciousness into the world of business that could have such a positive influence in our world today.

Business can be a great influencer for good when aligned with conscious principles.

However, her original project did not materialize in the way she had foreseen as the Canadian company lost interest in her project as soon as it became clear that the necessary changes to the company's own communications, relations, and behaviors must be a model for what the programs would involve. It became obvious to her.

The project did materialize in other forms and different delivery media with the great shift to online entrepreneur businesses, remote working, and the arrival of online video in 2013. It is interesting that this project was conceived at the time of the last great recession, 2007-2009. It must be even clearer by now that there is a rising tide of demand for change worldwide. The chaos and turmoil we see now in the corporate world is akin to the chaos evident in an individual as the ego breaks down and transformation beckons.

How we communicate with one another is fundamental to our existence at all levels and creates the experience of our reality. Integrating such a model into communications training for business will be a source of illumination and inspiration to those who are searching for solutions to the current crises and will be helpful in enabling a shift to the new paradigm for conducting global commerce with truth and integrity at every level.

An honest relationship with self and others is fundamental to all growth, success, and our very evolution. Whether at home or in the workplace, our dialogue with each other and our behavior towards each other is vital for our own self-development and that of our fellow man. And yet, we are much more than the words we speak.

We send and receive communication with our entire being constantly.

We possess multi-sensory antennae and are powerful transmitters of energy and life force. Through mindful interactions with one another, we can change not only ourselves and our businesses but also our planet. To be the change we wish to see in the world starts with us.

A Break at Hollyhock

After graduation, she took a one-year sabbatical and took herself to the beautiful Hollyhock Retreat Center based on Cortes Island, British Columbia.

Cortes Island is one of the Discovery Islands, an archipelago located at the northern end of the Salish Sea and the eastern end of the Johnstone Strait between Vancouver Island and the mainland of British Columbia. It can only be reached by sea plane or ferry. Interestingly, it was named after Hernan Cortez, the Spanish Conqueror of Mexico, by two Spanish naval officers who discovered it in 1792. The indigenous population of the island is Klahoose, who are known, by oral tradition, to be descendants of survivors of the great flood during the end of the last glacial period and the warming of the earth around eleven thousand years ago.

Cortes has gorgeous dense forests with excellent and beautifully maintained trails, pristine sandy beaches, inland lakes, and an abundance of wildlife. The Hollyhock campus is located at Manson's Landing and located on the traditional unceded territories of the Klahoose, Tla'Amin, and Homalco nations.

What a beautiful and loving place this was to rest and revive. Here, she met a lovely group for yoga and meditation and enjoyed the exquisite, fresh, and healthy food grown in the lush gardens and the delightful essence of the tall forests, beach, and sea that made this place an island paradise. Perhaps because she was with such a strong community vibration, as she walked the trails, she often found herself transported to another time and place, another bleeding of the frequencies, as she witnessed herself in Qumran and the Essene community she had belonged to there. This information would have much relevance for a future date and would become obvious why it was triggered here on this land. They say Hollyhock is all about nourishing those who work to make this world a better place. She felt blessed once again to be able to be there.

The energy at HollyHock was and is truly ancient and magical, and here she met a group that would take her on the next stage of her journey, traveling regularly to Santa Monica, California.

Sacred Energy Arts

One of the workshops she had signed up for was presented by a great Sifu or Master Practitioner. This was a combined program of Yoga, Qi Ging, and Tai Chi. Her love of Yoga and her desire to explore other modalities brought great enjoyment and anticipation of an opportunity. He was an extremely gifted teacher, and she was so impressed that after the workshop, she signed up on the spot to take his Sacred Energy Arts Yoga Teacher Training program in Santa Monica, USA. She had made good friends with a beautiful family at the original workshop who invited her to stay at their home in California during the school weeks so they could all attend together. All was perfect.

Needless to say, it was all about another major healing that would take place between her and the Sifu. He was/is an amazing teacher. However, throughout the program, for a reason totally unknown to her at the time, his treatment of her could be described as less than warm. It was noticeable not only to her but the other students also. Once, she had to walk out of the class because he was so rude and disrespectful. It seemed wherever she went, there was something to be uncovered. Her Being had triggered him in some way.

In this case, the realisation came about for both teacher and student when, during one of the classes, while holding one of the yoga poses, her body just collapsed and gave way. It was as if she had become crippled. In fact, this is exactly what she was reliving.

The scene moved from the yoga studio to a field of battle where the Sifu had smashed and broken both her legs (she was a young male in this scene). She came round out of the vision and found the class had been interrupted and she was now lying on her back and the Sifu holding and manipulating both her legs until she could stand once more.

It seems this was an opportunity for both of them to resolve whatever differences had caused the original wounding and was again a reference to a past life in China that had been revealed to her during her time at school. It will be no surprise that his own current prime instructor and teacher was in China and the Sifu visited him regularly. These were the two beings in the time capsule held in her knees. During the yoga session she had been transported back to an ancient battle between dynasties. She was a he, a young, inexperienced warrior. During a battle, the Sifu, now a great warrior in this time line, had broken both her legs and stopped her progression forward in that life. Now, he had an opportunity to repair them. She was healing his karma as well as her own by allowing herself to be there at all.

After this day, he completely changed his attitude towards her. He commended her for her persistence in continually showing up to his classes, although it meant monthly travel from Toronto to Santa Monica. At the soul level, he knew she was there to teach him something as well as to learn, and his ego could not accept this at first because he was the teacher. And so, he tried to make it uncomfortable for her to be there. He admitted this. In the alternate existence he was jealous of the healing powers of the young male warrior because he felt he was inferior in some way. This relational dynamic was bleeding through to the current scenario even though he was a most excellent teacher and she was a very willing student, her presence somehow brought up his own feelings of unworthiness and inferiority. She had given him the opportunity to get past the fact that she was also a healer, honor her as an equal, and allow him an opportunity to heal his own issues of stubborn ego and inflexible pride, fear, and the inability to give in and reconfigure the damage he had done to her legs in previous times that had stopped her moving forward in that life, all through compassion, forgiveness, understanding, bending, and flowing with ease. All's well that ends well.

At the end of the program, she passed with flying colors and a continued love of the physical body moving, more flow, and honoring the Sacred Energy Art of her masterful teacher. She presented the poem below to close her yoga class for her examination.

It was written by Yeshe Tsogyel   857-817 AD. She is the foremost woman in the history of Tibetan Buddhism.

Listen

O brothers and sisters

you who have mastered the teaching

If you recognize me

Queen of the Lake of Awareness

Who encompasses

Both emptiness and form

Know that I live in the minds

of all beings who live

Athena Melchizedek

Know that I live

in the body of mind

and the field of the senses

that the twelve kinds of matter

are only my bones and skin

We are not two

Yet you look for me outside

When you find me within yourself

Your own naked mind

That single Awareness

Will fill all worlds

Then, the joy of the One

Will hold you like a lake

It's fish with gold-seeing eyes

Will grow many and far

Hold to that knowledge and pleasure

And the creative will be your wings

You will leap though green meadows

Of earthly appearance

Enter the sky fields and vanish.

She celebrated her graduation from the program towards the end of 2010, just in time to return to the Advanced program at BBSH in October of that year.

Onward and Upward

She returned to the Brennan School for the next two-year segment of study, the Advanced Studies Brennan Integration Work. And my goodness, she was truly blessed by the gods to be able to take this program with such incredible teachers at this most auspicious time. The run-up to 2012 was underway. 2012 was a hugely significant date for humanity, earth, our solar system, and indeed the entire Milky Way galaxy as three specific cycles were all coming into an alignment.

The earth circles through the 25,920 great year cycle of its own axis, also known as the Precession of the Equinoxes, passing through each of the constellations for a period of 2160 years was considered to be moving out of the Age of Pisces and into the new Age of Aquarius.

The Sun's 230,000,000 years orbit around the Milky Way Galactic Centre – Black Hole Sagittarius A-had reached a perfect balanced alignment of the Sun, Earth, and Galactic center in 2012.

The entire Milky Way Galaxy was passing through a hi frequency belt of energy called the Photon Belt, which encircles the nearby star cluster, Pleiades. Earth entered this in 2012 and will continue this passage for approximately another 2000 years.

All galaxies, planets and stars have conscious awareness and are either following the Divine plan for this Universal matrix or resisting it. The planetary and galactic alignments in 2012 were all pointing to what we are now experiencing in 2024.

This is what people were and are still describing as the Ascension cycle. This happens over a long period of time, and we are really still just at the beginning, so it is worth revisiting what exactly is meant by the term ascension.

We have until recently been on a trajectory of involution or descension that has allowed our entire Solar System to explore all levels of consciousness, both light and dark. This has brought in a very high degree of perceived separation from our Source and from one another. Driven by lower, ego-based behaviors of service to self that created fear, conflict, and many different types of warring factions, all promulgating a distorted power structure. We must remember the original angelic human DNA blueprint was a highly prized and sought after attribute by other galactic beings because it is potentially directly connected to an infinite Source of energy. There are races in our galaxy and people on our own planet who have cut themselves off from this energy source by their distorted thoughts and malevolent actions. Ultimately, in this universe, it is a free-will choice.

We are now in the upward cycle of the return of evolution or ascension that is now moving the collective back towards wholeness and mastery and another free will choice to create a more beautiful, loving, inclusive, collaborative, unified experience of reality.

Every planetary body has the Holy Spirit at its core, just as we do.

The Divine plan for Earth is that it is a beautiful planet of redemption where we have the opportunity to develop unity consciousness by the joining of the positive, undistorted masculine and feminine polarities within and reclaim unity in our diversity.

These massive alignments and shifts in energy could be felt by all sensitives in 2012, even if they were not consciously aware of the real significance. It could most definitely be felt at the school Joan was attending, and it turned out to be a year of huge change. Her timing could not have been more perfect to do this deepest introspective work, for everything at the school would change the following year. It not only supported the raising of her own frequency but was completely synchronized with the earth's timing. Her next two years of study was an intensive deep dive that would be completed in 2012.

The previous four years would seem like a walk in the park in comparison to what was required of her in this forthcoming program. By now, she was working three days per week at her company, which was a blessing in itself. This gave her adequate time and opportunity to complete the syllabus. It was a phenomenal training. Not for the faint-hearted, very challenging, uncomfortable, with plenty of shadows, darkness, and copious amounts of love and light. The classes were very much smaller, only eight in her own class and ten in the year above, and absolutely nowhere to hide.

It was a full-on process: large group reflections, small group reflections, fishbowl reflections (as facilitator, client, supervisor, and observer), self- reflections, experiential reflections, practice facilitation sessions, process session write-ups, anatomy of emotions, and necessary reading material plus optional reading. This was just the homework!

The classes themselves involved full participation and use of all her skills: physical, auric (electromagnetic chakra system), haric (scalar field of intentionality) and core dimensions (quantum field and underlying awareness); listening skills; contact skills; wound;

higher self; lower self; mask; shadow; defense; beliefs; images; constellation; intentionality; transference; countertransference; boundary issues; ego; superego; witnessing; asking; experiencing, surrender; pleasure; cellular awareness; multi-dimensional core contact; higher sense perception; table work; process work; group participation; team building; reliability /maturity; awareness of ability with personal process; communication and self -expression skills. It was full-on. During these two years she would notice her clients were shifting from requiring hands-on work to remote healing transmissions. She was doing more and more work online and her guides were overseeing this process. They were now teaching her different skills, and this part of her training was completely guided by them rather than the school. The emphasis of the school was now on the psycho-energetic dynamics.

She recalls one of the most powerful processes that touched her deeply, which was the Anatomy of Shame she presented to the class. Once she had set her intention to do this, the material came in right on cue, and she was transported back to her days as a nun and the vows of chastity she had taken in several timelines. The body was bound so that any curves would be flattened. The head was shaved of hair. This had left an imprinting around any sexual impulse and sexual activity as 'bad' and the female body and physical beauty as something to be ashamed of. In this lifetime her oncoming womanhood had seemingly resulted in her father's rejection. Therefore, she registered her sexual self as evil. Her partners in this vignette helped re-bind her so that she could authentically access this part of her psyche. It was a very moving and cathartic process for her and others in her group as the deep and dark shame came up for transmutation.

Shame is the absolute lowest frequency of all human emotions and sadly runs deeply in the shadows for many people. For her, it had caused shyness, a tendency to introvert, an inability to truly love herself, a lack of trust in her own body, and, of course, the attraction of abusive relationships.

After this deeply transformational piece, she had been guided to a personal trainer in Toronto who helped her transform and strengthen her physical body while she underwent this transformative spiritual process. He was from South Korea, was raised Catholic, and had come to Canada almost penniless.

Through his own commitment and devotion to his craft, he became Canada's number one personal trainer. He was something of an enigma to her, and although they worked well together and she, for the most part, enjoyed her training with him, there was something about her attraction to this young man that alerted her to the fact that this was another 'special' karmic meeting. She worked hard and found this actually helped her spiritual process as the body released toxins and excess weight. He was delighted with her progress. Her chronological age was now fifty-nine, but his tests revealed that she had a biological age of thirty. She was beginning to like her body! He made her look at herself in the huge wall mirror in the gym. He would go away and come back after ten minutes and make sure she was still looking in the mirror. She noticed that he was recording on film every session. Her physical training ended up in a spectacular transformation of her physical body and it was no coincidence that it was taking place at the same time as her inner transformation. It was her suggestion that he set up his own gym. All their work together had taken place at the premier gym group at that time in Canada. Her results were astonishing, and he would use them as a testimonial and process of transformation to showcase his own skills and set up his own business. He married and had wanted Joan to invest in the business and work with him to bring Yoga and a healing facility to the new venture. His new wife also became a partner in the business, and it was Joan's intuition that any kind of partnership with her involved would not work. Her intuition was accurate as they parted after about two years, and he had to pay her out. He did, however, manage to survive this financial downturn and created an extremely successful fitness business in Toronto and online that now incorporates yoga and holistic practices.

Training-wise, he had pushed her to her limit, as her body results testified. However, their entire time together had worked beautifully in tandem with a new consciousness developing around her hard-won ability to truly love, honor, and care for herself. He had certainly enabled her to develop that absolutely necessary change of her inner perception of self as being worthy and enough.

When the time was in Divine order, it was revealed to her that he was the reincarnation of her mother. Her mother passed in March 1981. He was born in Aug 1981. Only Divine Love could have orchestrated this help for her to heal the guilt and, shame, and self-hatred she had carried as a result of her mother's death. They are friends to this day.

Her other Anatomy of an Emotion presentation choice was that of Joy. This was and still is a most sacred and memorable piece for the student Joan. She used her Yoga to present to each individual class member a particular pose that represented their own core essence. For her, this was an extremely joyful and divinely inspired process, to use the body that had caused so much shame and pain within her now as a tool for the expression of Divine Love. Expressed through her own core with the intention to mirror the core essence of love that is the other/s. Her body moved with wisdom and shone its light.

Her mantra through these school years was:

"Love is the most healing force in the world

Nothing goes deeper than love

It heals not only the body, not only the mind but also the soul.

If one can love, then all one's wounds disappear…

The innermost core of one being can be healed only through love

Those who know the secret of love

Know the greatest secret of life, "*Osho*

This is still one of her favorite quotations.

And from Hands of Light by her own beloved teacher, Dr Barbara Ann Brennan:

"Love is the face and body of the universe. It is the connective tissue of the universe, the stuff of which we are made. Love is the experience of being whole and connected to universal Divinity.

I want to encourage you to step out of the normal bounds of your life and begin to see yourself differently. I want to encourage you to live your life at the cutting edge of time, allowing yourself to be born into a new life every minute. I want to encourage you to allow your life experience to be lightly dusted with form."

The Canadian Rockies

The summer of 2011 was her sixtieth birthday, and to celebrate, she took herself off to the west once more, this time to climb and hike in the majestic Canadian Rockies.

On landing in Calgary, she found the hire car company had upgraded her booking to a spectacular red Corvette because it was her birthday! And thus, she began her time in the Rockies with a superlative drive on the Trans-Canada Highway to the Yoho Valley National Park, where her luxurious log cabin at the Cathedral Mountain Lodge awaited. Built close to the Kicking Horse River, this became her own private sanctuary in the mountains for the duration of her trip, and it could not have been more beautiful or nourishing on all levels.

She truly loved the Rocky Mountains of Canada. They are majestic, solid structures of the earth that helped her ground all the transformations occurring within her consciousness and also in her physical framework. She hiked for miles alone, without any fear whatsoever but with a solid knowing she was supported, held, and loved by this earth. Any time she was required to be in a group to take a particular hike, miraculously, people would simply appear, so she was able to join them. Some of the trails demanded only group permission because of the bears that inhabit certain locations. Her connection to all life intensified – the rocks and minerals, the kingdoms of the plants, trees, flowers and fauna, the animals and the birds, the translucent waters of the turquoise lakes, the sun that shimmered crystalline on their surfaces and warmed her as she walked, the sweet freshness of the air and the vastness of the space which held it all. She would forever bless and give thanks for these gifts of nature and the elements that painted a sublime picture on the canvas that is the earth. The whole trip was filled with beauty and magic and she felt so very blessed and grateful to experience this astonishing wonderment of the natural world and the elements from which it is comprised.

Her most beautiful and rewarding eleven days in the mountains included a visit to the ethereal Lake Louise in Banff National Park where, while floating in a canoe at the center of the turquoise lake, she received a vision superimposed on the steep walls of the mountain encasing the lake, of the face of Christ adjoined to the face of a strong and powerful Native American Chief. A stunning reflection for her and a most precious birthday present.

On return from the summer break in the Rockies, she resumed work in Toronto and threw herself into the final year of her time at the Brennan Healing School with great enthusiasm, commitment, and devotion. By the time 2012 arrived, she had a life choice to make: whether to stay in Canada and go west or return to the UK.

She had worked in Canada on a self- employed basis since 2009, and her project had shown her desire to continue with the company in some kind of partnership that could bring her work on communications into the mainstream eventually. She had spoken about this with the CEO, and he was always encouraging while there was a chance she would stay with them. He had supported her move from the UK, helped her with visa, permanent residency, and citizenship applications, and had been really helpful in accommodating all her travel needs for school. For her part, she had developed their global sales and, managed the staff, and had stayed much longer than originally intended. It had been a win -win. No one could doubt that.

However, relations had become frosty when several issues around sexual abuse of female staff arose and how they should be handled. For the first time, she realized that the veneer of support for women in business, which was always enthusiastically proclaimed by the company, was perhaps not as fully authentic as it seemed when it came to taking the right action in these situations.

A totally unrelated matter became the defining moment for her when, following the release of the current COO, a female member of her team was subtly threatened with disciplinary action and possible termination if she even attended his leaving celebration.

This was like a red rag to a bull for Joan, whose entire working life had been some form of a fight with an established patriarchal dominant energy. She reacted very badly in an unseemly outburst directed at the CEO, which shocked her as much as the recipient. She had to leave the building in order to re-compose herself, but it seemed irreparable damage had been done in that moment of anger.

This was, of course, was, the worst possible way to approach a rigid personality structure that closes down emotions, shies away from conflict, and is passive-aggressive in relational attitude. She knew better.

Even after all the work she had done around understanding these issues at school it sadly marked the end of her relationship with the man and the company that had brought her to Canada. She knew her work there was finished for now at least; however, it was her preference to leave in a more gracious way. To that end she agreed to do three final trips after her return to the UK on his behalf to Italy,

Germany, and Israel. At the time, this was not an easy decision for her. Once again, she was placing integrity before security. Her future was unknown. Most thought she was crazy for not staying and settling in Canada; she was now in her sixties.

After her graduation from the BBSH ASBIW program in 2012 she had hoped to continue her studies for an additional year and be enrolled for the teacher training in Europe. There was a teacher somewhere in her wishing to emerge. However, there was a great shift in the school that year. Many of the current faculty had already resigned. The school in Japan closed in 2010, and there was talk of the European school closing. It did actually close down in 2015. Her dreams of teaching at BBSH were not to be. The great shifting energies of 2012 could be felt by all. The energy was palpable.

Austria

It seems, as usual, her soul had its own plan and instead, she went on to do an MSc in Psychosocial and Integrative Health Science, a program that had been specially designed for the Brennan Alumni at the University of Graz, Austria. The university premises for her program was an old castle in Graz, and this time, the students were mostly from European schools, not the USA. There was plenty of fodder for additional process work. Plus, it was easier to travel there from the UK. Once again, there was a flow to the next step that made her decision -making process easy. Everything was always synchronous and obvious. She was very grateful for this opportunity as it was obvious to her, that she still required a vehicle for her to do more group shadow work after her disappointing contretemps with the business owner in Canada.

She also loved to learn and participate in groups. She did not know at the time, but this was all preparatory work for her future. Although this entire program was a much more academic venture, it had given her the impetus to really research the science aspect of energy and consciousness work. In many ways, this was a perfect opportunity for her to truly understand the material she would eventually download and bring into book form, as she was not a science major and was more inclined towards the arts. Throughout the research to which she was absolutely guided, she realized that there was a synthesis occurring between science and metaphysics that was revealing the amazing truth behind all life and physical reality.

Through her attendance at the University, she was inspired to create a book across all the disciplines for the newly emerging science that underpinned the comprehensive spiritual work she had been doing with energy and consciousness at school, and that incorporated ancient wisdom with a pathway for evolving consciousness. The process of downloading and writing her first book, The Quantum Keys, became a great gift that helped her own integration of the material as much as those who may be drawn to its frequency.

Germany

In Germany, she would find several more very interesting time capsules to integrate. By far, the most powerful of these was the impulse to go to Bavaria to meet an alumnus from the European school. When she looked at his photograph, his face literally transfigured into a shimmering light that resembled the Christ ... a strong signal to her there was something here for them both. Whenever these visions showed up it was an inevitable signal for her to follow without question. Her level of commitment to her path could never be denied. She followed these signals and the feelings in her heart and they always brought in miracles. Perhaps not the ones she thought she wanted, but definitely the ones she required for her and others' soul growth. This time was no exception. She planned a holiday week in the beautiful, historic spa town of Bad Tolz. The alumnus had agreed to meet with her. All on accomplished on social media, a miracle in itself.

They met, chatted, and had some lunch. He was extremely beautiful and interested in body building and obviously health. She had her new body at this time, and so they had this interest in common as well as their mutual studies at BBSH. As time passed, she became aware he was married. His social profile had not indicated this, and a little disappointment set in as she soon realized this was not to be about romance. Yet, he was a charming host and very intuitively suggested they climb a local hill known as Calvary Hill.

The Mount of Calvary was the site outside the gates of Jerusalem where the crucifixion of Christ had supposedly taken place. The scene was replicated around the world in numerous "calvary hills" after the Counter-Reformation and they are used by Roman Catholics in particular as part of their worship and veneration of God.

At the top of the path punctuated by stations of the cross 'doppelkirche' or two adjoining churches known as the crowns of this beautiful town. They entered and sat together on the wooden bench at the back of the church and went into silent meditation. Then, for her, the vision began. The altar of the church transfigured into a wedding altar with beautiful flowers. It then changed into a decaying scene with dust and cobwebs and the flowers had all died. They had been supposed to marry; he was deeply in love with her, but she had placed loyalty to her family before him. They had not wanted her to marry him and so she had not turned up for the wedding. This betrayal had compounded a distrust of women generally that had caused him to constantly be searching for recognition, appreciation, and validation outside himself. She required his understanding and forgiveness for compounding his original wounding but was also there to trigger the original cause of this through his own family imprinting.

She had also known him in Essene times, and their lives were simple and devoted. She was moved by what she saw but did not tell him anything. They came out of the church and went to look at the magnificent view below of the river that ran through this land and the town below. She also received another vision where they were had been some kind of nobility, possibly even royalty, and they looked out together across the land that was once ruled by them. They had been together for several lives, including a Native American incarnation. They did not speak. There was no need. Both knew something was unfolding. He took her back down the hill and back to her hotel. She now had to process this for herself before she could share it with him.

She spent the next several days walking beside the river that ran through the town; she fell on the road where she had fallen before in another timeline.

She was being shown opposites- a person with two dogs, one black, one blond. The light in her room was dingy and dark, in the shadows ....

The following day, after watching a group of white swans on the river, one lonely black swan came swimming straight towards where she was sitting on the river bank. Then she saw graffiti on the wall of one of the old buildings along the river path. It was projecting the word love in big, bold capital letters. The town itself reminded her of Bath, where she had lived. In fact, it was a combination of Bath, Bradford on Avon, and the Canadian Rockies. Her last three points of residence.

And then the knowing came in ... she was being shown the real reason she had come to this place. She was being shown another even deeper shadow within her. There were still traces of a requirement for validation from the external. The 'need' for love and validation from others is externalized when truly it can only come from the inner self. She was his mirror, and he was her mirror. All the work on the external body they had both done to create external beauty....and yet the real beauty was already there within each of them.

Like her, he was searching for something outside himself, outside his marriage, for validation and why he had not made as much progress in integrating the healing work with his fitness offer as he had shared. This is why he had agreed to meet her.

She was still looking outside herself for validation instead of fully giving herself the love that she 'needed.' There it was. This was what her Yoga teacher had told her and what she also knew from a cognitive understanding but had not yet integrated this knowing into a fully embodied experience that could be maintained. The true Love of Self. To know oneself as Love. It is a very necessary part of the full awakening process. To first fully love the self before one can realise there is no separate self. She had traveled all this way only to meet her mirror and perhaps to help him realize the same.

He had arranged to pick her up for a trip to his local gym. They did a workout together, changed, and then went for a coffee before he took her back. While they were together in the car, she was moved to ask him if he minded if she placed her hand on his heart. He agreed. As she placed her hand on his heart, she knew healing was happening through a transmission for both of them. When it was over, he thanked her and took her back to her hotel. He told her he would not see her again before she left as he was going to a workshop in the Black Forest about astral work concerning the Essenes. Ah, there it was, the synchronous confirmation for her of what and why she had received the information that had begun to be revealed at Hollyhock. She smiled and wished him well.

She knew that what had been accomplished was huge for her. Forgiveness was the key. She was there to shake up his process, perhaps, but more so to make an embodied realization for herself. She also was required to forgive him an infidelity of the past. These were the layers of that onion of betrayal by them both. Peeled away by her mere intention to meet her soul family and do the work that was needed. Powerful stuff.

It was a pivotal point for her to realize she no longer 'needed' validation of worth from any external sources. It was also a very powerful statement for her that the mirror of the external world is of the inner consciousness; she was really beginning to see and experience this more and more. No more would she need to search outside herself for that love she had felt during that very first awakening process in yoga. There it was within and would always, always be there. However, as she fully embodied this she would be guided to meet and heal the others in her soul family with the same issues. It was the actual healing of ancestral and genetic karma.

The next day, she was guided to take a train to a nearby mountain called the Brauneck, and she climbed to the top. There, she found a massive wooden cross at the summit, but it was empty. It had no body hanging there like all the other crosses in this place. And she finally got what the mirror was showing her. Time to come down from the cross .... No more suffering, no more searching for Love. All is within.

Turin

Next stop on her way back to Canada was Turin, a trip for the Canadian company. The significance of the place that housed the shroud of the crucified Christ was not lost on her, together with its message of resurrection. During her free time, she visited the famous Museo Nationale del Cinema. While there she managed to get an incredible picture on film. Somehow, she accidentally took a photo of the overhead camera that was facing the elevator door opening as she stepped out. To this day, she does not know how the image appeared on her phone, but it shows the opening of the elevator, her feet, and instead of her physical body, a full blast of an exquisite ball of iridescent pearlized light that filled the opening as she stepped from the elevator. A photo of her own core essence taken as she stepped out of the elevator at the Museo Nazionale del Cinema in Torino. A trick of light, mirrors, and reflection. Isn't that what a hologram is? Isn't that what the whole of the manifested form is? Synchronistically,this had all taken place in the Museum of Cinema. The Universe could not have been clearer with its messaging. External reality is simply a picture on the screen of the mind.

What was even more amazing was that the three places she had agreed to visit for the Canadian company had been pivotal in bringing all this information to her. At some level of their souls, she and her Canadian CEO and his wife had without doubt been working together. He had enabled this incredible soul journey from the very beginning by offering her a position in Canada, and for this, she was and is eternally grateful. Their soul contract with one another was about much more than any of them knew at the time. She had reached out to him several times after time had gone by, but he had never replied. Therefore, the memory of their time together and the deeper explanation of what it was all truly about is included in this book with great Love, Blessing, and Thanksgiving for all that passed during her time in Toronto and an acknowledgment of the Divine forces that conspire to bring us to whom and what we need exactly when we need it.

Only Love is real. Everything else is a story we make up caused by our hidden memories (karma) and imaginings that are often incorrect perceptions based on our conditioning by these memories.

Goodbye to the Americas

She returned to back to the UK in Aug 2013 via a trip to Asheville, North Carolina, to see her old school buddy for one last time. Shar was an ancient starseed like her so it was not surprising they had found each other at school. There were many starseeds at this school. They were also deeply connected through their Indigenous history and Atlantean memories, and they had actually done much beautiful healing work together during their time at the Brennan school. They spent an idyllic holiday week together in a most beautiful cabin in the Appalachian Mountains, enjoying the plethora of flowers and fauna of the forested slopes and the wisdom of the bees who were constantly showing up in beautiful ways, pointing them both to their future abundance.

This was followed by her much-anticipated visit to Cuernavaca, Mexico, to attend the first Children of the Sun Conference and to meet Tiara Kumara, Founder of the Children of The Sun Foundation. A reminder that this was a non -profit educational platform that offered opportunities for the evolution of consciousness. Its mission was to form a global group, Avatar, to serve all humanity and the evolution of the race. Together, they would link and focus their collective intention on the Crystalline Grid (the earth's energy field) and transmit their own codes of accomplishment to help trigger even greater levels of mass awakening. Through intention and their own frequency, they acted as human portals and extensions of the earth's own energy grid system and they were directing tremendous amounts of transforming energy from this grid to the emergent world. All human beings are, in fact, cells in the body of the earth and can have dramatic effects when consciously aware of this interdependence.

During this trip Joan was guided to do two excursions in her free time. Her first visit was to Tepoztlan. According to mythology, Amatlán, in the municipality of Tepoztlan, is the possible birthplace of the Mesoamerican god Quetzalcoatl over twelve hundred years ago, the feathered serpent god widely worshipped in ancient Mexico. She climbed the small pyramid there and meditated for a little while.

She was then guided to the larger pyramids at Teotihuacan, where the Avenue of the Dead links the Pyramid of the Sun and the Pyramid of the Moon. She was guided to lie on top of each pyramid just as the sun reached its highest point in the sky over each one. She literally was filled with the Sun amplified by the connection to the pyramids and, indeed, at that moment, became a true child of the Sun.

She had been working long-distance with Tiara and the group since the inception of COS in 2007, all through her school years. She had found this was a beautiful support as well as an opportunity for humanitarian service while she was doing the deep inner work. She felt very much attuned to Tiara. Through the conference and the confluence of souls that she had met there, she made new connections and was being prepared for the next cycle in her development. Among these connections there was a fellow, Brennan alumnus. He was originally from New Zealand and had attended the European school in Mondsee and Bad Ischl for four years. He gave a very impressive presentation at the conference and both he and Tiara would prove to be pivotal connections in her next cycle of life and spiritual development. But for now, it was time to celebrate, honor, and enjoy all that had been accomplished during her last seven years in Canada and the USA.

Back to the UK

S he finally left Toronto in Aug 2013 and initially stayed with her sister, who graciously helped her 'land' back in her home country. She was once again in the unknown, without income, a job, a car, or a home.

Winter brought her final promised assignment for the Canadian company, a trip to Tel Aviv, Israel. Here, she would meet the brilliant visionary, creator, writer, and entrepreneur coach Aviad Goz and his partner Roni. Together, they created the Momentum Group, now a leader in corporate coaching.

His current words echo all that is positive for the future of humanity when they accept self- responsibility and rise from victimhood into their sovereignty by free will choice.

"I was born in a time after the great wars. My parents were holocaust survivors from Dachau and the "March of Death." I was raised to believe in hope, in the ability of mankind to elevate itself by choice to be better.

Throughout my adult life, I dedicated myself to exploring and creating teachings, programs, and writings for human development now. I believe people can choose their future and even their state of mind. People can develop to have a greater consciousness and they can create the kind of life they want and the organizations they want to be part of.

I believe we are all born to contribute to our time and era to the best we can. We live in a most important time in human evolution.

The world must be a better place when we leave it after our short visit here. I am honored to have become a messenger of joy and hope for many." Aviad created his own Garden of Eden in Panama, where he now lives.

During her two- day stay in Tel Aviv, on her back appeared dreadful red impressions as if she had been whipped. Some kind of energetic imprinting that carried no pain or even memory of what this might be. The only thought that came to her was the scourging of Christ. Given the seemingly ever-ongoing troubles experienced in these lands, it is not surprising, as an empath, that she would materialize this in some way. She felt no physical pain, but the overall incoherent energy of the place was unmistakable, and she was more than happy when business was completed, and she boarded the plane back to London. As soon as she left the country, the marks on her back disappeared. She read this as an out-picturing of the low vibrational frequency present there that insists on replaying the 'crucifixion' of an opposing view rather than embracing and allowing freedom for all choices. Perhaps the marks on her back indicated the times in the past when she had judged others or had been judged by others. It was certainly congruent with the wounds to her back that had been shown to be inflicted physically by the many back stabbings and betrayals while working in the lower astral dimension during her second school year. Either way, it was all over now, and interestingly, in her present reality, she had been shown a new type of leader whose efforts were showing business leaders a new and better way forward.

It took several months of contemplation before she realized she was not meant to buy a property but to keep on renting as she had done in Canada. She knew she needed a place to settle in order to ''write, "and by Christmas, she had bought 'a small white chariot' otherwise known as a Hyundai i10, and her prayers for a suitable resting place were answered. On an impulse she had gone to the Iford website just to take a peek at the beautiful gardens and valley that had been her home before leaving for Canada and that remained in her heart. And there it was!!! The cottage again had just been put back on the market for rental that week! She called the agents the next day, explained she was a previous tenant, and booked an appointment. It was hers within the week.

They were delighted to see her return as she had been an exemplary tenant, and by January 2014, she was back in her old home with a full refurbishment and the beautiful stray black cat who had landed on her bedroom windowsill at her sister's place during the Christmas break. She tried to find his owner, but it seemed he was abandoned. She took him to Iford with her. She had so loved that place and it was a perfect location for writing and for cats.

She truly loved her ancient country cottage in Iford and its glorious location in the Iford valley. She had found it walking with her dogs long before the first time she rented the cottage in 2005. She had often wondered what it would be like to live there. The place held a certain healing energy, and there is no doubt each time she lived there, she had profound opening and healing experiences. This second visit was to last for seven years. She would find out much later that the cottage was actually situated on the main Mary / Michael ley lines that ran from Avalon (Glastonbury) right across to the other coast of Britain.

This ley line actually connected up with the main Athena /Apollo energy line that began at Solomon's Temple in Jerusalem and crossed southern and northern points in Europe, including the

Temple at Delphi, to eventually enter Britain at St Michael's Mount in Cornwall.

Its relevance will become clearer further into the tale.

Amazon, Peru and Casa Shipibo

Year 2014 saw the completion of her studies in Austria, and she celebrated by taking a trip to the Amazon with her friend Tiara and her group to Casa Shipibo, on the upper Ucayali River near the headwaters of the Amazon, on the eastern slopes of the Peruvian high Andes Mountains.

She would be taking part in Sacred Ceremony and her first introduction to plant medicine, facilitated by Tiara and the Shamans of the Casa Shipibo tribe. This was her first experience with the plant medicine Ayahuasca and the family who make their own mix of ayahuasca vine and chacruna leaves. It is considered a sacred ceremony where the group participants join the family to find the plants in the jungle and then prepare the ingredients for the pot, infusing them with their intention for the ceremonies.

"The first step is to clean the vine segments of moss or other plant matter that is not ayahuasca. This can be done by washing the vine segments or by scraping the bark with a knife to ensure that nothing other than the ayahuasca vine will be going into the brew. Making ayahuasca is a long process, so sometimes, the vines are cut and cleaned one day and prepared the next. Fasting is often practiced during the preparation of sacred medicine to maintain energetic purity.

Once the vine segments are clean, they are then mashed with a wooden mallet or hammer. This breaks the vine into thinner strands, increasing their surface area and allowing more extraction of their medicinal essence. The vines are hard, so it is important to strike them well but not so hard as to pulverize the segments. Sometimes, the curanderos sing icaros during this process to communicate their intentions with the spirit of the vine and make the effects stronger.

Once the vine segments are mashed into thin strands, they are placed in the pot along with the chacruna leaves, which are torn into small pieces. Then, water is poured in until it just covers the plant material entirely. The pot is put over a fire and brought to a boil. Cooking times vary greatly, as do cooking temperatures, controlled by the size of the fire, but the goal is the same: to reduce the water in the pot while absorbing the medicinal essences of the plants being cooked.

When the curandero feels the brew has cooked long enough, the water is removed from the pot and saved, leaving the plant material. This is called the first 'wash.' More water is then added to the plant material, and the boiling process is repeated. This procedure may be done several times with the same plant material. Each reduction increases the strength of the final brew because more medicine is extracted each time, and more liquid is produced for the last reduction, which is done without plant material.

Once all the reductions are done, just the liquid is combined and put back on the fire to reduce it further. The reduction is the final step in the cooking process and determines the strength of each dose. Therefore, the curanderos watch carefully as the liquid is reduced, making sure that it is at the strength he/she desires. The curandero stays with the brew the entire time during its preparation.

When the brew if finally done cooking, it is taken off the fire to cool. Dozens of liters of water are reduced into one or two liters of prepared medicine. The final step, when the brew has cooled, is to filter the medicine to remove any remaining plant material. This is often done with a fine cloth. The curandero then says a final prayer over the medicine to bless it. The brown liquid is then put into a bottle to save for the ceremony.

She was impressed by the care and love with which the medicine was prepared.

The Shipibo tradition is widely regarded as the most intact and profound of the indigenous traditions that use ayahuasca. While there are certainly numerous complexities within the philosophy and methodology of the tradition, there is one underlying principle that pervades the entire practice: cleanliness. The basic understanding is that within every living being, every cell is an innate movement toward wholeness and harmony. This motivating principle is a conscious force that acts on its own and forms the root of all life as we know it. It is an intelligent directive towards health and it works from micro to macro levels of existence. From cells repairing themselves to planetary and galactic movement, this mysterious energy constantly strives to maintain balance and achieve optimum health. This intelligent motivating principle that pervades all things, this divine directive at the root of all life, can be called God.

The Shipibo tradition is centered around the idea that if the obstacles to healing are removed, then God will take care of the rest. So, their healing tradition is based heavily on cleansing and purification. While the example of healing a cut is merely a physical process, the healing of most afflictions goes beyond just the physical dimension, for we are not just physical bodies. We are spirits, we are minds, we are emotional beings. Therefore, we must cleanse all of our bodies; we must purify ourselves on every level in order to achieve the most complete health possible. The Shipibo work to achieve this through the use of a wide variety of plant medicines, including ayahuasca, to assist the natural healing that strives to regain balance and harmony, and therefore, the tradition works closely with God." https://www.ayahuascafoundation.org/shipibo-tradition/

This first retreat was a truly wonderful experience. The energy of the land alone and the Amazon rainforest and jungle brought in such a magical combination and she felt so thrilled to be able to be there. Her experiences during the five ceremonies she attended during the retreat were very useful pieces of integration of more soul fragmentation. She had seen herself as a beautiful young man on this land, and he came to be with her to show himself during one of the ceremonies. He wanted her to know she had been there before and had lived and belonged there. This vision she was able to tie into the vision she had at school that showed her walking through a sea of blood. She carried the guilt of being the only survivor of some atrocity. The loss of an entire tribe, with her as she was then, being the only survivor. The loss of 'family 'was a deep and ancient wound she had carried for eons. This version showed her as the only survivor of some terrible happening and the guilt felt by the young man as being the sole survivor. At this point, she had no other information. Was this the root fractal of this awful imprint? Or just a layer of the onion?

She had also experienced herself as a beautiful insect of some kind just sitting on a huge green leaf in the rainforest, watching the large raindrops bouncing off her leaf. The forest was verdant, lush, and magnificent. She saw the roof of the temple simply open to the dark night sky where the moon shone, and a myriad of stars twinkled. Huge, gentle extra-terrestrial beings were just surrounding and looking in from the open temple roof, holding the space and guiding this beautiful process of unfolding for her. She felt their tender love and felt secure and safe. However, many in the group did not have the same experience, and this confirmed for her that we really do create our own experiences based on our own coding and consciousness.

Her consciousness was once more transported to her mother's womb, where she could feel again her mother's fear of giving birth to her but also her love. Perhaps because she had already done so much soul retrieval work, this experience was even more beautiful for her now as she knew she had nothing to fear. This entire retreat was a gift of a very deep connection to the plant kingdom, the earth, and its natural beauty, as well as the awareness of another layer of trauma and its cause. However, the awareness is never just enough. It needs to be processed in some way forgiven, and integrated into the now moment.

It was during this retreat she received the name Athena. She had no idea what this was about. When Tiara asked her name, she spontaneously replied her name was Athena without having any conscious awareness or even thought. It just came out of her without any thought process at all. She figured it was just another dip into one of the other dimensions that, by now, she was getting used to navigating. She would sit with this 'information' for the next two years before it came to mind again.

The Quantum Keys

S ettling back into the peace and beauty of the English countryside in her old home in Wiltshire initiated the downloading of the Quantum Keys through her fingers. The writing began, and every day continued non- stop until the book was finished.

The study for her MSc in Psychosocial and Integrative Health Science had prompted the research into all the incredible work across all disciplines that was trying to emerge at that time into mainstream science with some difficulty. There were so many different disciplines, all with incredible findings about the newly emerging quantum science, but the disciplines worked in silos that did not speak or refer to one another, so no -one of them really had the whole picture.

This realization brought forth part one of The Quantum Keys – Synthesis and Synergy that spoke to all the research from macro to micro across all the disciplines, from cosmology to cellular biology. It was and still is an encounter with the incredible newly unfolding science as revealed through fact, theory, and experiment and an exploration of the scientific revolution that demonstrates humankind's new understanding of the nature of reality.

It was quite an undertaking, and it has to be said she was guided infallibly by the scientists themselves who came through her one after the other to put these first chapters together. It is still a great reference point for this differing view from the old Newtonian physics and Cartesian theory that had guided the collective since the Scientific Revolution in the 17th Century.

The book was designed to describe the synthesis between science and metaphysics that reveals the amazing truths behind all physical reality, and whilst part one deals comprehensively with energy, part two, aptly named The Keys to the Kingdom, takes the reader into the realms of multi-dimensional consciousness and psycho-energetics as experienced by the author, and includes a pathway of practices others can follow in the final section, The Energetic Highway.

She self-published the book first in 2015 as Manifest Your Magnificence under her physical family name of Joan Walmsley and then republished with several amendments in 2017 under the soul family name Athena Melchizedek as The Quantum Keys: Unlock your Energetic Intelligence.

Although the book was written with the intention of helping others as a point of reference, particularly energy healers, the person it helped most was its author. It was a huge undertaking. However, she found it a very grounding experience as it brought her into a fuller integration of all the knowledge and lived experiences of her life to date and laid a firm foundation for all that was still about to unfold....

PART 4: A MORE ADVANCED

SPIRITUAL CLASSROOM

Spiritual Ego

The next couple of years brought her into wider contact with more members of her own soul family. That grouping had incarnated with a very similar energetic blueprint and soul contracts for this specific timeframe. Unknown to her, she was about to enter more fully the consciousness field of a group of souls called the Melchizedek. Please note this is not the same branch of the Priesthood associated with the Mormons and the Church of the Latter-Day Saints and should not be confused with them.

There was so much more she had to learn. Each time she thought she was 'done,' it seemed like everything kicked off again with very little time for pause. You may remember she had met a BBSH School alumnus at the conference in Mexico. She had done a little facilitation work with one of his very early online groups and some charity work for youth via a charitable foundation he was associated with at that time. While they were on the train to this venue, he had told her of his download and vision of his own Melchizedek heritage. While he spoke, she was also receiving a vision and information of a multitude of injured women this being was karmically here to serve.

They lost contact for a while when he headed off to Ibiza to set up a new life there, but their paths re-crossed via a connection who was doing some intriguing healing work online with his then-wife. They were doing DNA clearing work using geometric codes, which his wife downloaded and created into art forms, while he would provide the verbal commands for the clearing procedures. At this time, this was an entirely new way of approaching energy work, and she was genuinely intrigued. She became even more interested when she realized her new Melchizedek contact and his new business partner had also been his students.

Since she had left the school, she had noticed her own healing procedures had changed a lot as directed by her own guides. She was doing more and more remote energy transmission work rather than hands-on. She was, therefore, very intrigued by these new remote online teachings and so she enrolled as a student. It would only last a year. During this time, she met them both in Las Vegas for a conference for one of their own mentors and realised all was not well. The conference itself was about sales and money- making, and they were supporting their own mentor with this event. She met and spoke with Ivonne who was giving her a very clear vibe that all was not well in her marriage. She seemed hypervigilant and on edge. He, on the other hand, seemed laid back, non-communicative, and slightly flirtatious.

The red flags were waved and finally compounded by an email that was sent out by Toby to his students, which directly attacked the feminine. At first, she thought it was a joke and then a mistake to send this out to female students. When she brought this up with him, he told her it was her own issues with men that had not been resolved. This illustrates a very important point and why it is imperative that one does the deep inner shadow work that enables one to know when an issue is one's own and when it is clearly the other who has the unresolved issue. It was only through her own psycho-energetic studies with Brennan and the work that she had done to reconcile and heal her own issues she could recognize the dynamic that was going on, and for all the big talk, there was still deep inner spiritual clearing work to be done by this being. It was very obvious to her and equally obvious that she should not continue in his group. He had claimed to be a reincarnation of Kuthumi, a luminary called Shivananda Brahmananda, guided by Babaji. However, his teachings were actually from the Keylontic Science brought through by Ashayana Deane, one of the speakers for a group called the Melchizedek Cloister Emerald Order or MCEO, and published in her books Voyager One and Two. Joan never once heard him give attribution to this, their source. The codes of transformation used were created by his wife, Ivonne. He and his wife parted not long after this visit to the US. However, she was able to speak with Ivonne about the situation. She stated it was not her intention to be charging huge amounts of money for the codes/programs. His offers had all become very convoluted, on the one hand, selling codes and practices to clear the energy field and, on the other, teaching students how to present webinars and make money from their businesses. In her case, he was coaching her on how to present herself and her work and make money from this. At this time on her journey, she saw nothing wrong with either, but the most important piece missing was any reference or practice of the deep the inner work required, on the level of consciousness, to hold any energetic clearings permanently in place. She should have paid attention to the red flags and her own intuition. She did not leave before he, in conjunction with one of his associated groups, had extracted approximately forty thousand pounds of her savings and then later appeared to her in a vision dressed in a silver suit, smoking a cigar and sitting back smugly blowing the smoke in her face. She had allowed herself to be manipulated and had handed over her power to another in the form of her money energy. It was a very large amount for her. What was this showing her about her relationship to power and money? Could it be a hidden unconscious belief that money is power? She had been brought up in a paradigm that rewarded those who 'worked hard' with the benefits of being able 'to buy' anything they perceived would bring them happiness. She was beginning to see an old hidden pattern that believed money could buy anything and an even more insidious thoughtform, an imprint, that the more expensive an object /service is, the better and more valuable it must be. This is not truth, but an erroneous perception that is the cause of much of the world's current distortion around wealth and abundance. She had certainly initially subscribed to this gross misperception very easily. Perhaps this was what her encounter with part of her shadow was trying to show her. Her entire value system was adrift. Because her entire thoughts about her own value had only been based on what she could 'earn' and a desire to please rather than simply who she was naturally. This is indicative of the erroneous educational, social and political systems currently under deconstruction.

The whole episode brought up a consideration of money and how it should be used generally in life, and, in particular in conjunction with the healing arts. There was no doubt in her mind, this being had very confused boundaries, and whilst there is a place for healthy exchange for services, true healing cannot be bought for any amount of money because, ultimately, it is dependent on the self. This is a key point. This really brought up for her the whole question of the term healing, who actually does the healing, and how powerful the mind is when it can convince itself that something or someone outside itself can produce a change in either mind, body, soul, or spirit. Beware! You are the only person that can heal you! This process can be accelerated by an education of the mechanics of the creation of disease in the body, mind and soul, all of which can manifest in a variety of different ways. However, healing, or bringing back to wholeness will always begin with recognizing some kind of erroneous thoughtform or distorted feeling about the self and why ultimately an inner exploration is necessary for external transformation at soul level to occur. The most invaluable lesson ultimately is the empowerment the 'mirror' can provide when it is recognized by one's own conscious awareness.

Sedona

The one beautiful part of this trip in 2015 to the USA was the opportunity she got to visit Sedona in Arizona. Sedona is one of the most unique sites in the American Southwest and is known for its dazzlingly beautiful red rock formations and Cathedral Rock, which dominates the skyline. It is, however, best known for its large number of energy vortices that enhance meditation and healing. While there, she met a very beautiful indigenous woman with whom she was able to experience a Medicine Wheel quest. The Sedona Native American tribes active in the area include the Hopi, Navajo, Tonto Apaches, and Yavapai.

She lay at the foot of the great Cathedral Rock, noted as the only vortex in this region that greatly enhances and supports the feminine, magnetic energy, and suddenly, during this dry, hot, sunny day, the heavens literally opened, and there was a downpour of rain that turned the River Verde into a sea of red water flowing by where she lay. She was deeply connected to the earth in a meditative trance and felt this, and the vast amount of water indicated an emotional cleansing of some kind. Not surprising after being with such low-frequency energies in Las Vegas.

She left refreshed and renewed, as if the earth and the waters had combined to cleanse and impart information. Either way, she felt wonderful and blessed. Just another miracle, but it would point to the overarching theme of her life, the healing story of reclaiming her own powerful feminine energy and dealing with the distorted masculine that was continually being reflected to her in her external reality. Her dealings with Toby had cost her much financially, but she could only blame herself. She had made that choice. It was a very expensive year for her tuition, and she takes full responsibility for her own foolishness and gullibility.

She was still naïve and new to this next elevation of the 'spiritual game' and still had plenty of her own work to do, it seemed. Her private guidance and studies around this time demonstrated to her the fine line between what one might call white and black magic. Up to a certain point on the path, self-professed 'spiritual teachers' may seem to the student to be able to access heretofore 'unknown' information and speak of meetings with "Ascended Masters, "all of which to them may seem like a peak experience. However, their own resonance will invite in many reflections which are not of unconditional love and acting for the highest good, no matter what invocations are made. They will attract entities from what is known in 'new age parlance' as the false white light deception. These are reflections of beings from the lower astral realms that wish to keep human souls in enslavement so that the polarity on which they thrive and from which they gain energy can continue. When the necessary inner work has not been completed, these beings attract entities which are synthetic, not emanating from Source consciousness but from that fragmented consciousness complex that creates the drama of good and evil. There can be lower astral 'angels' as well as lower astral 'demons' and lower astral 'ascended masters' where the consciousness has severed into extreme polarity. There can be lower 'Galactic Councils' and 'Federations' all playing upon the inexperienced and naïve seekers need for external validation as opposed to trusting fully their own internal guidance and ability to directly access truth from the Quantum Field (often called the Akashic record). The higher we raise our consciousness, the more we have to raise our discernment in order to recognize what and who is in truth. It is well to remember everything that we experience externally is only ever a projection of our own interior landscape. We can be drawn into these co-created scenarios in order to correct our erroneous thoughts and beliefs. This is the great work of the soul family, and obviously, Toby had come along to reflect to her a huge lesson.

At first, the being will speak some truth and even teach what may seem real and probable, but then they give themselves away, as in the example below that materialized into an overly alpha presentation of the fragmented aspect, pathological and degenerate not in alignment with universal law, not in alignment with natural law and not in alignment with Divine Love, Divine Intelligence and Divine Will. There is, in fact, at each new level of consciousness a new 'devil' to discern, and it must be remembered that all is revealing one's own interiority. It is the next layer of the onion. This is why Earth is considered the School for Mastery. Below is the projection onto women of the distorted interiority of this being in 2015. This email was sent to Joan:

"Have you ever noticed that most men are extremely disempowered?
Like they are living their lives for their wives, walking on eggshells, afraid to enjoy anything, and feeling guilty if they do? If so, you need to be on my next training webinar...
Brand New CRUCIAL Masterclass This Week for Men ONLY:
Attention: Married and Divorced Businessmen
Discover How to Unplug from the Feminine Matrix, UNLOCK the Omnipotent POWER in Your Business and Sex Life, and REGAIN Your Alpha Status

In this Masterclass, you will LEARN:
How the Soul Mate Myth has you paralyzed in a catastrophic,
terminal disease called ONEitis
The ugly truth and reality of what drives women and men and the
definition of Hypergamy
How to kill your inner Beta and re-activate the Alpha you were
born with so you CAN at least DOUBLE your income and
influence in your life.
How to get OUT of the Feminine Matrix, stop sacrificing yourself,
and actually DO what you WANT to do each day
This webinar is for MEN ONLY and is very TIMELY and
polarizing...
I'll be sharing some MONUMENTAL distinctions I've personally
made in the last 14 days that will EXPONENTIALLY up-level your
understanding of the screwed-up situation you are most LIKELY in
right now...
If you want to get out of the Feminine Matrix that you've been
conditioned to and worked as a SLAVE for *since practically*
BIRTH and know the TRUTH about women, money, marriage,
monogamy, love, and sex, then get one of the ONLY 100 spots here
->
I will be verifying who is on the webinar by microphone, and there
will be an NDA to sign beforehand, so this is not for curious
women trying to sneak on, ONLY MEN.
There is nothing for SALE on this webinar, just a dispensation of
the TRUTH from actual, real-life, sometimes painful, yet
absolutely transformative experiences.
Talk to you on Thursday at 1:00 pm Las Vegas time.
To your freedom,"
Toby ----

The clue to the state of consciousness of this being, apart from the obvious tone, is

"This webinar is for MEN ONLY and is very TIMELY and polarizing..."

These cannot be the words of a true master or a true spiritual teacher. Polarisation is the very opposite of that which is considered healing. Healing actually means making whole or bringing to a state of wholeness. One can activate this process for another with one's own frequency and light and guidance, but ultimately, the person will heal themselves by doing their own inner work that expands their awareness and releases more photons of light into the system. A state of complete wholeness is Unity Consciousness, not dual and not polarized. How could she possibly continue to be mentored by this consciousness field as a woman who had been abused by men? It became obvious he had his own unresolved issues with women and knew nothing about the psychological process.

After a further conversation with his wife, it was confirmed they were experiencing challenges in their marriage, and she confirmed her husband had unresolved issues with his own mother at this time. It was now very obvious to Athena from the above text that this being was in a wounded and reactive state. She asked to leave his mastermind group and requested a refund, which was declined.

The ultimate gift it brought her was the realization of how easily she betrayed herself and gave her own power away and to be more mindful of those setting themselves up as spiritual teachers. It was a very expensive lesson in terms of money and energy. However, deep inside, she knew that could be replaced. Whereas her own sovereignty and power is her own choosing always. And so she walked away.

It seemed the more inner work she did the greater challenges from the darkness she had to face. It would take her some time to understand that the brighter her light became the greater challenge would arise from the darkness to diminish it. However, in her times of doubt and fearfulness, she was always uplifted by the miracles that would manifest without any effort on her part. As always, she made her intention to be aligned with the great universal forces of Unconditional Love, Will, and Intelligence and did her best to surrender all control and just follow her guidance. She never tried to manipulate the universe; rather, more and more, allowed it to just bring forth the next step on the path for her own highest good. It always did.

Conscious Business

Early 2016 brought in the Conscious Business Initiative offered by Humanity's Team, a growing non-profit online spiritual community founded by Steve Farrell and Neale Donald Walsch, intent upon creating a conscious learning community and transformational education to support businesses and entrepreneurs on their conscious journey to create a sustainable earth and flourishing at every level of life.

She had been a Humanity's Team member since inception in 2003, drawn by the wonderful and life-changing Conversation with God books by Neale, and this new initiative made it a natural interest for her given her long business background. Here, she met many like-minded souls and, through her project for this program, created her very first educational program, Energetics for Business-The Quantum Keys Quick Start, which was enthusiastically attended and truly wonderfully supported by her teammates.

Sadly, the CBI program was closed down due to what appeared to be some incongruence and discord within the group leadership at that time. She spoke out and named this in a meeting with the leadership and the community. It has now resurrected as the Conscious Business Innerprise. Still, much gratitude is extended as through this association; she developed several deep and meaningful relationships and another very important soul contact that would unfold in meaning further along the journey.

As you might realize from this record so far, her journey has been a process of stages, each bringing in new people, new learning, new wisdom, a new awareness, a new opportunity for a choice to either heal an old pattern, help another heal a pattern or simply walk away from an energy that was not in alignment, no matter what the perceived cost. All situations have served and played a part in the game of raising her awareness and vibrational frequency and required a continued dedication of intention above all else to find truth and freedom from what may at first appear gross naivety or misjudgement of a situation. It became apparent to her, eventually, that absolutely everything that shows up, even if created from an unconscious perspective, can be turned to an advantage if we do not react but rather respond with discernment rather than judgment and simply make a new choice. It can be easier said than done, and often, we need the concept of time and a distance away from the issue to be able to process it and come to a higher choice. It inevitably involves forgiveness and acceptance of self and others. We are never not supported if we align with the will for good and develop our ability for compassion, forgiveness, and love despite all attempts to extinguish our light by our own poor choices. Everything we experience is our own responsibility and how we meet each challenge is the making of our own Mastery.

We came to blaze new trails, to create new pathways, to leave each path we have trodden an easier and more beautiful experience than perhaps we found it. As these words pour forth, Joan acknowledges with love and thanksgiving the great beings who have guided the process for this soul and is aware, ultimately, that they are all aspects of her own being and awareness.

Ibiza

Hot on the on the heels of her encounter with Toby she was drawn to re-connect with Christof Melchizedek. He had invited her to attend a new retreat he was offering in Ibiza that summer. Ibiza seemed an interesting choice as it epitomized the duality of hedonistic extravagance and drug and alcohol abuse of its world-renowned party scene on the one hand and a burgeoning 'new age spiritual community' on the other. In many ways a reflection of the entire planetary consciousness.

''Since the 1930s, the (then) little-known, mainly untouched, and completely unspoiled beauty of Ibiza has been a magnet for artists, musicians, poets, writers, and painters alike, who all used the island's peace and tranquillity to feed their creativity.

During the 1960s, in the era of flower power, it was a place where many peace-loving Americans fled to avoid the draft into military service for the Vietnam War, and it quickly became the hippie capital of Europe.

The island is purported to have magical, healing energy, which wraps around you the moment you step off the plane or boat, arrive to endless blue skies and (almost) year-round sunshine, and traveling through the outstanding beauty and scenery that surrounds Ibiza, you can absolutely see why so many claim the island to have mystical qualities.

Especially after watching (what is declared by many to be) one of the most stunning sunsets on earth, in which one can see a magical vista that has, quite literally, been celebrated for thousands of years, ever since the original Phoenicians settlers worshipped Baal, the sun god.

Probably the most renowned spiritual point on the island is Es Vedrà. The holy island of the lunar goddess Tanit, partner to the sun god Baal and patroness of Ibiza, she is a deity of the moon, a symbol of sexuality and fertility, and a heavenly goddess of war and dance is located to the southwest of Ibiza and part of the Cala d'Hort nature reserve.

The small uninhabited rocky outcrop is claimed to be the third most magnetic place in the world (after the North Pole and the Bermuda Triangle). There are several legends that surround Es Vedrà. It is reputed to be the tip of the sunken civilization of Atlantis. It is claimed that UFOs have been seen in the sky above the island. It is said that it is home to mermaids, sea nymphs, and sirens (some of which tried to lure the Greek King Odysseus from his ship in Homer's Odyssey). With all the mystery and supernatural activity that surrounds the triangular-shaped rock, it is a popular site for spiritual practices of all types."

It seemed like an ideal opportunity to combine a break with some further spiritual exploration. Christof Melchizedek and Akasha Sananda were now doing their own work on DNA re-genesis and after a Zoom call with Akasha, she immediately booked to go. Akasha had an extraordinarily beautiful heart energy resonance, and she was looking forward to meeting him in person. She was intrigued to hear what they had made of their connection to her erstwhile 'mentor' whose training they had now reconfigured into an offer of their own. They seemed like an ideal partnership. Akasha was a very gentle and gifted soul and quite a lot younger than Christof, but they seemed to complement one another and work well together. Christof always liked to work with beings who could 'see,' she had noticed. Akasha had told her he had seen a host of angels around her at their first meeting and this was such a nice experience for him. Very nice for her, too, but perhaps a subtle flattery and making sure she knew his gift.

The retreat was a great success, and she began working with them. It had always been Christof's dream to create a Healing School of his own and as they both had attended BBSH, it made logical sense for her at the time to join them. Her extended training and experience at the USA school meant she could offer them additional psycho-spiritual, psycho-energetic, and psycho-somatic practices that Christof had not covered in his European training and that Akasha's yogic training did not provide. Up to that point, their courses were focused on energy healings and activations but very little in the way of serious introspective process sessions, as far as she could ascertain, other than something that was called the 'hot seat.' Not a very inviting description of a sacred and safe container for a soul's personal process.

Eventually, the Institute of Divine Potential was born, and she became a program facilitator, facilitating two of their flagship programs, The Divine Keys Certification program and co-creating and facilitating the Divine Keys Facilitation Certification. These programs brought her fully into the group work she so loved to do. During this time, she attended several of their workshops and shamanic ayahuasca journeys in Ibiza and it was here her own Melchizedek heritage was confirmed.

She officially changed her name to Athena Melchizedek on 1 November 2016.

The Melchizedek Story

"There are three prime sound fields that make up all manifested creation in our Universe. The sound fields produce vibration, then light, and through sacred geometry and mathematical formulae, become formed in matter with a specific energetic structure.

- The first Sound field produces the light Emanation of the Blue Ray
- The second Sound Field produces the light emanation of the Gold Ray
- The third Sound Field produces light emanation of the Violet Ray

The Melchizedek are the Blue-ray holders. Melchizedek is the sound tone of the vibrational frequency of the original Source family of the collective unity consciousness of this Universe. This means all humans are directly descended from this pattern and are, therefore, in truth, Melchizedek. Yeshua, The Christ, was a Melchizedek.

These founder races kept records known as the Emerald Covenant CDT Holographic plates.

This refers to twelve holographic disc records made of selenite quartz crystals that were created on a star called Sirius B that contain the evolutionary history of life throughout this universe and was originally sourced from the great cosmic hall of records /akashic field/morphogenetic field. They hold the wisdom of the divine original, organic creation blueprint records of the natural laws of God. They were also known as the Maharata teachings of the Universal Melchizedek Lineages of the Cosmic Christ.

These records reveal that there were originally twelve Tribes of Hibiru that are twelve Essene Tribes, which make up the entirety of the collective human gene pool or are the descendants of the beings that originally incarnated onto this planet from the future timelines of Tara (5D earth). These spiritual teachings were commonly understood during the Lemurian and early Atlantean timelines. Each of the twelve tribes are genetically key coded to their demographic Planetary Gates location and to that planetary dimensional sphere and its ley line network.

When we incarnate onto the planet, we have genetic time codes in our DNA related to the planetary stargates dimensional system that is a part of our main human tribal identity.

This is activated when we are able to access our inner personal Divine blueprint or inner Christ consciousness. This identity has had many lifetimes that have participated in the consciousness evolution cycles of assembling DNA codes in the angelic human root races evolving throughout the Solar System.

There are different families of Melchizedek within the lineage, one of them being a type of "cosmic management team" for planetary systems that are under threat or have experienced genetic digression, and thus, they are able to incarnate to support and assist in bringing in particular energetic codes that can heal and reconfigure the distorted genetic instructions. Initially, they sought to repair the genetic distortions on this planet by seeding the twelve Essene Tribes.

However, unfortunately, a group of Melchizedek became energetically imbalanced and denied the Law of One in order to choose service to self through hierarchical domination and misogyny. They co -joined with an invader race, the Annunaki, to become the Fallen Melchizedek.

The original teachings of the founder records were then hijacked by the Fallen Melchizedek, and these blood lines started to lose their connection to the Mother Principle/Divine Feminine Energy as they succumbed to the illusion of inequality between genders. This eventually distorted the DNA base code to ten and not twelve and became the prime root of all control of the distorted patriarchy down the ages and that we still see being played out today.

The Melchizedek's were the genetic hosting race of the earth's ascension cycle for the last thirty-five thousand years. They were to help the earth heal and evolve out from the lower dimensions.

As of 2009, our planet went beyond the Melchizedek Universal field to prepare for the return of the Mother Arc / Divine Feminine Principle and was replacing the fallen Melchizedek architecture on earth. In January 2013, Earth came to the time of the promised return of Cosmic Christ Consciousness and the externalization of Unity Consciousness. This was felt and recognized by many beings who now are actively helping to rehabilitate the organic timelines or the Ascension timeline made for preserving human sovereignty on the planet Earth, and many Melchizedek have returned during this new cycle to support and aid the great shift for humanity."

This historical material has been brought to us through Ashayana Deane's books Voyagers One and Two and The Ascension Glossary of Lisa Renee.

Athena finally felt she had found her true soul family and was so overjoyed as for all those years she had been without her own birth family. Each time she thought she had found the origin of this wound, she would go on to find another layer. She thought she had landed and finally overcome this karma and it brought in much joy and anticipation. She was ready to join this group and help them develop the Institute of Divine Potential or IODP. They asked her to be the CEO. She was initially taken aback but guessed perhaps it made sense because of her long business career and her move into the transformational space as she followed her own journey and guidance. It had brought her back to her undoubted soul family. To do the work she loved in community with her spiritual family seemed like heaven to her.

A heaven not to last too long, though, as it turned out.

At this point, she was still not fully aware of her true purpose and the meaning behind the work she had undergone so far on this journey. This took really another cycle of opening that was infinitely boosted by her time in Ibiza with the mirror of this section of the Melchizedek soul family. She began to work with them delivering programs and getting involved with the running of what was visioned to become a Healing School. She truly loved the work because she had trained in-depth for this type of opportunity.

However, once again, during this time, there were lots of red flags, which she ignored until they were impossible to miss and see what they were pointing to. She had developed a good relationship with the other younger Melchizedeks, who had been drawn to this space who seemed welcoming and happy that she would be joining the team. Through spending time with them, she learned that all was not as it seemed. By overseeing their first healing program, it quickly became apparent there was a distinct lack of enthusiasm and perhaps a lack of skill for managing the courses properly, and Christof had quite openly admitted to her that their preference was to get on with the creative aspects of the business.

One big red flag was the overall lack of inclusion that appeared to operate in this grouping. She was working voluntarily with the healing course team and overseeing the running of that program together with other members of the soul family. All were working on a volunteer basis. Yes, it was early days, and they were still attempting to establish themselves; however there was a distinct hierarchical approach developing with the younger members who had been recruited from various programs they had taken with the leaders. Indeed, she herself had come into the mix via a retreat program. Suddenly, they were asking her to be their CEO because someone in their inner circle had visioned this? It didn't make sense to her. She felt there was some incongruence but could not yet fully process what this was.

Later that year, they were doing a large retreat in Egypt but did not invite her as a co- facilitator, which seemed strange to her considering her skills and that they were asking her to take on a key role in their organization. She had no call to the retreat in Egypt. She had visited in the early 1990s and felt no soul calling to go again unless to help facilitate for others.

Mt Shasta

Instead, she chose to visit Mount Shasta in the USA, where she combined a delightful hiking vacation with a trip to set up royalty payments for her book. She was exploring working with an old school pal in California and stayed with her for a little while before making the trip to Shasta.

It was during this visit that the Ibiza group on the Egypt retreat were doing one of their main pieces of work from the Great Pyramid at Giza. She had no idea of their itinerary or when it would bring them there. However, during one of her nights in her friend's place in Sonoma County, she heard the continuous chanting of the Om echoing all down the valley past the house where she was staying. Not only this, but the ceiling of the room in which she stayed opened and began to reconfigure into the night sky, and she literally began 'seeing' the reflection of the configuration of the twelve Galactic Stargates* as the chanting gained momentum. She could hear the chanting now, like she was in the Pyramid with them. This went on for some time before she fell asleep. It was indeed a beautiful episode that proved to her you cannot ever miss what is meant for you.

*The Twelve Stargates are a reflection and representative of the twelve inner vortices or twelve chakras of the Divine Angelic Blueprint for humanity. They relate to the twelve-strand DNA of the original angelic human. There are Twelve Planetary Stargates that relate to Twelve Galactic Stargates that, in turn, relate to Twelve

Universal Stargates that open to the next Harmonic Universe. All is a reflection of what is held within our own memory and consciousness. As above; so below – As within; so without

She eventually got to Shasta and found her accommodation was a beautiful little house in the town at the base of the mountain called the Secret Garden. It was in the garden of this lovely little house she would encounter the energy of St Germain.

While meditating in the 'secret garden' of this lovely accommodation, she suddenly became aware of a shimmering violet iridescent light in the shape of a huge orb about four feet away from her.... It was shimmering amongst the flowers and communicated to her without speaking, and she intuited this was the essence and consciousness of the great St Germain, an Ascended Master who, according to her previous information from Master Djwhal Kuhl, is in charge of the New Earth Culture of the new Golden Age of Aquarius and is associated with the Violet Ray of Transmutation and Synthesis. Athena had already been guided in her meditations to use this Violet Ray for transmuting all low-frequency energies as early as 2015.

Just Another Soul Set up

Her meetings with the Melchizedek family of course, had been another soul set up. She had been working with them less than a year and soon after they had invited her to be CEO, they began private talks with Tiara Kumara about joining their two businesses. And so it began; while Athena was making plans to move to Ibiza to join them, it seemed they were already heading off in another direction without any notice or consultation. Tiara had a successful business that had been developed from her Children of the Sun days. She had also amassed lots of followers. Athena found herself excluded from several of their discussions. It became very awkward for her to be excluded from their private discussions when she was seriously thinking of making a big life move to be with them, and it was not clear at first what was unfolding. However, as always, all one has to do is wait and the mirror of events eventually unfolds for all, the true purpose of them being drawn together.

When they had finished all their private meditations and discussions, she was asked to join them to hear what they had 'downloaded. 'They laid it all out as 'the plan,' the framework within which she would have to work. Tiara had asked her quite pointedly if she was capable of managing something of this size, which, given her abilities managing global business trainings in her recent past and multiple global businesses in her far past, seemed rather an unnecessary question and demonstrated to Athena something was amiss here. She had thought they were friends as well as sister souls, but in this scenario, it became very obvious there was a pecking order, a hierarchy developing. She also felt a deep betrayal of their friendship.

She had also accidentally overheard a conversation about herself between Christof and his wife, which was not flattering, coming from a place of fear and definitely not inviting trust in this setup. She could not understand why they had not fully included her in the meditation and co-creation of the plan for the new offering, particularly if she was to oversee it. She was invited in to comment only after they had already met and discussed everything, implying an ongoing hierarchical structure. There were several other conversations where she was actually asked to leave the room and wait while they continued their conversations, all without the courtesy of any explanation.

It was only on reflection after it all came falling down that Athena realized none of them really saw her, and she was seen only through their own limited and sometimes distorted lenses. None of them really knew her at all or were even interested in her or her life or her contribution, only if she could fit into their visions and agendas. This is how it seemed to her. Although their media expert did provide her with the cover design for her book, and Christof had provided the main title for which she was most grateful. It did sit very nicely with their own programs. At the time, though, to her, it seemed that interpersonal, relational skills nor open and honest discussions were considered part and parcel of, and a necessity for, a successful and thriving team, never mind their own harmonious personal relationships.

Christof and Akasha always seemed to have lots of 'advanced' new information to share, but in terms of actions, like many professed 'new age' teachers and so-called gurus, still had some way to go on their own inner journey to fully integrate and embody Mastery. There was never any reference to either of the Voyager books by Ashayana Deane or the Ascension Glossary of Lisa Renee, where most of their information came from. This is called appropriating knowledge. She had been looking forward to perhaps being able to help facilitate one of their Amazon retreats with them. She had experienced multiple incarnations as an indigenous Native American in both North and South America. This had become revealed during her school years and was one of the reasons she had spent so much time on these two continents, even in recent years. She was also an expert in personal process and integration.

She was still in shock at being excluded by the three of them, and of course, the pain of this triggered right into the scenario of loss and betrayal of her own human family all those many years ago all over again. Here it was, another repeating pattern, but now at a higher spiritual level. This was an ongoing process of healing for her, and it seemed her soul was determined to guide her to the roots of this trauma. As usual, once the piece was triggered she began receiving downloads as to the full meaning of what was truly happening. As always, she was given the full picture shown on her mind screen of the previous existences with the current players: who they were, what parts they played, and why she was here with them now, not only to create an opportunity for healing her own karma/ wounds but also an opportunity for them.

For her, this demanded a lot of forgiveness, understanding, and compassion as it finally revealed the root fractal of all her family losses down the ages. Her time spent at the Brennan Healing School had revealed several major tribe losses and other family losses going back to Atlantean time. It also revealed the roots of the recurring betrayals of love and trust in intimate partnerships and friendships that had carried over into the present time and been the cause of recurring patterns of betrayal. It was all being recycled once again for her to plainly see in this movie show, and the members of this group played their parts admirably.

The opportunity for healing was immense, and it was only a few years later that, as she underwent even further consciousness expansion, she was able to fully 'see' and accept the whole setup as a mirror for herself and the opportunity for resolution this opportunity had offered. This is the true purpose of the soul family – to provide the stage and setting for a new choice to be made so that the cycles can be terminated once and for all. Often, the realization comes much later after there is recognition of the immensity of the challenges the souls take on when agreeing to do this type of work together. She never was advised by any of them what was unfolding in their own awareness. There was no true sharing because the ego present in all prevented this. She had to process this all alone as and when the guidance came in. By the time the information came fully in, they had all gone their separate ways.

Eventually she was able to fully forgive and release. For a number of years, however, she struggled with watching the players play their part on the world stage as 'sages' and 'experts' while she struggled with the hurt and pain this whole episode had brought her. This resulted in a very passive-aggressive attitude and parlance from her whenever they came up in conversation in different groupings of mutual contacts. Of course, this was entirely the wrong way to deal with what it had brought up and the way we often react when the wounds that cut straight to the core fractal have been deeply triggered by others. The blame gets projected out because it is too painful to accept the responsibility that, in some way, one has created this oneself in order to heal.

After the deep and lovingly held sharings at the Brennan School, this all felt quite brutal in comparison. But she was in a different and more advanced classroom now. It only continued the conflict as various people she spoke to in confidence and thought she could trust reported back to the parties concerned. She had brought this on herself by not being mindful of her speech and trusting the wrong people. This was another huge lesson for her about the right use of language and her ability to use projection to deflect from taking responsibility. A mistake many make when faced with these difficult pieces of personal process. It all only brought in more suffering for her and more alienation from her 'family.'

She felt very alone. It had cut to the very core wounding of being abandoned by her family, the betrayal by both masculine and feminine reflections with no one around her with the skills or frequency to either recognize the true situation for what it was and help her and themselves through this.

It took her a long time to realize the lack of authenticity in this grouping. Everyone around her talked of spirituality and healing but no -one could actually truly understand or facilitate the deep inner work required when faced with it in a live situation in which everyone had their own part to play. She had been 'given' the information but needed support and help to process this in such a tight group. But no one it seemed, could own their own part because they could not yet see their own distortions. This also frightened her as she had trusted her guidance to be with these people and looked up to them at the time as more knowledgeable, more experienced, and more conscious than her. Another huge misconception on her part.

It was a steep learning curve for her that brought to the forefront more shame and guilt. And touched into the deep unworthiness that the betrayed 'victim 'always feels. She continued to co-create and deliver a facilitation program for them, but this was the last time she would be with them all together. She was, however, truly thankful for the short time she worked with them to deliver their training programs. Her own extensive exposure to all the main human core issues had given her expertise in this field that was enormously beneficial to her own process and to any who became her students /aspirants. She loved this work and truly loved helping others really 'see' what the mirror of their manifested reality was showing them. However, it is often easier to see this for others than deal with it for oneself. It requires a deeply safe, tender, loving container and this she definitely did not experience while with this group at this time. She was only with them for one year, but before she made an exit, she was at least, due to her extensive training in psycho-energetics and psycho-spiritual 'gymnastics,' able to fulfill one of the soul roles which she had been called to this group for and this was to illuminate the various co-dependencies within the grouping and the hierarchical behaviors prevalent. Whether they were able to acknowledge and integrate this or not was another matter, but at least she was able to bring this into the open for contemplation by all and felt she had completed her task in this particular 'family Melchizedek matrix.' Unknowingly, they had also completed theirs by bringing into her awareness all that still required healing and integrating within herself. Shortly after this, the whole group and the Institute itself was disbanded, and they all went their separate ways.

It was a massive learning curve that began with her own ego that was secretly thrilled to receive the invitation to be CEO. To be seen, to be validated, and to belong once again to a family, when, in fact, later, she would realize that this top-down structure is the very structure that does not serve the human race. She was placing her own need for validation and to belong in front of what would serve the whole collectively. Always easier to see in hindsight, of course. In the future, they were all heading into, she could not and would not be CEO of any company. This was diametrically opposed to her own inner coding. She had even downloaded the New Earth organizational templates during their own ceremony! She remembered Christof asking her immediately after she came around after the ceremony what she had downloaded about the IODP, totally oblivious to the fact this was not something to be processed in a few minutes.

This could not yet be processed because she had been confused by their conflicting vision and because of her longing to belong and to be loved and valued after learning how she had been abused and betrayed by the protagonists in her visions. She would never make the same mistake again. This in itself was a beautiful gift and realization for her. It had also demonstrated an opportunity she took to step into her own power and speak her own truth in the presence of those who 'seemed' more powerful than her. Despite the loss once again of her family group and the loss of income from the program facilitations, the 'real work' she had come to do was begun.

Slowly, she became aware that her whole working life had been a battle with this structure of elitism. She was not conscious at the time of keeping these structures alive by complying with them and enjoying the benefits of being a leader in her various positions in her early business life prior to going it alone, but nevertheless, she had spent a portion of her life complying with an old hierarchical business structure. So, it would seem, in some way, she had played her part in developing and keeping this structure in place for a time, and why she was now guided to support leaders who would build new, more equitable structures in the coming times. It had brought her attention specifically to the new business structures that would be the hallmark of any New Earth society and the change in leadership style for any structure that would be required as more and more people awakened and were ready to take full self - responsibility and move into sovereignty. Like all change, this requires inner transformation first before external manifestation can take place. It was a hard lesson for her. Yet the purpose of the soul family coming together was to do this very work.

More recently, as more and more truth around this whole situation emerged, it prompted her to publish the following piece about her own experiences with this type of situation on social media and an important piece to be shared in this book concerning 'new age spirituality' and the multiplicity of beings now stepping forward as 'spiritual teachers.'

Avoiding False Teachers, Gurus and Cults

❝It is very easy to impress the naïve spiritual initiate with all the trappings and reputations of spiritual figures and the charisma of those with many followers. Having many followers does not mean what is being presented is correct. Those who do not have spiritual awareness of advanced states of consciousness, and even those who do, often have no means of guidance except their intuition that says something is off, particularly if their discernment is clouded or else their own unhealed wounding causes a blind spot. (i.e. third eye not functioning properly) Claims of supernatural powers, paranormal feats, and fanciful titles and dress can often impress the naïve but actually have little to do with the real soul work.

The hallmark of a true teacher is humility, simplicity, lovingness, compassion, and peacefulness. It doesn't really matter to them if others join them or not, and there is most definitely avoidance of a personality cult. There is no desire to control others or coerce or persuade.

There is no financial charge for delivering Truth, as there is no interest in money, personal power, or gain. However, there may be an appropriate and reasonable contribution to cover administration costs. There is no attempt to appropriate knowledge (using sources without the appropriate reference) or force it on others as it was freely received. All shared should be from one's own lived experience.

Please note there are a multiplicity of astral realms and universes, each with its own teachers, masters, spiritual hierarchy, and belief systems. It is easy to be entrapped by fascinating esoteric knowledge and doctrines. However, the ultimate state is not reachable by the level of forms.

People can be intimidated by what appears to be complexity, rituals, requirements, commitments, and money. Some groups/teachers insist applicants are initiated and go through ceremonies, pledges, agreements, and activations. In reality, there is nothing one has to do, join, or study. Some misleading figures claim special instructions from God, or their spiritual guru, etc, and become self-proclaimed prophets and visionaries. These are distractions and all rely on form and to varying degrees, specialness.

Then we can get into referencing spaceships, UFO'S, extra-terrestrials and prophecies, galactic federations, guardian alliances, etc, and none of this is really relevant to the spiritual process. In effect, it can become an astral circus and mislead folks into thinking it is real or spiritual. There are a whole range of babas, masters, and legendary figures, many of whom have sold out their spiritual integrity in order to either have power over others or extract large sums of money for their delusions of grandeur."

Reference copyright "THE EYE OF THE I" Dr David Hawkins M.D. PhD 1927-2012 and confirmed as the last reincarnation of the true St Germain.

I repeat, the ultimate state is not to be reached by any level of forms. All manifested form is a result of either memory (karma) or imagination. None of it is real. It is a projection of your/our consciousness! All of it. What you see with Ayahuasca, DMT, or any psychedelics are astral projections. All the various 'beings' that inhabit the galaxy/multiverse are projections of individual and collective consciousness. This includes Satan, Lucifer, devils, and demons. It is the consciousness of the projector that requires attention.

The most important work that changes your vibrational frequency, your DNA template, and your energy bodies is the inner introspective work that finds the root fractal of your repeating patterns and cycles and brings it to conscious awareness so it may be consciously transmuted permanently. This means the charge connected to the memory is erased. When this is done alongside the relevant energy work, this is optimal. Doing energy work or activations alone will not transmute it permanently unless the consciousness that has created it is addressed.

What is present in form is not real; it is merely a projection of our inner world created by the mind. We have an individual mind and a consensual reality created by a collective mind. We also have a soul and the highest emanation of form, which is spirit /essence. The essence does not carry blemishes or wounds of any kind and is fully connected to the Source Mind.

Energy Work and Activations

The type of energy work is very important and must be directed by the person's own higher consciousness. The inclusive energy that animates the atom/form is stimulated and strengthened until, through its own internal potency, it burns up its sheaths and escapes by radiation from its orbit, creating photons of light. The fire within burns up all else, and the electric fire escapes and; therefore, the true alchemist will seek in all cases to stimulate the radioactivity of the atoms and will level attention on the positive nucleus, increasing its vibratory activity or positivity.

The master does this in connection and conjunction with the human spirit and does not concern themselves with the material aspect. They work with the soul within the form and produce results that are intelligent, self-induced, and permanent.

An energy worker who is of a low frequency or, even worse, ego-driven by service to self basically has not done their own inner work, centers their attention on the form or the combination of atoms in order to allow the central life force from the atoms to escape. They bring this about through external agencies; they burn and destroy the material sheath of the atoms in order to imprison the escaping essence as the form disintegrates. They attempt to produce specific ends by manipulation of the matter of the form. This hinders the evolutionary path of the life involved.

So do it! Do your inner work now!

If you don't know how to find someone who can help you do this until you understand and finally experience. All manifested form is an illusion and based on your own consciousness.

What is within you at the Core is God / Source /Presence /Awareness. It is formless.

Everything else is a memory held in your DNA, energy template, and physical body. It is held in your form or is created as a form by your thoughts and imagination.

With no distortion to your awareness, you will most automatically create love, joy, peace, compassion, gratitude, humility, abundance, reverence for all life, reverence for your planet, reverence for all the manifested worlds on all levels /dimensions, and frequencies and healing within the physical form.

Muscle Testing

This important work is mentioned here because it is such a valuable tool in discerning truth from falsehood in a world that is currently moving through a major transition in consciousness.

Dr Hawkins was director of the Institute for Spiritual Research, Inc. and founder of the Path of Devotional Nonduality. He was renowned as a pioneering researcher in the field of consciousness as well as an author, lecturer, clinician, physician, and scientist. https://veritaspub.com

Through his vast studies and experiments in kinesiology, he has been able to make a map of the levels of consciousness and calibrate through muscle testing. Through this work, he devised a reliable way to determine truth from falsehood.

Over 250,000 muscle testing calibrations spanning thirty years of multiple research studies conducted by Dr Hawkins for the Institute for Spiritual Research, Inc. resulted in a defined range of values that correspond to levels of consciousness, which include well-recognized attitudes and emotions. With a logarithmic scale of 1-1000 and the Map of Consciousness® format that he developed, Dr Hawkins explained the classification and characteristics of these energy fields to make them easily comprehensible and useful in daily life.

It is most important to realize that the calibration figures do not represent an arithmetic but a logarithmic progression. Therefore, the level of three hundred is not twice the amplitude of one hundred and fifty; it is three hundred to the tenth power! An increase, therefore, of just a few points represents a major advance in power.

The ways various levels of consciousness express themselves are profound and far-reaching.

Levels below two hundred are detrimental to life in both the individual and society at large; those above two hundred are constructive expressions of power. The decisive fulcrum of two hundred divides the general areas of force and power and truth from falsehood. Dr Hawkins has been able to show that until 1987, the collective consciousness of humanity calibrated to below two hundred points, corresponding overall to negative states of consciousness.

(Pride, anger, desire, fear, grief, apathy, guilt, shame).

After the Harmonic Convergence 16-17 August 1987, the collective consciousness rose to two hundred and seven, and this important upturn on the spiral upward marked an important turning point as it denoted courage and empowerment and an upward swing in the overall level of consciousness.

In 2012, it was two hundred and seventeen.

In 2024 it is two hundred and twenty- five. Given this is a logarithmic progression this represents a huge shift over the past thirty-seven years. The collective has some way to go but is most certainly heading in the right direction. However, never assume that you as an individual cannot make a huge difference to the whole. In his book Power v Force in 1995, Dr Hawkins cited research to show:

- one individual at 300 counterbalances the negativity of 90,000 individuals below 200
- one at 500 counterbalances 750,000 below 200
- one at 600 counterbalances 10,000,000 below 200
- one at 700 counterbalances 70,000,000 below 200
- one avatar at 1000 counterbalances the collective negativity of all humankind.

You can learn how to find the truth of anything using this procedure. It is a great gift to humanity in these times of confusion and chaos. When you have learned how to do this simple test properly, please calibrate this article and calibrate the truth level of this book.

Map of Consciousness
Developed by David R. Hawkins

The Map of Consciousness is based on a logarithmic
scale that spans from 0 to 1000.

Name of Level	Energetic "Frequency"	Associated Emotional State	View of Life
Enlightenment	700–1000	Ineffable	Is
Peace	600	Bliss	Perfect
Joy	540	Serenity	Complete
Love	500	Reverence	Benign
Reason	400	Understanding	Meaningful
Acceptance	350	Forgiveness	Harmonious
Willingness	310	Optimism	Hopeful
Neutrality	250	Trust	Satisfactory
Courage	200	Affirmation	Feasible
Pride	175	Scorn	Demanding
Anger	150	Hate	Antagonistic
Desire	125	Craving	Disappointing
Fear	100	Anxiety	Frightening
Grief	75	Regret	Tragic
Apathy	50	Despair	Hopeless
Guilt	30	Blame	Evil
Shame	20	Humiliation	Miserable

PART 5

THE LAND BECKONS

Nepal and the Himalayas

Athena had already booked to go on a retreat to the Himalayas facilitated by Tiara and Akasha towards the back end of that same year. After what had transpired in Ibiza, this was going to be tricky for her, but it had long been a dream to see and experience the Himalayas; she was not about to cancel the trip. Years earlier she had studied the vast amount of Ascended Master teachings of Djwhal Kuhl and had promised herself one day she would visit their playground in the Himalayas. She was just turned sixty -five, and it seemed an appropriate time. It was supposed to be a spiritual retreat for her, and she was a paying participant, not a facilitator.

However, as it turned out, there was very little facilitation. She had overheard a conversation of the facilitators with Akasha talking about her 'pride' being her issue, not realizing she was sitting behind them on the coach and could not avoid hearing the conversation. It seems they totally missed the deep re-wounding that had occurred for her in Ibiza or even seeing that there was perhaps a projection of their own pride and inflated ego going on. It was as clear as day to her now. This topic was never mentioned to her in any session or brought out in a group. Akasha advised of the positive feedback they had received from the groups she had facilitated on behalf of the IODP and acknowledged how lovingly and tenderly she had held all her group members throughout the year. This was easy for her because this is what she loved doing. Learning and then helping others through her own experience. When your soul's purpose is in alignment with your action, it becomes a joy rather than work.

The entire trip was basically more of a physical challenge than anything else. They began in Katmandhu, and flew to Pokhara to make the sacred intentions for the long trek. Here, Athena made her vow to continue to serve all humanity in whatever way she was guided and took the name Sananda as part of that vow. In Sanskrit, the word means joy and happiness. She had always associated the name with the Christ Consciousness that was always present within her and was now growing in intensity more and more each day. Waves and waves of this Cosmic Christ energy kept filling her physical body. It seemed fitting to adopt this name on this sacred culminating journey. There was also a little negative mischief she enjoyed with this by taking the name also held by Akasha. She felt the pride of this identity was an issue for him, and the pride she had overheard him suggesting was hers was also actually his own. A clearer sight would have shown him she was beginning to more fully embody the Divine Feminine Principle and why she had come to this place. Her vow was sacred to her and for her, it meant the embodiment of the consciousness her name stood for and had absolutely nothing to do with identity. For her, Athena stood for wisdom and truth, Melchizedek for the cleansed soul blueprint of the Divine Angelic Human, and Sananda finally recognized the liberation from the cross of suffering as the inner experience of the Christ Consciousness that had been with her all along and now fully experienced as joy, bliss, and happiness. This is why she came to this world and why she had lived the life she had lived. To do the inner work of clearing the karma (ancestral, genetic and archetypal wounds), she had brought in and be a model for others. How could Akasha possibly see her clearly when he was still dealing with his own mother wounding and the recent loss of a relationship? However, it was not her place to become his facilitator in this particular scenario, and whatever had been revealed to her about the entire soul grouping and its real dynamics was not to be shared at this juncture.

The trek was long and really quite difficult in places, even for the very fit and healthy female she was. The roads were very treacherous, even in mild weather. The buses really challenging if one had a queasy stomach, which happened from time to time. The accommodations were sparse and cold, but the people of the area were all just wonderful to meet. The sherpas were amazing and carried miraculous weights of baggage. Bless them. And their energy certainly made up for the general physical discomfort. However, the mountains did not disappoint; they were nothing less than spectacular. She got to see Annapurna at dawn. The energy was undeniably and palpably beautiful and indeed, Athena got to meet the masters on the way to Muktinath. Six of them appeared to her in the snow-capped mountains just outside Muktinath, and she was able to capture their images on film. Miraculous and stunning.

However, even more magnificent is what she felt in her heart. It had literally been a long, hard path through the life lived to date and now echoed in the physical experience on this trek through the Himalayan mountain towns to their final destination of Muktinath. She felt such gratitude, love, and peace as she registered the faces of those who had gone before her in the snowy caps of the Himalayas. She had read and studied so much about their lives never dreaming that one day she would get to see them as a reflection of her own inner landscape. But here they were. She felt humbled and blessed and wept.

Muktinath itself is a sacred place for both Hindus and Buddhists alike. This shrine area is very special, situated in the lap of the remote Mukthinath Valley area at an elevation of 3,710 meters (12171 ft), near the Ranipauwa, at the base of the Thorung La pass, a part of the famous Annapurna circuit in the Mustang district of Nepal.

The term Muktinath is derived from the Sanskrit words Mukti and Nath. Mukti implies liberation, and Nath stands for master or God. The temple of Muktinath lies at a higher elevation since it is also known as the sanctuary above the cloud. The mesmerizing scenic view of its surroundings engenders a feeling of complete otherworldliness. The sacred Muktinath temple area is also widely known as Muktikshetra.

The term Muktikshetra is derived from the Sanskrit word called Mukti means Moksha or liberation, and kshetra refers to the place, which represents the site of salvation. Despite being in such a challenging, remote region, thousands of pilgrims from different corners of the world come to pay homage here. It was one of the most blessed moments of her life.

This would be the last time she would see any members of this part of her soul family in person. She felt very grateful for this opportunity. It had been a strange and wonderful trip for her, even though the main issues were never approached, discussed, or processed. It didn't matter to her, for she could do that for herself. It was further confirmation of what she already knew, and all she could do was not allow this to spoil what was such a life-affirming trip for her. For this, she gives great thanksgiving and appreciation to and for her soul sister Tiara for organizing this wonderful pilgrimage. Akasha would spend a little more time in the Himalayas and then go on to facilitate another Egypt retreat with IODP and Tiara was heading back home to the USA. Athena made her way back to the UK.

She would hear later that year, after the Egypt trip in November 2017, that the IODP disbanded, and Akasha and Christof each set up their own individual enterprises for the public. Tiara also gave up teaching a few years later to create her homestead. Athena began setting up her own group online mentoring still based out of the UK.

Processing her Melchizedek Soul Family

The Himalayan trip had allowed her to process much around the distortions that had been mirrored back to her by the various situations she had found in Ibiza. She was being shown patterns of distorted masculine energy and the results of the deep wounding of being objectified, i.e., loved for what one can achieve or what one can do, rather than what one simply naturally is, which creates the egoic need to be better or higher than another (the seeds of hierarchy) in order to be seen, heard and validated. This is an egoic defense practiced by many leaders in current times. Athena had processed much of this distortion before arriving in Ibiza and knew it was an opportunity for her to stand up for herself, knowing she was worthy and 'good enough.' In doing so, she lost her family again. The pride taken in expressing higher knowledge aggrandizes the ego and keeps hierarchy in place if it is not tempered with humility and compassion. She had finally discovered the root, the core fractal of the wounds that had caused all the various family losses and betrayals on all her timelines down the ages. It had all started with this group of Melchizedek souls.

In this incarnation it had begun with her father. Now, it had been revealed to her he was also a Melchizedek. One of the few adult conversations she had with him about his own family concerned the early loss of his own mother, her grandmother Mary apparently, a great psychic and adored by him, who had gone before she was born. She (Athena) had been his mother (Mary) who had passed and then reincarnated as his daughter Joan. This was why she could recognize him at birth and why there was such a strong bond between them in her early years. He had been her son, and she was his mother on this other timeline.

However, the biggest shock and most difficult piece to come to terms with was the realization that Akasha, in this new timeframe, was the reincarnation of her father. She had recognized the energy signature again when they first met, it was unmistakeable. Athena had been the mother of her father. Remember, his mother had passed long before Joan arrived, and her early loss had caused his deep wound of abandonment. She was then reborn as Joan, his daughter. After his passing, her father had subsequently reincarnated as Akasha, who would suffer the same imprinted wounding in this new incarnation and continually be searching for the mother. She recalls the family meeting in Ibiza, which she had been guided to set up and where there was an opportunity for all to work on these issues. She had brought the issues of co-dependence to the attention of all. She can remember being in tears and apologizing to Akasha for she knew not what. But her soul knew. He was in tears, also. They had all suffered the same wounding and the same issues, the loss of the mother, which, of course, symbolizes the Divine Feminine Energetic Principle and is the great balancing archetypal energy that is required for the entirety of humanity as the distorted patriarchy collapses and reconfigures into the positive Divine Masculine expression.

As the new information came pouring forth, it revealed the being now called Christof had been (Athena's) husband eons ago and was unfaithful to her with Tiara. One has to be careful here because, in many ancient cultures, men had more than one wife. Whatever was the norm on this particular timeline, Athena had perceived the situation as a betrayal then, and it certainly had been replayed, perhaps unconsciously, who knows, with the players in this vignette with the IODP. She had received this information at the time.

Toby had been hijacked by a false light entity calling itself Babaji and also suffered this deep mother wounding. In fact, all the Melchizedeks in this family grouping, including Athena herself, have/had in common a mother wounding of some kind of perceived loss and abandonment. This was one of the great archetypal configurations they had come to heal collectively.

Another shocking revelation that unfolded during this period was the experiments undertaken during the time of Atlantis by the Fallen Melchizedek had somehow wounded the womb of Athena and had played out in many ways on many timelines to affect her sexuality. This may or may not be literal; it often is the only way the mind can process horrific information from another timeline. More important is, that it serves as a metaphor for the Divine Feminine that became subjugated to the Fallen Melchizedek.

These revelations help give understanding to the patterns and processes; the soul contracts we take on to transmute, and the challenges we all face when we are committed to deep spiritual work. Remember, we are making it all up. It's all a story that seems so real when it hits our wounds and emotional bodies. We will keep reincarnating with the same soul family and play out these dramas until someone within the soul group breaks the cycle. Please note none of this is personal. It is all part of the soul contracts of all involved. How we choose to work with this in the present 'reality' is the key. In order to do this deep work, we have to open our awareness and be willing to admit we have something going on. Ego and fear often prevent this. Forgiveness for ourselves and others, along with unconditional love and compassion, resolves everything. It became apparent to Athena this was one of the reasons they had all been brought together again. The Melchizedek returned to earth during this time to do this very work.

Once again, she was so grateful for the experience she had gained in the deep psychological /spiritual process work of diving deep into the darkness of herself that enabled her to continue to do her own inner work now. All her hard work and devotion had paid off. This enabled her to differentiate and evaluate what was her own baggage and what was another's projection. Invaluable tools and knowledge for navigating this physical dimension and what it presents to us. Even more valuable, this work brings us a deep understanding of what is truly going on within one another and allows for a much deeper understanding and compassion for the human condition. As we bring these fragmented parts of ourselves back out of the shadows and integrate these pieces into the wholeness of our being, we realize it is merely a construct to expand our consciousness and raise our frequency. When we can take this higher perspective about what the external world reveals to us about ourselves, then we can honor all and love all. But we must have humility and be willing to go there, which can be hard to do when you set yourself up as a teacher with a 'superior' knowledge. Beware this use of intellect and emphasis on knowledge rather than true spiritual process; this is a typical defense mechanism used by many 'spiritual teachers' to bypass their issues.

It became clear to her after some time that the entire depiction was showing the ongoing imprinting of hierarchical, patriarchal patterning within the 'families' she had been associated with down the ages. This entire construct is one of the major challenges now for humanity overall, as rising consciousness involves a move away from top-down structures of leadership and into the concept of individual sovereignty, freedom, and shared leadership. This means each becomes fully responsible for all their own choices and their consequences and each becomes their own leader. From this perspective, we move and behave in community and communion with one another very differently.

To come into a state of full forgiveness for them and, in particular, for herself and her own part in this story took some time. But the willingness to visit and retrieve these shadowy parts of herself was always deeply rewarded through grace and the support of her guidance with completion eventually and a further expansion in her own consciousness.

Cosmic Connections

Since her visit to Muktinath and the beautiful reflection of the 'masters' she was blessed by, a new aspect of herself had come into her awareness. She continued to develop her own programs of transformation and empowerment based on what she had studied, but more so, what she had fully experienced and integrated within her own body, soul, and spirit.

She had willingly made a contribution to the IODP coffers to have use of the beautiful codes created by Akasha. No one had asked her to do this.In doing so she did not truly acknowledge her own coding and that all true healing is enabled by the will of the recipient. One cannot 'buy' codes of healing. This is an erroneous precept. Her longing for the acceptance of her soul family had totally blinded her to the fact she was, once again, giving away her own soul sovereignty. It was not so apparent at first because they were truly beautiful pieces of artwork, and she seemed to transmit the codes successfully, as did many others. But it was not necessary as she already carried the codes within. Art can be beautiful, and beauty can transmit a frequency, of course. However, this became an important realization and clarification for Athena.

One must also remember that in the work of healing, it is the client/aspirant that always enables this. The facilitator can use their own clear field to empower and quicken this process by entraining the client's energy field into harmonic resonance with their own field that holds the codes pertaining to the client's specific architectural configuration. However, ultimately, it is the willingness of the soul and ego to let go of all that is not real and not in alignment with the Source that completes and integrates the process. It is better described as empowerment rather than healing.

Since her early years, she had always been assured by her connection to the Christed One/Christ Consciousness that the embodiment and guidance of this energy and consciousness would be with her 'even until the end of the world.' This guidance came through in 1992, and had overseen all her training and process work from the very beginning.

Her first vision experiential of the Christ energy appeared in meditation in 2005 at her home in Iford. A huge and glorious being of shimmering light golden iridescent light appeared to be standing in her field in front of her. It was as if she had become the sun. It would completely overshadow her physical body and infuse her entire energy field, so it felt as if this energy was an extension of her own field as, of course, it was and is. In her work she would always invoke the name of this consciousness field. As time passed, she became aware this golden field encompassed her entire physical body and energy field.

However, since her return from the Himalayas in 2017, the energies of the great alchemist, Master St Germain, and the Bodhisattva Lady Master Quan Yin have joined her energy transmission sessions in the light forms of violet/amethyst and turquoise/aquamarine blue iridescent light fields respectively and guided her speech. She did not and does not see them as 'personas' but simply experiences of different light frequencies rather than 'personalities' and was given field descriptions telepathically. She was given the information through a download during meditation that St Germain had reincarnated in 1927 as Dr. David Hawkins MD, PhD. You can calibrate the truth of this information when you learn and use his method.

Apart from an incredible life of contribution to humanity, he bestowed a most gracious and timely gift to us all in his development of the Map of Consciousness© mentioned earlier and the method to determine truth from falsehood using the body's own innate Source intelligence. This beautiful gift to humanity was developed over many years of scientific experiments and thousands of patients and clients. In times such as these, when there is so much confusion, chaos, and clutter in the collective field, this is a true blessing for humanity to have access to such a powerful tool of discernment while we are busy developing and honing our natural skills of higher sense perception and direct knowing. All three aspects continued to guide and oversee Athena's own personal process and all her work, and they are most definitely not from the lower false light matrix of the lower astral world but from the higher dimensions of spirit. One could ask how can she be sure of this. Answer: their guidance has never contravened Universal Laws; has always been loving and affirmative; concerned for her wellbeing and growth, moving her forward into evermore challenging situations that have developed her own Mastery, yet always for the highest good of all involved. Her tests have been extreme, and ultimately, she came to realize these are all different aspects of her whole being reflected back to her, just as her own shadows were illuminated by their light until they transmuted and integrated.

St Michael's Mount, Cornwall

A thena continued to live at Iford for the next two years and enjoyed the great beauty of the nature that she was immersed in there. These years were not without incident. For the land once again beckoned.

Michelle, one of her American friends from the online conscious business group, visited with her in 2018. She was on vacation in London, and Athena invited her to stay at her place in the South West so she could see the ancient Roman Spa city of Bath and explore some of the other ancient sites in the South West of England. It was an opportunity for both of them to take a break.

They visited the stone circle and Henge at Avebury, and it was here she saw the map that showed the details of the great Mary /Michael ley lines through Glastonbury and out across the southwest of England. As part of their tour of the southwest, she was also inspired to take Michelle to Marazion in Cornwall, the access point to the famous St Michael's Mount. Athena wanted to see and experience this herself, and Michelle's heritage was Jewish, and there had been a Jewish enclave there at some point in history. For centuries, tin and copper had been exported from these two locations. Here, the great Apollo/Athena ley line, originating at Solomon's temple in Jerusalem and traversing the continent of Europe, enters the UK and eventually crosses the Michael/ Mary Line at Glastonbury. All of these grid lines carry energetic intelligence and they certainly had information for Athena and Michelle.

During her visit, Michelle was on edge and seemed troubled. She was not a relaxing person to be around at this time and snapped at Athena several times as well as castigating her for what she perceived as a lack of compassion. When Michelle first arrived, she was in tears about the loss of her dog while they sat together sipping tea in the garden. Athena was picking up a disturbing energy from her that was not only connected to the loss of her dog. Michelle was a guest in her home and had been invited for a fun visit. What was really happening here?

Over dinner Michelle had tried to shame her again over the listening incident. Athena did not wish to argue, but this did not sit well with her. She was uncomfortable; what was all this about? It felt to her as if something deeper was wishing to be revealed. She could only wait and allow things to unfold. She had not expected this visit to be a working session but that was the way it was heading. The next day, she drove them both to Marazion, where they stayed overnight so they could catch the causeway to St. Michael's Mount before the tide came in.

From as far back as 495 AD there are tales that tell of seafarers lured by mermaids onto the rocks or guided to safety by apparitions of St Michael. Apparently, St. Michael is considered to be the patron saint of fishermen, and it is said the Archangel Michael appeared on the western side of the island, just below where the entrance to the castle is today, to direct fishermen away from certain peril. It is a legend that has brought pilgrims, monks, and people of faith to the island ever since.

In 1066, the island came into the possession of the Benedictine Abbey of Mont St Michel in Normandy, and construction of the church and priory began in 1135. The mount has weathered many times of battles down the ages, and eventually it reverted back to British ownership. Four miracles are said to have happened here between 1262 and 1263 would have only added to the religious magnetism that drew pilgrims from far and wide.

It is now owned and still stewarded by the St Aubyn family and is still an important landmark for those spiritual seekers who say its unique energy is thanks to age-old ley lines that course under the sea and cross at the heart of the Mount.

Whether it is religious beliefs, spiritual energies, or simply the opportunity to take a breath and reflect, many people from all over the world are drawn to pause and become immersed in the uplifting atmosphere of the Mount.

They visited the castle and the church without any incident. It was a welcome contemplative time for Athena where she could simply experience the land, the sea, the fresh air, the lovely gardens and simply tune in to herself after the long drive and her friend's erratic energy. However, when they returned to the car, Athena accidentally caught Michelle's foot with the car door as she helped her into the car. It was a sheer accident with no hurt and certainly no intention to cause harm, and yet Michelle had reacted in terror as if she had been literally attacked and severely admonished her forlorn and long-suffering chauffeuse. Athena could not make any sense of any of this, and she began wondering what was really going on here with her visitor.

Before setting off for their return journey, Michelle began complaining of pain in her neck and back and was very apparently in great discomfort. Athena did an emergency hands-on healing in the lounge of a nearby hotel to alleviate the symptoms which it seemed to. From here, they went shopping for some mementos and dined together that evening in a nearby restaurant, and she did her best to remain centered and grounded. She wasn't looking forward to the drive back but all went ahead without any problem or misadventures. Eventually, they arrived back in Wiltshire, and the following day, everything became clear.

They were both meditating in her meditation room at the cottage and the energy movement in Michelle began again. Following the trip to Marazion, plus the 'quick fix' healing she had done with Michelle, she had received more information and could see more clearly what was happening in Michelle's energy field. They did another healing together, and Athena removed a huge wooden stake that had been plunged into the center of Michelle's back, causing death in that particular timeline. The implement was from ancient times and astral vision indicated an incident of betrayal that had killed her during some kind of battle in that timeline.

There was no information on how this got there other than it happened in an ancient war zone. It was Athena's intuition that the war zone had been Marazion in some ancient time. Athena had the skills to see it and remove it, she did so without question or pause. She checked in with her guidance if she had been the perpetrator and the answer came back no. She was merely helping a friend who was in need. But they had needed to go to Marazion for this energy to be triggered. Also, the energetic signature of betrayal was a common denominator for both women and had no doubt triggered the energy and enabled Athena to do the work of removal. Now she understood Michelle's behavior and why she was truly here, and it allowed her to feel deep compassion for this soul whom she had at first experienced as a rather prickly visitor to her home.

The incident had pointed to the fact that in order to facilitate the healing of this piece in Michelle's energy field, Athena's own healing of this particular wounding needed to have been accomplished. She could not facilitate for another a vibrational frequency change such as this if her own conduit still carried the same unresolved patterning. So, in many ways, this setup had been beneficial for both of them and brought in information for both, even if not understood immediately. Athena had only facilitated an energy healing on the astral level of Michelle's field, but still the deep psychological inner work needed to be attended to reveal and heal the fractal core of this deep wounding. Because of their past relationship, Athena was cognisant of Michelle's family background, and this needed to be further explored and resolved in the present day with true love and forgiveness. If this was not attended to, it would eventually cause physical disease in the body. Energy work without consciousness work is not a complete solution. There was no time or inclination for this at this stage. Michelle was leaving the next day.

Athena took her to the train station the next day and would not hear from her again until a few years later when one of their mutual contacts from the past got in touch with her to inform her Michelle had cancer. She contacted Michelle immediately and was guided to ask if Michelle would like to meditate with her online; she agreed enthusiastically. She already had a team of other healers in place, apparently, as well as her medical team. Athena did several online transmissions with Michelle and heard later from the same group member that her operation and treatment was successful, and she was clear of the cancer.

Very often, our karmic healing work involves just holding space for an event so that the other person can make a different choice. There have been many instances in Athena's life where her actions or non-action have been about a soul contract to play the 'role 'she offered to play in order for a healing of some kind to occur for another. The healings often were often masked as something else or what Athena would call a 'soul set up' that would bring her to a situation of working with another despite what either party 'thought' their meeting was about. It became apparent to Athena that wherever she went people would be triggered in some by her energy so that an opportunity for healing could occur, or at least symptoms could be brought to the forefront. It was the universe showing her she was indeed a healer, but not in an apparent or orthodox way of setting up a practice and working formally. Her true gift to share was about the embodiment of a frequency. She was slowly becoming aware that wherever she went holding clear loving intentions, there would always be disruption of the status quo in some way. She did not even have to 'do' anything.

We make the entire story of every incarnation up because we are powerful creators of reality, and we choose, before we come, the various roles we will play to either further or lessen our own evolutionary process. Athena was beginning to notice how many of these events were specifically time-coded and how events synchronistically arranged to bring her into these soul contacts. None of this is about blaming or shaming another for in effect we are meeting a part of ourselves; it truly is all about learning to love ever more deeply and unconditionally. How we can best do that, but more importantly how we best be that for one another. Sometimes, it is just about showing up without knowing the outcome. If one needs to know for the highest good, then the universe will structure events so one will always get to know somehow.

Betrayal of any kind is painful, and yet the true value of the gift is the shadow consciousness it brings to the surface of a deep lack of self-love and self-worth, just as it had all those years ago for Athena. Only when we have true love, compassion, and forgiveness for the self can we authentically extend this to another, and it seems this whole soul setup provided that opportunity for Athena once she could 'perceive' the situation clearly. She was once again being shown her healing work on this planet did not have a straightforward or orthodox format.

Another most beautiful gift this unexpected occurrence brought forth was the deeper information about the energy grid upon which she lived. Michelle's visit had revealed important information about the great ley lines on which she had lived and worked for many years for which she was hugely grateful. The earth's energy grid itself was reflecting the balancing of the male and female energetics that had been her lifelong mission. The soul is immensely innovative in not wasting any opportunity for as many as possible to reap the benefit of its healings, including the earth itself.

Michelle's visit had brought in much for Athena. It was not what she was expecting but nevertheless profound and she treasures the two beautiful china plates, each depicting a hummingbird, that Michelle gifted to her when she first arrived at her home. In many indigenous cultures, the hummingbird is revered as a messenger between spirit and the physical world and represents joy, freedom, love, and healing and reminds her daily of the reciprocity that only the universe itself can orchestrate. Every day, the plates remind Athena of this and the unconditional love she extends to Michelle and all beings. May all beings be Happy and Free!

San Diego 2018

Later that same year, Athena would go to San Diego to attend a group event held at the Paradise Port Spa there, which beautifully illustrates the delightful, synchronistic ways the soul guides us. She had been attending an online marketing course for some months, and this was an event where the course members got to meet one another physically and network. An altogether uplifting event enjoyed by all, as so many of them worked online just like her. For Athena, it was extra special for here she would meet Mimy Wong. It was a very powerful meeting for them both. Mimy was from Hong Kong, although she also had homes in Los Angeles and Vancouver when they first met. You will perhaps remember Athena had connections with Hong Kong and China in her early life as a business director in the import industry and later connected to her first soul guide, the Chinese Master Huang Po. (Huangbo Xiyun)

Like Athena, Mimy had a business background and was a healer, and also, like Athena, not typical. There was an instantaneous soul recognition between them and Athena began receiving information almost immediately that this was an important karmic meeting and one day they would work together. Around this time, the Quan Yin energy was coming through strongly for Athena, and this was also strongly present in Mimy's energy field. Indeed, Mimy became her client for a while and when the shadow work was complete, they continued to be friends. Here was another strong, powerful, and successful business woman who was also a healer in an unorthodox way. The Quan Yin energy and consciousness was also a profound reflection for both women. Her life was filled with much hardship and abuse, and yet she is a beautiful example of forgiving the great transgressions against her person and choosing wisdom and spiritual growth. She did not bury her anger, but instead simply chose to let it go and find within her heart peace and compassion. She used any irritation and suffering to transform negativity into light through her compassion. She was present to illuminate the way of the great Divine Feminine energy and the effect this energy can have not only on individuals of all genders but also on our world.

Athena would stay at Iford for another two years and continued her work in the South West of England. Since the time in Ibiza, she had maintained a connection with several other members of the Melchizedek family who had also left the group, and it was now these relationships that would return to the forefront of her life as she began to assimilate more and more information from the land on which she lived. She still had within a longing to create some kind of healing retreat or pilgrimage on this sacred land. According to the law of synchronicity, when a soul's longing is aligned with its Divine Purpose. Miracles happen.

Gabriel, whom she had met in Ibiza, had offered to help her with the technical support she so badly needed with getting stuff done online, and together they made a fair exchange arrangement for his services. Through his friendship with Tony, whom she had first met in Glastonbury during a Melchizedek family visit to the UK, she had found two delightful partners with whom to co-create. Gabriel and Tony joined forces with her to explore the creation of a retreat in Glastonbury, where Tony was currently living. Perhaps, unsurprisingly, given her track record, it turned out that the real work was nothing to do with a retreat and everything to do with each of their own soul's individual work.

As mentioned several times already, the soul is ingenious in setting up its next task, and for Athena it had been full on without pause. She was so excited about what they might develop together.

Avalon

O n his own path, Tony had been living in Glastonbury for some time and had amassed a great knowledge of the Avalon story through his diligent research and, in particular, his own Druid ancestry.

Gabriel she 'knew' more deeply from their time together in Ibiza. He had been part of the IODP scenario until it disbanded. Apart from being a beautiful soul on the seekers' path, he was also a tech wizard and was able to create wonderful web pages, and Athena could provide the initial written outline proposal for them all to consider. It seemed a perfect combination.

Until, of course, folks began to be triggered. It slowly became clear to Athena that something was being played out here. These issues became projected out onto her as both her partners' physical family patterns began to be played out in this scenario, Tony's particularly. It quickly became apparent to her that neither had done enough work around their family conditioning at this time that allowed them to own their projections and sadly, the project never really got off the ground. Athena was bewildered as her enthusiasm and willingness to collaborate had brought in such great joy for her but this particular collaboration was not meant to be at this time. It had simply been a mechanism to bring them all together.

She was so grateful for all the inner work she had already done around her own distorted male energy and her growing relationship with her newly found feminine power and was able to distinguish quickly what was being projected out on to her from a still wounded consciousness. It was an opportunity for all to heal these outworn family dynamics, but it was not an opportunity to be embraced at this stage.

She was, however, appreciative that this scenario had brought in an opportunity for her to accept and stand in her own true feminine power. When one is growing spiritually, sometimes this evokes lower vibrational responses, which might be fearful, insecure, jealous, or even angry, and these responses arise so they can be transmuted and integrated. For Athena, it was an important test to allow herself to shine and not be diminished by the healing process of others. And to be able to recognize it for what it was without taking any of it personally.

Once again, the men of her "family" where unable to truly see her and accept her as she held true to her own feminine power. She had spent years and years healing this rift within herself around the distorted masculine energy and bringing back the true feminine within herself, and it really only dawned on her through the gift of the research and grid connections this project had brought in why she had lived on this great energy grid for so long. For this, she was so grateful to both her soul brothers.

After the visit to St Michael's Mount at Marazion with Michelle, she had realized the intersection of the grids from Solomons Temple in Jerusalem that ran right across Europe from Mt Carmel, Athens, Delphi, Assisi, Sienna, Genoa, Mont Michel, and finally entering the United Kingdom at St Michael's Mount created an axis with great Avalon Grid at Glastonbury and out to the great Druid Stone circle at Avebury and across the Celtic Sea to Ireland. The map that she had kept from her visit to Avebury showed her that she lived directly on the Mary / Michael ley line. The great Michael / Mary line conjunct with the Apollo/ Athena grid coming in from Jerusalem across all the axis points in Europe. She had memories of living and working at Mt Carmel, Israel, Athens, Delphi, and Assisi, Siena, and Lyons – all points on this grid. Flooding in came various connections from other known parallel lives with the Essenes, the Templars, The Druids, the Celts, the great Arthurian legend, the priestesses at Delphi and the Knights of the Round Table, Guinevere, Merlin, and the visit of the young boy Yeshua to Avalon and St Just, Cornwall with his uncle Joseph of Arimathea. Her research into this to set up the retreat had brought in a cascade of new energy and consciousness and connected many of the different visions she had received at other times, which was very beautiful. The information and realizations came in as she was sitting alone in her garden contemplating in solitude, and suddenly, she was aware of the golden Christ energy that once more enveloped her as she watched the daylight fade across the old orchard in front of the crystal river that flowed on and on always…. her tears spontaneously joined that flow as she sat transfixed in love and bliss as she experienced once more the unmistakeable presence of the Christ Consciousness within.

Her dreams of a collaborative retreat were not yet manifest; however the great gift she had received from the episode with Gabriel and Tony was the opportunity to own her own power and not be diminished by any projected perceptions. She knew for sure she had entered this opportunity with them with love and joy and the intention of sharing. Nothing more and nothing less. Tony had perceived she was making it all about her; this could not be further from the truth. He had told her on a visit to her home she was very powerful while quizzing her on her starseed status. This was not her issue. At this time, Gabriel did not support her, and the project could not move forward. Although never discussed, Athena intuited he was between a rock and a hard place and his own family issues were being mirrored by this family configuration as indeed, for sure, were Tony's. However, perhaps for them, it was an act of showing up for her, whether consciously or not, so she could realize how far she had come. Sometimes, we don't always get to know the gift our mere presence is for another. And so, to Gabriel and Tony, she offers her deepest appreciation and love.

India

It was her dear brother Gabriel who had introduced her to the work of the Indian Yogi and Mystic Sadhguru. Athena had never been to India in this incarnation and she was fascinated by the whole Guru phenomenon. What was it all about?

Synchronistically, that very year, he was hosting a very large event in London, which, of course, she attended. From this point on, for the next twelve months, she became a follower and flew to the Isha Foundation in Coimbatore for two lengthy stays in order to complete all his programs, culminating in the Samyama program in March 2019.

As soon as she had stepped onto the land of the Ashram, she was enveloped in a field of such great love that was such a stark contrast to the busy and sometimes frenetic energy of the outside world, and she felt exhilaration and deep joy. It was a time of sublime happiness to experience the simple life of an Ashram, living with the most beautiful beings whose lives were so uncomplicated and yet created such a loving container. She made wonderful friends from inside and outside India. It was a meeting place for all nationalities and a most wonderful and memorable experience that she would recommend to any seeker. This mighty land, with its enormous spiritual legacy, enchanted her.

Sadhguru himself is a powerhouse, full of passionate action and has done much to forward the spiritual process for many of his followers. It must be said he is not warm and fuzzy but direct and matter-of-fact. "He believes liberation as the fundamental longing in every form of life. Truth, for him, is a living experience instead of a destination, a conclusion, or a matter of metaphysical speculation. The possibility of self-realization, he strongly believes, is available to all.

He has a unique ability to make the ancient yogic sciences relevant to the contemporary mind." https://isha.sadhguru.org/uk/en

To support her own ongoing personal process, she attended the programs offered by the Isha Foundation and enjoyed her time at the Ashram immensely. However, it was the basic teaching from the very first program that she experienced before even going to India that was indeed the most profound for her: the great Shambhavi Mahamudra.

For her, this practice sums up the core teachings and have stayed with her and are now deeply embodied. She had not really needed to go to India. But it was a wonderful experience.

"I am not the body

I am not the mind

I am responsible for everything

My ability to respond is limitless

I am Mother to the world

This moment is the only moment there is."

This simple practice is experienced evermore deeply as an embodiment of truth. When we can fully live the essence of these simple but profound statements, we have realized the true I AM Presence.

In recent times, she has heard many criticisms of Sadhguru from several people who have brought attention to various statements he has made about population control, vaccinations, and connection to the World Economic Forum.

From Athena's perspective this being has done much to alleviate the suffering of humanity. She had once heard him say that if he had an opportunity to bring world leaders together in the same space for a period of days, it would contribute to rapid change for the wellbeing of the world, and perhaps this is why he was guided to address the UN and the WEF when given the opportunity.

Any comments about population control may perhaps refer to family planning methods that help overpopulated families regulate their number of offspring rather than referring to genocide via MRNA vaccinations in the country that has now overtaken China as the most populated in the world at 1.4 billion. The size of the population may be a problem for India given the food and nutrition problems, housing problems, starvation and famine, infectious diseases and epidemics, increasing population pressure on the cities and development of slums, heavy burden on most resources; decrease in agricultural areas; continuous destruction of forests; threat to the environment including wildlife; ......

At the same time, it is her view that the guru model is rapidly becoming a structure that will eventually not be viable as more and more step into their own sovereignty and become their own leader, trusting their own inner 'guru.' This is the meaning of liberation and incidentally, is the true meaning of the word sadhguru. It means 'inner guru'. The guru model has been much abused down the ages as power and influence over many inevitably can and has corrupted many, and they often fall from a high altitude.

There is no doubt that Sadhguru is well-loved across the world, but he has never demanded to be followed or worshipped and has always taught the true essence of sovereignty, freedom, and liberation. He is a person of much influence and is fair game for maleficent influences. Only he knows what he is about, but rather than criticize and create polarity better to accept all make their own free will choice, even gurus, and honor that. You can always calibrate his energy as per the Hawkins model.

Community

It was not her soul destiny to stay at the Ashram; however, her experience of being in this community had stirred within her ancient memories of living in an active community, and on her return to Iford, this was at the forefront of her thoughts

Athena had recognized the possibility of creating some kind of sanctuary of wellbeing at Iford as early as her first stay in 2005. The location had such a peaceful and beautiful ambiance, and the stewardship of this special land and gardens had now been passed from the original owners, Elizabeth Cartwright-Hignett and John Hignett, to their only son, William, and his new wife, Marianne. William particularly seemed enthusiastic and keen to help something materialize. During this stay at Iford, she also met a new friend, Alena who was/is a very talented artist with an equally talented young son, Timbalee. There seemed to be the makings of a community here for her at last.

Unknown to her at this time, there were bigger plans to renovate and add a full restaurant and workshop rooms adjacent to the estate, and they asked her if she would be interested in providing well-being workshops for their clientele using the newly built facilities. It was a perfect space and opportunity and she was truly thrilled that a vision she had of a healing sanctuary in this space the first time she lived there in 2005 seemed very close to becoming a possible viable proposition. William had discussed this possibility with her several times, and now he had the help of Marianne, his new wife, and so he asked Athena to put together a concept proposal and discussion catalyst. She was very excited.

Her appointment to discuss the concept and possible workshops with Marianne was canceled several times. When they did finally get together, Athena had felt something was off. It turned out the building program had to be put back a year due to some problems with the foundations of the new proposed construction next door to her cottage, and there seemed to be a marked withdrawal of enthusiasm for the whole idea. Perhaps this was understandable, given the delay and the issues they now faced. No one ever mentioned it again to her. She never received any feedback. It was such a disappointment as everything had seemed so perfect to create a win -win for all.

There also seemed to be a distinct change in the energies at Iford at this time. None of the staff were their usual happy selves and several had come to Athena to voice their concerns. Of course, she was only a tenant, and it was not her place to comment. But she could read the energy, and it was not good. Something for sure was not wholesome or beneficial.

And so it began, the slow realization that her future would not be at Iford. It took a while for her to process this, for she had spent some of the happiest and most profound moments of her life in this beautiful valley. This beautiful place of healing where she had done so much of the preparation for her own personal unfolding. The place where she had truly connected with the earth and nature and where she had taken so many wonderful walks with her beloved labradors, Josh and Sammy, whose ashes were scattered on this land.

The home of the abandoned cat she had brought to shelter.

The home that was her very own sanctuary amidst all the madness of the outside world.

She had listened to the birdsong every single day and fed so many different varieties of our feathered friends. The resident kingfisher was spectacular.

The crystalline river almost ran past her door, where the sunlight sparkled like specs of crystal light just for her.

The one hundred and fifty different species of butterflies and the spectacular dragonflies that filled the meadows and riverbanks, the flower and fauna, the horseshoe bats ... in terms of biodiversity and natural beauty, it was a paradise, and here she had made profound connection to the plant and animal kingdoms. She truly loved this place and its eccentric but delightful original owners, Elizabeth, and John Cartwright- Hignett who had first offered her this shelter from the storm that had been her life after her break up with Frank.

The whole area of Iford, Freshford, Brassknocker Hill, and the Frome River Valley was and is one of the most beautiful spots in the South West of England, and she felt blessed it had been her home for so long. She had experienced a profound connection to the natural world and awakenings to her own nature there.

Since leaving Bath in 2005, she had never felt any need to own another property, and she had lived there happily for a total of nine years, with extraordinary times of profound awakenings in between her adventures in Canada and the USA. However, as always when a move was coming in, she could feel the energy of change approaching.

Dorset

At this time an opportunity arose for her to buy the property next door to her sister in Dorset. Another beautiful spot in the South West of England, where her only sister June had settled and made a beautiful home.

Athena was in a perfect position as a cash buyer and she did make an offer that was accepted. However, for some reason this purchase would just not happen. Again, she could sense something was not right, and after five months of backward and forwards with legal issues, it became clear to her this was not meant to be, and she rescinded her offer. What should have been simple and straightforward became so complex, and she saw this as an omen for a possible future existence there. After years of not owning anything, she was reminded of how onerous we have made this process of living and finding shelter and simply let it go when it became apparent this was not in flow.

There was a restlessness within her soul.

At the human ego level of her being, she just wanted to find a place that she could call home that would be a base for her travels and where she knew she could stay and be safe. She had thought Iford would be the perfect place for community but it was not to be. She did not yet understand what her soul was now asking of her and was being asked to learn to be comfortable with the unknowing and the unknown once again.

PART 6 A BEAUTIFUL

COMPLETION

Vancouver Island

December 2019 had brought in the 'covidiocy', and by February 2020, she had come to terms with her disappointment over the Iford project and took a trip to Vancouver Island, BC, to visit a friend she had met online at the Conscious Business Initiative. Gail had just recently lost her husband and had offered Athena her basement to rent.

During this visit, she was able to get her Canadian passport very easily, as she had been granted citizenship in 2014. By early April 2020, she had packed everything up and, with the help of her sister, managed to get a flight out of the UK before they closed travel down because of the 'pandemic.' She left her home and country again to become a wanderer once more.

She was now 69 with no real fixed abode and a world gone mad. She was still as healthy and fit as a thirtysomething. Unlike her female ancestry, she looked set to live a long and healthy life but where? It was not lost on her that after leaving Toronto, she had had thoughts about heading west to Alberta, as the happy memories of her adventures climbing the Canadian Rockies were still fresh. However, circumstances at the time had urged the alternative decision. Her soul had guided her back to Europe and the UK, and it was now clear why. She had also noticed that her guidance tested her almost beyond the limit, as her soul was still in the driving seat of her life. There had been many times she was just bewildered by her soul's promptings, and as she surrendered once again to her soul's urgings, this was one of those times.

It turned out there was profound work for her to complete on this beautiful island, but as usual, she was only given one step at a time, demanding full trust and faith in the process and the unfolding.

She felt a deep empathy with her friend Gail, who was still in mourning and also was suffering from health issues. Gail was a gentle soul. Athena recognized her as a fellow starseed from her poetry and other confidences she had shared. Athena was deeply moved by her kindness. One of her family properties included a beautiful log cabin on Pender Island, one of the Southern Gulf Islands located in the Salish Sea, British Columbia. They took regular trips there together, and Athena was able to help with the garden maintenance of both the house on Vancouver Island and the cabin. She loved gardening. She had always loved gardening. For her it was a meditative practice and a connection with nature and the land. The sea air at Pender was sublime, and the views were so beautiful that sometimes when the mist rolled in, one could not differentiate the sea from the sky. Looking out across to the mainland felt almost surreal at times, as if she had been transported to another planet. Their arrangement was certainly beneficial to both at this time of great change in both their lives. For now, Athena meditated, gardened, walked, wrote blogs, and took trips to Pender with Gail. In a state of surrender, she asked for guidance as to why she was there. Perhaps it was to collaborate with Gail in some way. She still had dreams of working in some kind of wellness center with others. What a beautiful location this would make. What was all this about? Soon, it would all unfold.

Gail had a son and daughter and four grandchildren, as well as an adult stepson who was diagnosed with autism. There seemed to be some family friction that had developed between her and her now-deceased husband's previous wife and her daughter. Plus, she also had her own ex-husband, the father of her own children, who had recently been moved into care to consider. It seemed like a lot of pressure for one person who was still in the process of grieving. She also had at least four different family properties to look after. Although Athena was grateful for a place to land, she still had no clue what was unfolding here. As usual, she was once again in the unknown, just following her guidance. She did her best to be a friend to Gail at this strange time.

After the terrible demise of her own mother, Athena had simply vowed never to be ill, and she never was. Her studies had demonstrated clearly it was always a choice at some level by the mind to suffer in some way that was not necessary. She had no intention of being vaccinated and had a strong intuition this was not a healthy option for anyone. She was contemptuous of masks and the whole hullaballoo around the supposed 'pandemic.' None of it computed for her at a very deep level of her being.

She had been very surprised to find the family, and particularly Gail, all were following the rules set out by the Canadian government and that the situation in Canada was much the same with regards to this situation as in the UK. She noticed how easily the Canadians did what they were told, just as most of the rest of the world at this stage of the game and also noticed Gail's tendency to go along with the narrative of the authorities. Perhaps she had expected her to take more of a stand and perhaps this was unfair of her as Gail had some physical health issues at this time.

The house was in a wealthy neighborhood. For Athena, the complexities of home ownership had long been dropped while her host was juggling the responsibility of multiple home ownership. She felt once again out of step with her environment.

However, it must be said the property she now inhabited had a most beautiful view of the Salish Sea and an even more beautiful giant wooden carving of the Goddess Quan Yin, her very own guide, in the hallway on the upper floor. It was good to know she was there, keeping watch above her. As time passed, she began spending more and more time on her own in the basement as Gail's time was filled with her family matters, managing the carers for her stepson, and trips alone to Pender. Athena felt isolated.

And then it began. One evening, when Gail had left for Pender, she tried to settle to watch a video but could not. She became aware of a presence in the room. She went to get a wrap from her bedroom and inadvertently, as she threw it around her shoulders, disturbed the small china statue of Quan Yin that Gail had so thoughtfully placed in her room. The head of the beautiful miniature was knocked clean off. She was totally mortified, but on checking the damage knew she could be easily repaired. On reflection, the break in the statue's neck was reflective of what would unfold. She sat to watch the video and almost immediately felt as if she was being strangled. There was some kind of malevolent energy in this room. Thank God she had the tools to deal with this. She cleared and transmuted the energy and her own field, but in doing so, had opened up her vision and realized there had been some kind of fierce battle on this land. She also intuited Gail's husband was still roaming present in the property in etheric form. It seemed he needed help to pass over, and of course, she could help with this process.

Gail had told her of the terrible arguments between the two families of her late husband that had occurred on this property. Also, from the house next door, she could often hear the raised voices of mother and daughter fighting. What was being shown to her was the energy imprints of conflict present on this land and in this home. She felt as if she was being 'used' in some way to sort out the mess that existed here energetically. She had thought there would be an opportunity for her to spend more time with Gail on Pender but here she was on the mainland, in the basement, while she and members of her family and related friends and carers spent summer time over there. This didn't feel right to her somehow. She had plenty of time to explore her own feelings about being left behind. It seemed entirely reasonable that Gail should prioritize her family and her own friends and Athena did not understand her own feelings. They didn't make any sense to her.

Then, suddenly, the entire vision dropped in. She was transported to a time and place where Gail was a shaman and also her mother. In this time capsule, Athena had felt neglected by her mother as all her attention was placed outward to other members of her family and her duties to the tribe. It was the origination of the abandonment wounding that had been continued by her own mother, who could not connect with her as a baby, who spent much of her time helping her own family rather than being with her children and husband, and who finally left her under appalling circumstances, being replayed. Here it was, she was being shown the recycling of a story that had not yet been resolved within her and she had crossed the Atlantic once again in order to bring the light of understanding and resolution to this situation. The guidance and continual reminders of the presence of the Divine Mother, beloved Quan Yin, was palpable and the role she had begun to play in guiding Athena's life. The Mother of Compassion itself, whose Presence was unmistakable. She finally realized she had been brought here to break yet another cycle and heal yet another space/place within. She could not share all this with Gail immediately. It took time to process. While she took her time to evaluate everything that was being presented, she continued her gardening duties and started to explore the issue of abundance. What she had thought may have developed into some kind of working partnership had now clarified itself, and she realized she needed another plan.

Victoria, BC

S he had been on the island for five months, and coincidental with the arrival of her furniture, she moved to a convenient apartment in Victoria, the capital of British Columbia, situated almost right next door to the Parliament Buildings. Her apartment was on floor nine, appt 911, and had a beautiful view of the harbor. She had not lived in an apartment since she was five, so this was going to be another new adult experience. Her apartment was modern, clean, and functional, with enough room to house what was left of her earthly belongings. She had been an avid reader in her early days, but now not so much. Her library was limited to the writings of the great spiritual masters, poetry, and her own journals. Nevertheless, to a certain extent, it was comforting to have them near her, and she was glad to receive her books. She did not need a car. Everything was nearby so that she could walk easily enough to all the amenities. What was next, she wondered? She had leased the apartment for one year, so there was time for the next steps to unfold.

She came across an advert on social media for a group that had been created by a local woman in Victoria looking to create a community in Mexico. This attracted her interest, and she joined them. She loved the name of the group more than anything – "Eco-Villas de Amor." She definitely was open to some 'amor' in her life and started to follow them.

It was here she would meet a young German fellow who seemed very savvy and clued into what this group was attempting. He was very impressive. She liked him. They had an easy rapport. Somehow, she got to chat with him, and it turned out his wife was Mexican, pregnant and they were planning a permanent move to Mexico. They began chatting about the project, and in so doing, his energy information began to flow to Athena.

What came through was a shock. He was the child she had aborted in her youth. She recognized his energetic signature because they had a soul contract. Oh my God, how was she going to handle this? This connection would never have been made if she had not been picking up the Canadian group, which she would never have done from the UK. This is the miraculous way the universe works in our favor to heal all that is required to heal. All we are required to do is follow the promptings of our soul no matter what or where it leads us. Here was another piece of her karma to resolve. She had halted a life process, and this had caused her untold grief and sorrow and brought in much guilt. It does not mean what she did was wrong or that she was bad, but to prevent a life from coming into being is not necessarily in alignment with the highest will of the creator that wishes to experience itself. That is the simple fact. It had taken Athena many years to deal with the guilt and shame this incident had brought in for her and fed into the 'religious conditioning' she had built up through various lifetimes of religious service in varying capacities.

As for the child, the incoming soul, if rejected, will simply find another familial set up that will provide what it requires for its own progression. And so, the challenges will inevitably be the same and as she got to know this young man, she could see this very clearly. What she could do in the meantime was clear this for herself and give him an opportunity to understand his own wound, particularly at this crucial point as he was bringing a new life into the world with his beloved.

He liked to talk with her, and upon checking in with her guidance if it was in alignment to share the information that was unfolding through her higher sense perception, she arranged a Zoom call to share. He told her that he had been drawn to her in the community group, and she knew once again the universe was weaving its magic. She arranged a meeting for them where she could create a safe field and share her findings.

He received them remarkably well. He was only a young man but on his own path of soul discovery and was most assuredly one of the beings here to build a new and better earth. At this time, his energy calibrated quite high, and she recognized him as a Starseed and wanted to help him as much as she was able, given the circumstances. They had a beautiful online meet up where she created a safe and loving space for them both to share and completed this with an energy transmission as guided. After this session, he asked her if it would be alright to share the information with his wife, and the result of this was a beautiful online ceremony for them all, including the baby Maximillian who was still in utero.

Following this, Athena worked with Dirk and his partner Erik for a little while to support their project, The Paradise Syndicate. Their connection to the original opportunity in Mexico eventually fell through, as did an attempt to build out her own work with them through their platform. They were not ready, and Athena still felt that this move to Canada was temporary but was not getting clear guidance as to where the next port of call would be. Dirk and Erik had dreams of moving to Mexico to create a community there, but this was still only a dream. However, Dirk was intending to move to Michochuan with his Mexican wife and new baby to be nearer to her parents soon after the birth, which he did do eventually. Again, she was at the point of just allowing life to flow.

The Unfolding

The first thing that struck Athena about Victoria was how exceedingly British it seemed despite the beautiful indigenous totems placed strategically in downtown locations. Perhaps it was the preponderance of the highly manicured gardens that fronted the Legislature Building. To be honest, this was not attractive to her. She preferred the more natural spaces of nature she had found in the wilder, forested parts of British Columbia. Tourism, technology, and public services dominated employment, and by all standards, it was a thriving city that would ultimately be adversely affected by the covid nonsense like many other places on planet earth during these few years.

Many of the totems describe the legendary demise of Mu or Lemuria, and Vancouver Island has long been associated with this cataclysm through the legends passed down by the totem carvers of the Pacific North West. Lemuria was a matriarchal society where women were highly respected and had an equal voice with men. Perhaps now, as her own inner masculine and feminine energies were balancing, there was another piece of soul retrieval here for her.

She explored everywhere on her feet. She loved walking and, almost every day would walk to the nearby waterfront and often several miles following the coastal path around St James Bay. On a clear day the majestic Olympic Mountains formed a powerful and constantly changing backdrop to these coastal pilgrimages. This mountain range is found on the Olympic Peninsula of the Pacific

Northwest, located in western Washington of the United States, and forms part of the Pacific Mountain System. Visually, they are truly spectacular, and she found their benign yet constantly transforming presence comforting, strengthening, and grounding.

The other most delightful place she loved to walk was located further out of the city, the locals called '" Mount Doug." This is a most beautiful forest parkland of around one hundred and eighty-eight hectares with more than twenty- kilometers of trails. She had first found the park while living in Saanich with Gail who had also recognised the reverence of this place. She had found her feet were just drawn to this most magical site, and she had many mystical experiences there where her heart would simply explode into love and gratitude for life as she climbed the various trails. She felt a deep love of this land she could not explain. Of course, it would all unfold in time. For now, she was content to walk the trails. Trails that would lead to the summit where there is a three hundred and sixty-degree panoramic view, and one could see seals and orcas. In the lush forests, she could smell the sweetest pine of Douglas Fir and Cedar trees that towered above her, collect wildflowers amongst the abundance of ferns, and be accompanied by the birds and animals on her path.

On one of her walks, silence fell across the forest and she was guided to stop and sit on a nearby tree trunk that had fallen near the trail. Suddenly, she was transported to a different dimension and was being shown visions of all the events in her life that had been painful but had now changed into loving memories. The scenes ran like a film show, clip after clip of events that had been painful but were now all changed into beautiful images and memories. She was smiling and laughing she felt incredible. The mountain forest was showing her all that had been resolved and healed in her own life to date. It was astonishing.

Mount Douglas was first known as the "hill of cedars" to the local Songhees people. The aboriginal and Songhees people call the hill Pkols, meaning "white rock" in their own Sencoten dialect. According to traditional history, the mountain grew after the Creator tossed four white rocks that mark the borders of the different first nations territories. This most sacred space was a culturally significant gathering and meeting place of the Sencoten and Lekwungen peoples, a site for ceremonies and sharing important news. Later, after the Songhees harvested lengthy cedar planks from its forests to construct palisades to create Fort Victoria, its title was formalized as "Cedar Hill."

This beautiful parkland was set aside in 1858 by Sir James Douglas, who, as Governor of Vancouver Island and British Columbia, led the British Colonisation and negotiated land deals with the First Nations. Cedar Hill was placed as a Government Reserve (the creek and hill were both named after him) and was protected as a crown trust since 1889. In November 1992, it was transferred to the Saanich Municipality

The Douglas Treaties, as they were known, promised the protection of the way of life of the First Nations people. Yet the Saanich treaties have never been properly honored. It has been put forward they were legalized land theft and part of a devious tactic to force the indigenous peoples off their land and into designated Indian Reserves. This is what actually happened.

Dispute over the hill and its name was ongoing: in 2013, Chief Eric Pelkey led a group of Coast Salish people and hundreds of local supporters up the mountain to place a hand-carved sign at the summit. First Nations' reclaiming of Mount Douglas as Pkols represents a small piece of decolonization on Vancouver Island. Athena visited this place often.

Soon after the arrival of her belongings, she set up her home altar with the crystals she treasured and her own stone statue of Quan Yin. This period was an intense time of inner reflection for her, and she meditated for an hour daily, sometimes twice, in front of her altar and the panoramic view she had of Victoria and its harbor.

One of her most treasured crystals was an aquamarine, an elongated shape that she had found in a market long ago near her home in Iford. It meant such a lot because, in it, she could see her mother as she was in her youth, beautiful and smiling, with her hair long and dark before the ravages of the disease that took her. Every time she looked at this crystal, she could see this image of her mother quite clearly in its reflections. It had helped her through many dark moments. This type of occurrence was not new to Athena; she could see a lot of different beings everywhere she went, particularly when she was in nature. In trees, in mountains, in gardens, in flowers, in photographs (other than the subject). In every home she had ever owned or rented beings appeared on the walls, on the curtains in the carpets, on the tiles, in the shadows. This had been ongoing for her since she was a young woman and she accepted it as her normal.

This particular evening Athena sat to meditate and picked up the crystal as she often did before going in deep. It dropped onto the rug, and as she bent to replace it in front of the altar found it cracked open, wide in half, completely severed across its center. Her mother had disappeared. It didn't make sense as it had dropped to a soft surface and yet had shattered. How had it broken? Athena felt that the energy of her mother had completely vanished.

What had appeared now in the bottom half of the crystal was the face of her father enveloped in the beard of another larger being that looked like some kind of 'priest/shaman /wizard who was wearing a strange tall hat. Something very strange was happening. She asked for guidance as she sat to mediate upon these messages and then went to bed. As soon as she awakened the following morning, she knew instantly what she must do.

Ancestors

The story her father had told her when she was only a young girl, when he was still in a loving relationship with her, was how he had longed to bring her mother and his young family to Canada to settle and begin a new life. His own elder brother Tom had already emigrated and was encouraging him to do the same. This would have been shortly after the death of her mother's own father. It was one of the few confidences Athena's father had shared with her before he could or would no longer communicate. Her mother had declined with the reasoning that she still had her younger sisters to look after and needed to be there for them, as she had always been. Athena could only imagine this may have started the decline in their own relationship, although Ken always stood by Grace and supported her. But she knew, somehow, this was an important piece of family history. When she herself arrived in Canada for the first visit in 2005, she found that the man who had offered her the position that would bring her to Toronto lived on Walmsley Boulevard. Walmsley was her human family name and actually carries the same frequency as Melchizedek. It seemed what was unfolding here was some kind of historical tie to this land she was not yet privy to.

By now, Athena had long been able to forgive her father. There had been many times, particularly when she lived at Iford, that she was able to feel into his deep pain and sorrow. She cried for his desperation and all the loss he had encountered. As she began to heal her own wounds this had opened up for her such deep compassion for the suffering of the human condition. She could feel her father, a bright, sensitive young man of nineteen years being shuttled off to fight a world war only to find himself a prisoner of that war at the end. All she felt for both her parents was deep sadness but also total unconditional love, forgiveness, and compassion for the tragic early loss of them both and for all the losses they had both incurred in this incarnation. She simply loved them as she does now. Instinctively, she knew what she must do.

That weekend, she took the broken crystal to the Hill of Cedars. It was January 2021. This time, she took the bus to the base of the park trail and began the long climb to the top. Very close to the top of the hill, she stopped at a clearing on the trail; there was a kind of gateway created by two huge evergreen bushes (either Salal or Evergreen Huckleberry) with a pathway between them to the top. Such a peaceful stillness there. There was no one else around or even on the trail it seemed. Beside the shrubs and the gateway, there was a natural clearing of undulating green mossy grass and white rock. The White Rock of Pkols! She sat there for some time contemplating and then took each half of the crystal and buried each one at the foot of each shrub. Finally, she had buried her father on the land he had dreamed of coming to all those years ago, beside the woman he had loved so deeply. Athena sat again to contemplate and bless this ceremony. She felt a deep peace as the memory of them both was put to rest. There was no weeping just a lightness of being and knowing that all was well and as it should be. She set off to take the trail path down with a sense of completion.

As she got about half way down the trail, a huge bird came flying past her left side. So close it almost touched her head. The trail opened out to a view of the forest and she could see the bird had landed on a branch and seemed to be facing away from her. She was mesmerized as the bird turned its head to look straight at her. It was a beautiful Barred Owl, and it stayed with her for approximately twenty minutes. They locked eyes, and she could feel the bird communicating with her. Somehow, it was a part of Grace, her mother. She was saying she was flying free, liberated by the ceremony, by the land, with the spirit of the man she had loved; they had come home together in peace. At this point, Athena did weep with no knowing why, the what, or the how, with no need to know, other than the knowing of the great love of this universe and its many wise and wonderful ways and how blessed she was to witness and be aware of such connection to it all. And she remembered that Gail's place on Pender Island was called Owls Nest. Another mother from another time that she had loved.

Freedom

F reedom, it seemed, was the name of the game.

On August 15, 2022, the Saanich Council approved a request from the Wsanec Leadership Council to move forward with a municipal park name restoration for PKOLS (Mount Douglas)

This had been an incredible journey across all dimensions of her being. All timelines are actually happening now in the present, just at a different frequency of light and, therefore, not always visible. Her many journeys to foreign lands had entailed rooting out and transmuting any residual pieces still present within her energy field that possibly could prevent the highest outcomes for all in the now moment. And finally, Athena understood what she had been doing these many years and why she had come at this time to be here now. To find what still required the grace and blessing of forgiveness for actions (karma) taken either by or against this being in any timeline.

These time capsules were embedded in her DNA and often time-coded to be unearthed at the appropriate stage in the current life experience when she has already done enough work to be able to connect the dots with conscious awareness and had reached a stage where forgiveness and grace could be forthcoming without reservation. When we can do this at the deepest level we clear every timeline, we clear the land and the places we visit of that distortion. We bring love, forgiveness, and compassion into the collective field. Often, we need to be in a certain place on the earth's grid for these to trigger. It can be a circuitous route to truth and one has to commit one's life to this. She had committed her life to this prior to incarnation and she had formally committed her life to this at her 'formal 'training at school when she committed to reaching the highest potential possible in this body, this lifetime. She had retaken her vow in the Himalayas.

When we are able to do this, it shifts the frequency of that particular complex within the entire hologram and why she is always encouraging everyone to do their inner work.

Athena's own inner work has been an ongoing life process and has been phenomenal in its scope. She actually spent nine years in total living and working in Canada and the USA. She had returned in 2020 during the Covid farce, which all must realize by now was about much more than a virus and everything to do with freedom. She had returned to do the work of liberation. She had no idea why she had been directed to Victoria, but slowly, it was unfolding. It always did in time.

The Residential Schools of Canada

❝❝Before the country was settled by Europeans that, includes the British Crown, England, Scotland, and Ireland, Indigenous peoples were organized in hundreds of distinct territories. The First Nations is the name given to six hundred and thirty- four distinct communities across the mountains, plains and forests. Canada's constitution also recognizes the Metis, descendants of unions between the Europeans and First Nations people between the 17th C and 19th C, and the Inuit, whose territory consists of 51 communities in the Arctic Circle.

Between 1871 and 1921, the British Crown entered eleven treaties with some First Nations members. Members of all these communities would eventually be sent to the schools.

In 1876, parliament passed the Indian Act that imposed strict control over the lives of Indigenous people. They were made to live on reserves and couldn't leave without permission, and the children were sent to institutions that had the explicit aim of stripping away their culture, language, and identity. For most of the 20th C, at least 139 schools were run by Catholic, Anglican, and United Churches.

It is estimated one hundred and fifty thousand Indigenous children attended.

They were prevented from speaking their native language and had to adopt the school's religious denomination. Many were beaten, verbally, and sexually abused; thousands died from disease, neglect, and suicide. The schools were designed to be deliberately far away from where the children lived, preventing their parents from visiting. Children were beaten for using their own language and told it was the devil's tongue. The Church and the generations of officials and politicians knew of the conditions in these schools and did nothing. The current official number of children that died is 4120, but this is likely only a fraction of the total".

The Guardian

https://www.theguardian.com/world/ng-interactive/2021/sep/06/canada-residential-schools-indigenous-children-cultural-genocide-

Kamloops, BC

In April 2021, Athena awakened one morning in deep, visceral grief. She had no conscious awareness of what this was about. Shortly after this incident a fellow student from BBSH whom she had met while she had been studying in Europe turned up a couple of blocks away from her in some real distress about her accommodation and was reaching out on Facebook for help. As soon as she visited her, she knew she had to help her get out of her dismal and dark apartment, and so Athena invited her to stay in her spare room until she could get a new accommodation sorted out. Blanche had been working with the Indigenous people in the Northwest Territories.

Rapidly, the story unfolded. Within a month, Blanche invited her to join a ceremony being held by the Indigenous Tribes of that area on land adjoining the Parliament Building. The ceremony was to honor all the children of the Residential Schools in Canada. Blanche was very clued into all these events as she had worked closely with the First Nations people for some years in the North. She had first met Blanche in Austria when they studied together, and indeed, Blanche had even visited with her at Iford. When they met again here in Victoria only two blocks away from each other, Athena had sensed another soul set up. No such thing as coincidence, and everything to do with a soul pre-plan.

And so, Athena prepared herself to attend the ceremony with Blanche to honor the victims of the Residential Schools of Canada. The Parliament steps were filled at this time with signature Orange T-shirts of the movement and Teddy Bears of all sizes to honor the children. Athena carefully selected three small red sandstones that had naturally formed into rose-shaped carvings. They had been gifts from the Trail of Tears ceremony she had attended while at school. She placed them into a small lavender-colored gift purse with leather ties and gently placed them on the Legislature steps before moving on to the land where the ceremony would take place.

Athena was drawn to stand under a very large spreading oak tree on this land, and the ceremony began. Blanche was some distance away. Nearby but not next to her. As the drumming and chanting began, she could feel time proceeding to dissolve as it brought in a vision. It was her brief life as one of those children. She saw a baby being incinerated in an ancient furnace. The baby had been a product of sexual abuse. It was her. She broke down into uncontrollable grief as this time capsule was released. Her whole body was convulsing, grieving, and in shock, but she knew she had to allow it to pass through her and out from her.

This was the memory she had tapped into all those years ago during her termination. The body's cellular and energetic DNA holds all the memories of every incarnation. Her body does not lie. Athena did not even know about the residential schools of Canada until she arrived in Victoria in 2021, and at this specific time when the Indigenous tribes were gathering to honor the lost children so close to where she lived now.

She had been brought up in the UK. Even though she had lived in Canada for seven years prior, this topic was certainly not then on her radar. The schools were not part of her conscious history.

As she allowed the release of grief through her body, another vision began of the souls of the children arising upward.

Shortly after this occurred, the news of the Kamloops Indian Residential school BC was released in the press.

In May 2021, Dr. Sarah Beaulieu, an anthropologist with "about a decade of experience searching for historical grave sites," surveyed the area with ground penetrating radar GPR and observed "disruptions in the ground," which she concluded *could be* 200 unmarked graves based on "their placement, size, depth, and other features Indigenous community had long suspected that unmarked graves were located at the residential school, but no proof existed to support this." Sadly, Dr Beaulieu's findings have now been discredited.

In order to conclusively prove this specific allegation, full excavation is required, and no -one has to date authorized this. However, the knowing that children went missing from the Indian residentials schools has been recognized by the Indigenous communities for generations.

The Kamloops Indian Residential School was part of the Canadian Residential School system. Located in Kamloops, British Columbia, it was once the largest residential school in Canada, with its enrolment peaking at 500 in the 1950s. The school was established in 1890 (the Church-run schools had begun as early as 1830) and operated until 1969 when it was taken over from the Catholic Church by the federal government to be used as a day school residence. It closed in 1978, but the building still stands. Pope Francis visited Canada in 2022 to apologize on behalf of the Catholic Church. Since there has been no further advancement in this matter. However, On October 27, 2022, Canada's parliament unanimously recognized the country's residential school system as genocide.

For Athena personally, as she went back into the quest for truth, this matter arose once more, and she wept again. Grace, her mother, had been at one of the schools, and she had been subject to sexual abuse. It was her baby that was incinerated. This is why she had been so fearful of giving birth in this current incarnation and why she had always been fearful of allowing her girls their freedom. She was unconsciously terrified for them. Also, why she had issues with her own relationship with sex and her eventual conflict with the Catholic Church; she carried all this within her own energy field without ever finding the means to bring it out of her unconscious mind and process her fear. It was no wonder cancer had devoured her.

The Healing of Genocide

How do you forgive cultural genocide? How do you forgive this atrocity and the atrocities that continue around the world today?

Obviously, there was still personal and ancestral grief to release, and this memory was triggered by being part of the ceremony that took place in Victoria at this specific time. However, if she stayed that grieving victim, it would not be possible to break the cycle. And this she must do; otherwise, it will only replay and replay in some other timeline. She was here to break another cycle.

First, she expressed the deepest love and compassion for herself and her family and friends of that time and all the victims and families. All must have been so traumatized with so much grief to process. She realized the roles of her mother and father, then and now, why Ken had wanted to bring them all to Canada in the early years, and why the ceremony of laying them to rest on the Hill of Cedars was so significant.

She held unconditional love from the core essence I AM in her field now in the present moment. Now, she is aware. She is even more present and stronger three years on.

It means she will no longer carry this memory with her in any part of her field or her DNA template, for she allowed the grief to expose itself for cleansing. She fully allowed the emotions to flow rather than pushing them away quickly, thinking or hoping she had already dealt with the pain of this. She releases any cord or attachment to this memory that might currently be draining her energy.

To all those with whom she has unfinished business, through all time and space, she now declares to the perpetrators;

"I acknowledge you are a soul learning as I am. I forgive you. It is my intention to forgive you. I choose to free you and myself from the past by disconnecting myself from this memory. May you and I be blessed with mercy and grace."

She watches her core essence light burning all cords and attachments to this memory, and she visualizes all the cords snapping back into her own field now. She finally forgives to empower herself, and it is done. She is free.

The perpetrator/s still have their own work to do in this or another cycle. But Athena will no longer carry this burden and will never recreate that victimhood. This is liberation from that cycle of karma, from that piece of victimhood.

Before this chapter is completed, she is guided to remind the world also of the Trail of Tears in the USA as all is connected. She had also worked with this horrific piece of American history while attending her third year of study at school in the USA.

The entire third year had performed the ceremony and a very profound group healing for the poor souls forced to take this journey, which was, of course, for their own healing in this current time. From this ceremony, she had kept three small pieces of sandstone rock that had formed natural surfaces, each with the appearance of a rose. For her, the stones represented her own heart and her own tears for the suffering of all these poor, displaced families. These were the stones she placed on the Legislature steps to honor the children.

The Trail of Tears was the forced relocation, during the 1830s, of Indigenous peoples of the Southeast region of the United States, including the Cherokee, Creek, Chickasaw, Choctaw, and Seminole tribes, among others, to the so-called Indian Territory west of the Mississippi River.

The routes used by Indigenous people as part of the Trail of Tears consisted of several overland routes and one main water route that stretched some five thousand and forty-five miles (about 8,120 km) across portions of nine states. According to estimates based on tribal and military records, approximately one hundred thousand Indigenous people were forced from their homes during the Trail of Tears, and some fifteen thousand died during their relocation.

Athena had been guided to place the three small stones on the steps of the Parliament Building in Victoria immediately before attending the ceremony for the residential school children that took place on the land right next to this building. This was symbolic of the invitation to the current power structures in both countries to accept responsibility for the part that the British Crown and both Governments had played in these atrocities against the Indigenous peoples of North America.

Athena had been part of both the powerful healing ceremonies and could once again witness the ways in which the universe works in a miraculous fashion to orchestrate events. If it hadn't been for Blanche and her predicament Athena would probably not even have known the gathering of the indigenous tribes was happening. And most certainly if she had not invited Blanche to stay, her own personal work may never have been accomplished. Once again, she felt blessed by providence.

Blanche also was blessed by the benevolence of the universe as it only took a month before one of the apartments in Athena's block was vacated. As she was staying with Athena, she was able to get an early warning of this and was delighted to move into her lovely new apartment with a spectacular view of the waterfront Victoria Harbor.

They continued to explore Victoria and the waterfront together until Athena was prompted by her guidance that her work on the island was complete. She had been in her apartment exactly one year and knew deep inside her time there was coming to a close. Those of you who are open to their own higher sense perception will know exactly how this feels. You know something is afoot but have to wait for clarity and further instructions. These important steps cannot be rushed.

She had not seen or heard from Gail during this past year and was delighted to be invited out for a birthday lunch with her and a friend in late August 2021. It seems there had been big shifts in Gail's life also.

She had sold her property in Saanich and moved to a smaller place further north. Alex had moved into a full -time care home facility, and she had also purchased another property on Pender Island. She took Athena to see this new property right next door to Owls Nest. Such a beautiful spot, but a lot of work to be done on the house.

Athena had fond memories of the island. She had cared for the garden at Owls Nest as if it had been her own. There was something about planting, growing, and harvesting she loved and still loves. Her connection to the land and also to the plant kingdom brought remarkable states of joy for her. She had wondered if somehow this was the place she would stay. However, during one of her visits, she had looked over the balcony as she often did when gardening and seen two beautiful orcas swim by the cabin and knew, like them, she was just passing through; her work was complete, and she would leave.

Searching for a Home

A thena knew she would not, could not stay in Victoria, but was not yet getting a clear indication of the next steps. In her state of inquiry, she decided to visit Canmore and the Rockies in September 2021 once more to see how this felt for her. She booked a convenient lodge to stay, took a flight to Calgary, and picked up a hire car at the airport. Within a week, she was in Canmore.

She loved this vibrant mountain town that was nestled in the Bow Valley and surrounded by mountain peaks. The Three Sisters Mountain peaks always reminded Athena of her mother and her two sisters. She had been drawn there originally by this name while still living in Toronto.

In 1883, Albert Rogers named these mountains the Three Nuns after a storm left a heavy veil of snow on the northern face of all three peaks. They were renamed the Three Sisters in 1886 by George Dawson, and they are referred to individually as Big Sister, Middle Sister, and Little Sister. They are also known as Faith, Hope, and Charity. Athena was reminded the reason her mother did not come 'home' to this land was because of her two sisters and their respective families. And she was happy she had brought her mother and her father to their final place of rest.

Canmore is situated in Alberta's Rocky Mountains, west of Calgary, and an area known for its stunning natural beauty, abundant outdoor recreational opportunities, and laid-back lifestyle.

The Grassi Lakes Trail weaves past a waterfall to two turquoise blue lakes, and there is a provincial park for cross-country skiing and mountain bike trails. All such a delight for the nature loving Athena after a year of apartment living! The weather was perfect, and she spent the week between here and in Banff, climbing mountains, exploring, meditating, and feeling as if this was the place to settle. She revisited Lake Louise, and this time, she saw the most beautiful huge merkaba made from the light resting upon a quiet part of the lakeside hidden from the crowds.

The Merkaba is a star tetrahedron with its two geometric shapes spinning in opposite directions. It has the power to create a perfectly unionized and balanced energy field and creates balance and stability. These are the first of the platonic solids, and with four triangular sides, the sides sit flat no matter where they lie so that structure and stability become an unshakable force. The tetrahedron is also linked to the energy of the solar plexus – and related to personal power.

The top tetrahedron represents the masculine energy, the lower represents the feminine. This can also be applied to the earth and the cosmos, the top being cosmic and the bottom earth. It can be applied to the physical realm and the spiritual realm or the existence of dark and light. It is all about opposing forces coming together to create harmony. These two energies spin in opposite directions but together create balance, strength, and harmony. It becomes a vehicle to carry the body and soul into higher consciousness. The upward point takes us higher, while the lower point keeps us connected to the earth and grounded. It was such a very beautiful message from the sacred turquoise lake at Banff for Athena to receive after these past two years of work. It always held such wonderful confirmations for her.

Although she had spent an idyllic week in these most exquisite locations and felt revived and rejuvenated after the intense soul work she had been doing almost non-stop for the past two years on Vancouver Island, she had a deep knowing she would return to the UK.

Gail had helped her arrive and she also helped her to leave. She was the gatekeeper to this realm for Athena. Gail had created a beautiful sacred ceremonial circle in her garden at Pender, and together, they planted the breathtakingly beautiful Japanese Maple Athena had bought for her first 'garden' in Saanich at Gail's house and then later for her balcony at her apartment in Victoria. She had also grown a huge Pieris, which now adorned the balcony of Gail's property next door. It felt so good to offer these plants to the spaces there. To leave expressions of her life and love there.

So much had been accomplished, and if she did not leave now, she would not be able to for some time as Trudeau was closing down all air travel for the non- vaccinated. Her apartment lease was finished in Sept, and by 12 Oct, her furniture and belongings went to storage again, and she left James Bay for the last time.

And so it was; she spent her last days on the island of Vancouver with the person who had made it possible for her to come there and do this deep and important work.

What Now?

It occurred to her that we may think we know what we are doing and why, but the Universe has an intelligence far beyond our mere mortal minds ...... it orchestrates synchronicities and synergies that we cannot possibly comprehend until we do ......

The flight back to the UK was complicated by testing and then retesting because of an admin mistake by the doctor in charge, all ridiculous as Athena knew she did not and would never have Covid or any other virus. She complied only to be able to board the plane and leave before flying was forbidden, and the ever-increasing signs of the democratic dissolution of the Canadian government seemed imminent. Of course, the state of affairs in the UK in 2021 was not much better, but at least she could get back in without too much trouble. Before she knew it, she was in a taxi driving west to her sister's place in Dorset.

This was a delicate situation for both sisters. Athena was very aware that her sister was under a lot of stress working part-time in a local supermarket for a couple of years to ensure survival until her pensions kicked in. The government had put back the dates of the claim, and unfortunately, her sister was caught by this after taking a forced early retirement from the company she had served faithfully and well for around twenty years. It must be said in this situation, her sister had been doing her own freedom work, no longer complying with a denigrating and demeaning authoritative misogynist.

Athena just needed a place to land and was sure it wouldn't be for long, but she was acutely aware that for her sister, it was not an ideal situation. She knew June did not really understand why she had made what looked like crazy decisions at the time to leave and then to return. Athena barely knew herself what was going on but just had to trust her instincts and her guidance. She understood fully why she had to be in British Columbia as the unfolding history revealed itself, and as it did so, she realized it was never about actually going to live there permanently. The whole event was an orchestration to see if she could do what she had to do and trust the process. For now, she was just so very grateful for a place to land and to be with someone she loved, even if mayhem was the best descriptor of the British Isles at this time.

For three months, she did what she could to keep a low profile in the small living space of June's cozy country cottage and helped as much as she could. It was hard to find reasonable accommodation as the rents had increased even in the short time she had been away, and she had no idea where she wanted to live. Dorset, although lovely, was not calling to her. Her soul was telling her either Scotland, Ireland, or Cornwall. She had been receiving these messages still while living in BC. She knew, somehow, she needed to be near water.

And so it was; after spending a lovely Christmas with her sister and a trip to Bath to see a few old friends, she moved to a spot just outside Newquay in Cornwall that turned up just as miracles always do when she needed them to. She visited a tasteful urban community development on 22 November 2021. Stayed at a hotel at Bedruthan rocks and fell in love with the stunning coastal path at Carnewas. She had breakfast at Shiva Café at the top of the road where the property was situated. She signed the lease in November. Her sister had been using her old car, which she duly handed back after purchasing her own, and by the first week of January 2022, she had the keys to a lovely new house in the development of Nansledan, so close to the beautiful, but wild north-western coast of Cornwall, the Celtic Sea, and the Atlantic Ocean. Somehow, it felt important to be on the Atlantic side.

Cornwall, UK

A thena was once again in the unknown, yet there was something about this land upon which she trod now that brought a warmth to her heart, a feeling of remembrance that she had spent joyful times here at some point in "her story." She actually felt like she was coming home. Whenever and with whomever it was, she had been happy here. This is all she knew and could feel.

It would take five months for her belongings to arrive back in the UK. She slept on the floor of one of the bedrooms and lived without a TV or radio. It was a profound time for her as she built a new garden in the derelict space behind the house. Walked the coastal path most days and meditated for hours on end, journaling all that was unfolding in her awareness. She had no books other than a paperback, *A Step Away from Paradise by Thomas K Shor,* and an online version of I AM THAT by Sri Nisgardatta Maharaj. They were the perfect company for her soul and spirit at this time. She communed with the elements daily, particularly the water, as she walked this land. She had always wanted to experience this specific coast, and indeed, it spoke back to her lovingly.

A few weeks after her move on 22 January 2022, the great and beautiful Thich Nat Hahn passed over, and as she meditated with the worldwide grieving community on this day, she felt an energetic explosion occur in her heart that brought in both the greatest joy and sadness and everything in between. It was such a memorable heart expansion as she experienced the vast compassion and love of this great and humble master teacher and felt sad for the world at the leaving of this beautiful being of light and love from this physical dimension. He was such a gentle master with an iron strength and formidable courage. His creation of the Buddhist Monastery at Plum Village near Bordeaux in France during his exile from his homeland, Vietnam, left such an impressive yet simple legacy for us all to learn from. Athena truly loved him with all her heart.

This precious time was akin to being on the mountain tops for her. She had nothing except a laptop, a few clothes, and the new garden project. A kindly neighbor loaned her a beach chair and table, and for months, she worked on this. At this time, she had no real interest in creating a home again. She had been through this process of moving and shifting articles around the globe many times now and it was getting to be arduous. The great expansions that had taken place in her consciousness had left her without worldly desire of any sort except for shelter and food of some sort, and she noticed how hard it was to be interested in getting back to the basics of life on the physical plane. It was quite disconcerting not to feel the desire of any kind for material things. All she wanted to do was immerse herself in the writings of Sri Nisgardatta Maharaj, and of course, she had the magnificent nature afforded by this stunning coastline of the British Isles. The only real desire she had was a deep longing to create and plant a garden.

Her neighbors were an elderly retired couple who gifted her enough rocks, left over from their own garden, to create a small rockery, which became the garden's focal point, and she collected more from her trips to the beach to supplement this stash. Before long, she had spent far too much money on beautiful pots and many exotic plants in order to create beauty where there had been a barren and empty view from her window. But it didn't matter to her because this is what she had done with every place she had ever lived. Whether she owned it or not, there was an impulse to create beauty that she would enjoy while there, and others would enjoy when she departed. This had been one pattern of hers she was happy to keep. Even when she stayed with her sister, she was always willing to tend the garden /allotment. It was in her genes. She knew she came from somewhere where she had loving correspondence with nature and all its beauty. It had been one of the greatest joys of her life and she remembered how that memory was first triggered at her Yorkshire cottage when she had time to breathe again after calamity and look into the beautiful columbine flowers outside her kitchen door. Such purity and innocence they conveyed to her heart.

She had not realized it then, but only on reflection she understood the move to Cornwall was in some measure about grounding and embodying the new higher frequencies of her field that were descending into this dimension. She was literally being forced to think of the mundane again. It was all an exercise to fully ground her, and what better way than to place her hands and feet into the soil and build again?

By the time her furniture actually arrived, she could put her mind to setting up another dwelling with as much comfort as she could muster. She was always good at adapting the few pieces she had left and was able to add to them tastefully to create a comfortable but modest place to live.

2022 became a time of nesting: the experience of a kind and caring landlord, getting to know the community, a further spiritual expansion, getting a grip on financial possibilities, receiving a very unexpected forty-year-old, financial windfall which after changing her name and traveling and living on different continents, could definitely be classed as a miracle. This actually paid for the recent double shipping of her goods across the Atlantic. There seemed to be a lot of sunny days and a long, hot summer.

She knew she had to address her financial situation as the money was going out at an alarmingly fast pace without any coming in. She had made investments whilst in Canada but had not really earned anything since 2017 with all the travel her guidance had led her to.

In April 2022, she was offered what she perceived as a gift of the opportunity to earn passive income from a group that appeared to be spiritually minded. It seemed all was well in her world, and solutions to her long-term financial setup were coming in.

By now, she had joined several other online communities that seemed awake and spiritually aware. Given what was playing out in the world, this seemed a good way to support those who were committed to creating the new, particularly the youth, and yet there was a sense of accelerated change in the air.

She had greatly enjoyed planting her seeds for her new garden, buying pots and plants, and generally creating a space of beauty where there had been none. Her sister came to stay for a couple of weeks in the summer and brought her cat, Jessie Pinkie, who, it must be said, settled down very well without any fuss.

They went to see Coldplay perform their Music of the Spheres concert at Wembley Stadium together on her birthday in August, and June came back to celebrate the Christmas break in Cornwall. Then the year was gone. It had flown by.

Connecting the Dots

2023 brought in an entirely different energy. The energy of the collective was oppressive as the results of various perceived hidden agendas and inept handling of the covidiocy became apparent and as more and more people were becoming aware of the challenges that currently face humanity. She had seen no improvement in anything the government were doing, and it was becoming increasingly clear the world was now heading for some kind of huge breakdown in structure. Like many, she had already felt this as early as 2012.

This was Athena's guidance at the beginning of the lunacy around Covid:

It is repeated here in the hope it can be used as an example of the fractal nature of the hologram in which we exist and how everything is a reflection of our collective consciousness ......whether there ever was a virus is really of no consequence. What we believe is true is what causes our reality to emerge within our physical bodies and externally as our experienced reality.

A virus is a packet of DNA or RNA genes that are looking for a cell to dominate. Viruses can only exert influence by invasion as they need a host cell to replicate; they cannot thrive outside a body. What is being reflected to us is a dominating parasite that cannot live on its own. For those of you familiar with deep psycho-energetic work you may be able to see this as a reflection of consciousness as we are being shown our collective shadow at a cellular level. Shadow is consciousness that we are unaware of that is projected outside the self. It cannot exist without us, the host, just like the virus.

It is a pre-condition already built into the DNA. The virus invades the cell boundary.

At its very core level, this is about victimhood and the consciousness of the cells, allowing themselves to be overcome without the adequate power to create the antibodies to prevent this. Dis-ease within the lungs and possibly death may be manifested as the physical outcome. Only if you believe it is so.

Can you see how this cellular picture simply reflects the larger picture of how the victim/perpetrator dynamic demonstrates all that does not work on our planet? Essentially, this is about the use of power. If we approach this as a war, sadly, this is the expression of our fear, and this exacerbates its proliferation and likely resurgence, despite any measures that are adopted, and why we think we will always require vaccines or something or someone outside ourselves to rescue us.

Our fear will create more and more undesirable darkness because we are either not aware of our own power to create it or are afraid of it. It is why we are afraid we will be attacked by aliens, demons, devils, and so on. Why we are afraid of Armageddon, and why we are afraid of climate change. Why we are afraid of starvation, poverty, and unfilled lives.

If we adopt the approach of moving out of fear and into holding Unconditional Love in our energy system, this creates a resonance that brings in coherence, harmony, and balance into the physical body and promotes the consciousness that is a higher frequency (power with) than that of domination (power over) and the body can return to homeostasis and health. We can transmute all distortions with the power of our unconditional love for ourselves, our Source, and each other. At this moment in our history, most do not live with this high level of consciousness continuously, and is why this is now being reflected to us in this most powerful way.

It is interesting that even just the thought of the presence of a virus actually opened the hearts of many, and the whole pandemic created havoc and chaos in many of the systems of the world that require revision from the way we govern ourselves through to our healthcare systems. Perhaps the experiment has backfired?

Even great darkness can be used to create much light when we know how to use its presence wisely. Just like Athena has.

You may also wish to consider where in your own life do you behave as a victim and where you might be a perpetrator. Where do you not take responsibility for your own creations and where do you always project blame out onto others?

Collectively, we hold this dynamic in place when we do not take responsibility for the outcomes in our lives or when we use control to dominate others.

Some of you may recognize this, and I have revised the words to more fully reflect the consciousness of the one unified field we create when we come together as One in love and service for and to one another, our planet, and all sentient life.

With this, we can create a very powerful energy field of Unconditional Love that can be used to transmute all dysfunctional energy and consciousness within our DNA, our physical bodies, and our multi-dimensional energetic anatomy.

This brings our energy systems into equilibrium, harmony, and balance through harmonic resonance so that any dominant energy joins the whole and is no longer a threat to healthy functioning.

This is a very different approach than "killing" it. And also a profound example of how we can bring peace, harmony and balance at the macro level and the micro level into our lives and into our world.

The Great Invocation Revised

The Great Invocation is an ancient prayer, now revised by Athena in recognition of the Unity Consciousness that joins us with the Source of all life. This revised invocation now recognizes there is no longer separation between humankind and its creator.

From the point of light in the One Mind
Let light stream forth to all life
Let Light descend upon Earth

From the point of Love in the One Heart
May the Consciousness of the One stream forth
And be ever-present on earth.

From the center where the One Will is known
Let purpose guide this will infallibly to
Fulfill the plan for Earth.

From the center of light of our One Unified Being

Let Love, and Light, and Power transmute and raise all low-frequency energy into harmonic resonance with the whole and bring peace to earth.

May Love and Light and Power restore the plan for Earth
Because I AM. Therefore, it is.

PART 7: THE NEW EARTH AND ITS

STRUCTURE

Group Work and Abundance

A thena had begun to align herself with groups who appeared to have an intention of bringing forth solutions to the problems rather than fuelling the problems. It has become apparent that the distortions on this planet have everything to do with poverty consciousness and victimhood and the corrupted power structures that create and hold these abominations in place. But still very few are capable of committing to the deep dive inwards required to bring external change.

She had maintained a connection with the group in Mexico, and her contacts in one of the financial groups she had joined seemed ready and willing to start some inner work. She enjoyed contributing to all their different schemes and to their plans for building a new future for themselves and Planet Earth. She created an online social group called Visionary Leaders Rising and contributed whatever came through her to share. Essentially, she was slowly becoming active again in the community after the required hiatus in order to settle back in the UK. But in a new way. Her perception of time was changing as she really only marked it by whenever she had a group to run, a meditation to offer, or an article to write. Otherwise, it did not exist for her. It passed in a blink.

She also knew that in order to change external realities and shift timelines, the inner work must be done, and yet convincing the masses of this has proved somewhat challenging for her. Plus, the fact that many who have specifically come to do the work of helping this planet heal and expand have often themselves become part of the problems rather than the solution. She knew she was amongst those souls who were here to aid the great shift in consciousness for the planet and humanity, and she was not bothered by the fact that, over the years, very few people had paid her for her service.

She held the knowing that her income to live could come through prudent investment in the new conscious businesses of the future which meant she could offer her services freely and without any prejudice to those who needed them the most. It seemed like a sensible comprehension of what she had hoped would be of service to those who sought her help.

She had never in her life not been abundant. One can see from her story that money was never an issue, as the universe provided an abundance of infusions every step of the way to support her journey. But now, there seemed to be a different dynamic in play as she explored ways to create abundance that were not directly attached to her work.

She was very disturbed by a session she had done with one of the group leaders of a passive income investment proposition she had become involved with and the information that had come in around this session. It turned out that the group itself was deluded and in great distortion headed up by Masonic interests and dark, polarised, distorted energy. It had seemed like the answer to all her prayers and yet she would be feeding her energy into the very structures that oppose freedom and sovereignty. This is, of course, the way the dark forces work under a mask of doing good while harvesting member's energy (money). She was shown this very clearly when she worked with one of the group directors who had sought out her expertise in these matters.

Athena had learned much about the intricate workings of the levels of Masonic activity that are in distortion and knew she carried the coding to overcome these gross distortions. They can never overcome the light of the true Christ within that has nothing to do with religion or any other man-made institution and everything to do with the wisdom of the I AM Presence. The Christ/Unity Consciousness within.

She publicly renounced this group and formally detached her own energy field from all contracts, vows, and curses associated with this dark setup peddling pseudo-Christianity at all its leadership levels. This is how energy can be siphoned into supporting low-frequency and negative projects through financial contribution. Your money is merely energy. Be careful where you spend it!!!! Her own guidance had warned against sharing this opportunity until she had seen proof of all the great claims made, and once again, she would see how her guidance protected her from negative karmic implications while providing a lesson and its accompanying wisdom. She had lost the money but not her soul. Here is what came through for Athena 's contemplation around this whole debacle:

Humanity is in the process of a major shift in consciousness, moving away from victimhood and compliance with hierarchical structures and into sovereignty and freedom. This is a choice each is responsible for making. Any structure that is not in alignment with this shift of frequency will not be sustainable and will eventually collapse.

Multi-level marketing schemes of any kind are dependent on ongoing subscriptions from those at the bottom of the pyramid to those at the top; otherwise, the whole thing comes to a standstill.

Whether or not they are set up in good faith, they still favor those at the top and, of course, like any other venture, are open to corruption. This could also be considered as the mirror of the current financial structure of the planet, which is basically a huge Ponzi scheme run by the central banks. This is not a structure that is in alignment with any 'new earth' frequency. Wake up!!!!

The entire financial system of the planet is in chaos and volatility as the old breaks down and the new is finding its way. Where money is concerned, the lack of consciousness and understanding of how this universe truly works with regards to abundance creation leaves many open to continue to be the victims of those who can use these forces for good as well as for corrupt purposes.

One does not help another to become sovereign when they are 'dependent' on a hierarchical structure in any way. Of course, each is responsible for their own choice. However, when you choose to lead any group in this kind of framework, you take on a responsibility and karma that cannot be discounted.

Here is how to disconnect yourself from any business or financial concern that you may intuit is not in alignment with the highest frequency.

"Invoke the I Am Presence. Of my own free will and as a sovereign being of light, I now dissolve and disintegrate any contract of permission that I have given any being associated with this venture or this group to be attached to my energy field.

I release all such beings, entities, attachments, and inclusions from all dimensions of my energy field and my body now.

I release these now with love and peace and burn all contracts I ever made associated with them through divine grace and my own free will, so be it."

This is published in the hope it will serve any who are embroiled in this kind of mess.

A New Leadership Model

It is in our DNA to work in unison, harmony, and love allowing ourselves to trust and surrender to the creative, evolutionary process of life.

The current organizing principles of life are in hierarchy; this is an inescapable fact. Our evolution as a species is the passage from Hierarchy to Synarchy.

Definitions:

HIERARCHY

Is a system in which members of an organization or society are ranked according to their relative status or authority.

HETERARCHY

Is a system of organization where the elements of the organization are unranked (non-hierarchical) or where they possess the potential to be ranked in a number of different ways. Authority is distributed.

Heterarchies are networks of elements in which each element shares the same "horizontal" position of power and authority, each playing an equal role.

SYNARCHY

Is a system where there is joint governance, harmonious rule, and collective leadership. No ranking.

Ultimately, the difference between hierarchy and synarchy is about the level of awareness.

Hierarchy has produced competition and control and is based on a fear of anarchy. It is really about relationships and group dynamics. Its distorted versions are typically first experienced in a family situation where individuals either accept the rules and are either overwhelmed, submissive, and repressed or find a way to manipulate the rules and externalize the fear by being reactive through anger and control. Either way, the overall frequency of fear generally generates resentment that leads to discordance in families and organizations to fail.

When we can embrace these shadows of distorted perceptions that create fear, then over time, we begin to draw in our fractal family and begin to self-organize. These group dynamics become more heterarchical and are based on our higher life purpose rather than control, manipulation, and fear. Organization is based on creativity and service in an expansive heterarchy where the individual elements within the system are given their freedom. In a heterarchical system, control is distributed organically- horizontally rather than vertically.

Individual uniqueness becomes service to the whole.

Heterarchical processes can carry more information than a hierarchical design, as the scientific breakthroughs in how the brain and Artificial Intelligence work now demonstrate.

Control is placed in the hands of the creative evolutionary impulse itself, and life starts to self-organise using the inherent divine intelligence inbuilt into the creative process of life. It allows life to rise to its genius level by downloading truth from the quantum holographic field.

But first, this must be unlocked in individuals who are still coded in the old hierarchical ways. This means transmuting anything that prevents the self from knowing itself as One with all life. There is a need for total Surrender and Deep Trust to find the true human fractal where there is more support for the higher purpose. We were never intended to operate in isolation.

Individual uniqueness becomes service to the whole.

Synarchy means collective leadership. We all lead together. This does not mean we are all the same. It means our uniqueness has its own place in the orchestra, and we begin to play in harmony with everyone else. We become aware of the conductor of life from every molecule of DNA waiting for us to follow its lead.

At this level, there is non-interference. We see everything as it is and leave it where it is. We know all life as self-organizing. The shadow eventually organizes its own breakthrough. Our underlying nature is synarchy. This involves hierarchy, heterarchy, and synarchy. It transcends and includes all previous levels and steps. It is the realization of the perfection in all beings and circumstances.

Synarchy is specific to these times and is a group of beings who have incarnated to catalyze the next phase of human evolution. It is a collective genetic instrument where communal awareness will breakthrough through humanity. It is a living spirit waiting to be awakened within each human being. A synarchy is where it will be first experienced, demonstrated, and manifested. Remember, everything in manifested reality at whatever level is a projection of consciousness.

As above, so below; equally as below, so above. Everything shifts when we do.

When we realize the truth of our own synarchy, we will create the world in our own likeness.

Reference Richard Rudd the Gene Keys. 44 Gene Key Synarchy.

St Agnes Head, Cornwall

The failed investment had alerted Athena to the fact that deep within her was something connected to money that required her attention. She knew it would come into her awareness when the time was right.

During 2023, she was working with three separate groups of young people who were all exploring ways to create abundance outside the regular system, and she truly wanted to support them. All involved had much inner work to accomplish, and in this, she was an expert. As visionary pioneers for the new ways of living and being on this earth, it must be expected there will be much for us all to learn together, including Athena, and so late 2023, at the time of the Winter Solstice, she took herself into a Vision Quest for what she wished to create.

This took her into another deep dive to explore anything that might be holding her back from her highest form of creative expression. This took one month of dedicated meditation and inner exploration around any of the issues her numerous past (simultaneous) incarnations could be responsible for. She had asked for illumination of specific lives that had not yet been fully resolved and integrated.

And bingo, as soon as the quest was completed, she was guided to enter a competition for a house in St Agnes Head, Cornwall, that was being run by a large national charity. She was attracted to the property, and the charity that would benefit was the WWF or Worldwide Fund for Nature so it was a win-win either way for her.

The week she placed her contribution, she drove to St Agnes Head in Cornwall, just nine miles from where she lived currently to see if she could find the house. She could not find the property. However, St Agnes Head is an area of outstanding natural beauty on the western Cornwall coast, and so she took a long walk in the glorious sunshine that was gracing the day of her visit. The sky was the bluest blue and cloudless except for one cloud that hovered above the Head, a rock formation at St Agnes. It was surreal. The cloud actually looked like the shape of an angel. As she looked at the cloud, her vision began, and she was taken back to the past as a young girl in Rome. Athena was thrown into a time capsule, and the remembrance of having her throat cut had begun at school in 2008 when she had started doing a lot of deep astral work. However, the entire story had not fully emerged at that point. All she knew was it had caused fear issues around speaking her truth and speaking out, particularly in public. The throat is the location of the 5th Chakra and is about expression and the Higher Will of the creator. She remembered clearly how desperately frightened she was of public speaking when she was younger and why she volunteered at both her school graduations to deliver the graduation acknowledgment on behalf of her class to help her heal this fear. She certainly now held no fear of speaking her truth to anyone. However, the incident brings attention to the suffering and martyrdom that is revered by the institution of the Roman Catholic Church and rewarded with sainthood. This is the wrong message. Suffering and martyrdom are not required and never were. This is an important message for humanity in these current times.

Simultaneously, she was recalling another vision she received in 2005 of being an abbess of some kind of institution where her yoga teacher had been the chaplain. She had picked this up by being with him. In a later vision, while living in Toronto, when she had moved into a new apartment on St Clare Ave East, she had been shown her membership of the Franciscan Order of the Poor Clares. While standing on the Cornish land of St Agnes Head, she was being shown both visions again, and both were resonating deeply in her physical body as she was being guided to research St Agnes without delay. She drove back home with some alacrity in order to check this out on the internet. She found two St Agnes.

Agnes of Rome

Agnes was a member of the Roman nobility, born in AD 291 and raised in an early Christian family. She suffered martyrdom at the age of twelve during the reign of the Roman Emperor Diocletian on 21 January 304.

She was an attractive young girl from a wealthy family. She was also a devoted follower of Christ and noted for her resolute embodiment of purity. She had many suitors that she turned away, and the young men who were slighted by her devotion to her faith submitted her name to the pagan authorities as a follower of Christianity.

The Prefect Sempronius condemned Agnes to be dragged naked through the streets to a brothel. In one account, as she prayed, it is said her hair grew and covered her body. It was also said that all of the men who attempted to rape her were immediately struck blind. The son of the prefect was struck dead but revived after she prayed for him, causing her release.

There commenced a trial from which Sempronius recused himself, allowing another figure to preside and sentence St. Agnes to death. She was led out and bound to a stake, but the bundle of wood would not burn, or the flames parted away from her, whereupon the officer in charge of the troops drew his sword and beheaded her or, in some other texts, stabbed her in the throat.

Agnes of Rome is, among other patronages, a patron saint of young girls, virgins, victims of sex abuse, and gardeners. The irony is not lost on Athena, who in this incarnation has suffered sexual abuse and is a keen gardener.

Agnes of Bohemia

Born in the year 1211; Princess Agnes was predestined by birth to live a life of luxury at one of Europe's royal courts. Yet, instead, she dedicated her life to service and sacrifice.

Historian Vít Vlnas from the Czech National Gallery wrote:

"Agnes was a princess born into the royal family. Her father was King Přemysl Otakar I., one of the most important monarchs in Czech history, a man who was behind the rise of the Czech state. And therefore, Agnes was a much sought-after bride. She decided not to follow this secular path and joined the religious order of The Poor Clares. She herself later established the religious order of Knights of the Cross with the Red Star, the only religious order to originate in Bohemia which exists to this day. As a member of the order of Poor Clares, she founded a convent in Prague and became its first mother superior."

She devoted her attention to charity and care for the sick and poor, working in two hospitals in Prague.

"For centuries, she has been perceived as a moving character because she did not see the meaning of her life in earthly goods, political power, and material wealth but rather in the spiritual sphere. She sacrificed herself for the sake of others and tried to improve the world in a different way than rich people and politicians usually do."

The convent Agnes founded was the first convent of the Order of Poor Clares north of the Alps and, at that time, also one of the most modern buildings in Prague.

"Agnes founded the convent and hospital in the 1230s. Apart from the Poor Ladies convent there was also a monastery of the Friars Minor on the premises, whose cloister still exists.

After a life of service, poverty, and illness, Agnes died at the age of 71 in 1282. She was buried in the convent church, but her remains were moved in the 14th century, allegedly to be saved from floods and later Hussite attacks. All attempts to find her remains over the centuries have failed. The most recent investigation in the nearby church of St. Castulus in early 2010 brought no results.

Despite the longstanding efforts of her compatriots, Agnes of Bohemia was not beatified until almost six hundred years after her death. She was finally canonized by Pope John Paul II on November 12th, 1989, just five days before the events of November 17th triggered the Velvet Revolution, leading to the fall of the communist regime in Czechoslovakia; for some people, that was a confirmation of an old legend.

The act of founding a convent and a hospital was unique in that it introduced the ideals of the newly established Franciscan movement in this country along with its cardinal idea of respect and love for every human being, especially for the poor and suffering. Princess Agnes set up the first charity service in this country which eventually led to the establishment of the only originally Bohemian religious order of the Knights of the Cross with the Red Star. And so, more than seven centuries after her death, the legacy of St Agnes of Bohemia still lives on.

Why Now?

So here it was, the imprinting that had not come to full light until this part of her life for two reasons: she knew she was in the process of consciously creating the new and had asked if there was anything that would prevent the highest outcome. She needed to be in Cornwall at St Agnes Head to trigger the process of bringing in the intelligence and information of what required transmuting. She was being asked to fully clear these imprints now because the horrors of child abuse and death and the vows of poverty, obedience, enclosure, and renunciation of all earthly goods were still in operation in her field and had actually resulted in canonization by the Roman Catholic Church, an institution that has long been corrupt and rewarded these two versions of herself with sainthood for obedience to their perverted version of the requirements for this as outlined in the history of the Church. Do you see how these histories and teachings are perverse? One version of Agnes was a child martyr, and the other died from illness and poverty, and both were then beatified by the Church. Both versions are no longer congruent with the being Athena, and therefore, this consciousness had to be brought to her awareness and transcended.

Jesus /Yeshua, Buddha, Krishna, Mohammed, and Zoroaster all came to free us, not enslave us to a dogma. They came to show us the way, not to be our saviors but to show us how to save ourselves. The elements of a new earth do not include poverty, obedience to a hierarchy, enclosure, renunciation, or abusing children. By reviewing these two shocking time capsules, she was being shown once again the time of suffering is over and this will not be part of any new conscious collective creation. The transmutation of this energy ensures this will not be part of the new timeline and was purposely held in her field until this very chaotic time on Earth when the planetary systems are breaking down, and many people are still living in poverty consciousness. It is really the underlying imprints of unworthiness, compliance with victimhood, shame, and guilt hidden by these two old archetypal constructs in these specific neural memory banks that required her attention and full transmutation.

As a collective, we are facing numerous challenges, such as poor access to healthcare, education and safety, sex trafficking, child abuse, wars and military conflict, water contamination, human rights violations, mass media manipulation and corruption, global health issues, global poverty, a corrupt global financial system, hunger and food access, migration, accessibility of weapons, climate change, planetary degradation ....

We may wish to consider deeply the state of the collective human psyche when we realize everything we perceive as external is a projection of our own collective consciousness and a result of our own actions or our own compliance.

Athena had personally experienced the great power of group energy to effect rapid transformation through witnessing her own personal process and the work she has done with groups over the years. Through this deep inner work and the monitoring of all she was able to co-create, she came to realize that her darkest challenges were, in fact, the source of all her greatest gifts and, through this realization, learned how to truly love herself and others unconditionally, have deep, deep compassion; forgive fully without hesitation; move through fear bravely and courageously; developing a deep trust in the guidance and benevolence of the inspiration that runs through her fingers when she writes; through her voice when she speaks; and through her body and field as photons of light as she stands in space. This is shared now to inspire and provide a model for others. The heavy lifting has already been done by her and others like her who came to specifically to shift these gross ancestral patterns and archetypal energies.

She holds deep gratitude and appreciation to those "beings," namely aspects of herself from the higher realms, that had supported, held, and led her with such grace and love. And above all, the trust and commitment that allowed her to connect with these parts of herself. Her own descent into darkness had been an opportunity to truly choose time after time, the light over the dark. To choose freedom, sovereignty, and full self -responsibility. It had afforded her opportunities to overcome self-hatred, shame, self-judgment, jealousy, envy, fear of being alone, of not fitting in, of being different, fear of failure, of not being good enough, or being too big, and even worse the deeply hidden fear that she may be really evil somewhere in the depths of her being to have experienced those awful situations so early in life. And finally, to realize none of it was real, merely information that had been distorted by the senses down the ages and recycled over and over again to prevent the knowing of her true Self and final liberation.

Her ability to see across all timelines afforded her the understanding of what karma truly is…. a bunch of memories that simply recycle and recycle endlessly until that cycle is broken. Breaking the cycle involves first recognizing the cycle, understanding the patterns, and then transmuting their energy with

Love, Forgiveness, and Compassion. Through this process Wisdom is developed and fed back to the whole of creation for furtherance of humanity's evolutionary progress.

And then, at the even deeper spiritual level, further testing came when she realized the personalized God she had been brought up with did not exist; the God she had prayed to and found comfort in her darkest moments actually did not exist in the way that she had thought, but was, in fact, a much vaster experience than she could ever truly comprehend. She had felt alone again for a time and missed the 'comfort' of a personalized God who had represented for her the father she had lost. Even far along her path, there was a tendency to reach outside herself to those who it seemed had gone before her and now guided her so brilliantly, patiently, and lovingly: Yeshua, Mother Mary, St Germain, Quan Yin; Huang Po; Dr David Hawkins; Sri Nisgardatta Maharaj; Thich Nat Hahn and the many others who had contributed to her final knowing that she was indeed the all of it. All of them existed within her own Beingness, and this was the one aspect that was the most required to truly fully embody to bring change to a world of suffering. This Beingness. The Balance of Beingness. The Allowance of Beingness, The Acceptance of Beingness, the Discernment of Beingness, The Non -Judgement of Beingness. The Full Surrender to Beingness. The Trust of Beingness. The Humility of Beingness. The Unconditional Love of Beingness. In essence, the full return of the Divine Feminine Principle to create, in conjunction with an undistorted Divine Male Principle one unified field of consciousness.

A disconcerting effect of all her inner work was the absence of all desire and fear. It had all disappeared. She was not sorry to wave fear goodbye, but desire fuels creation, and for a time, she could find a desire for no-thing. It was a bewildering and unnerving state until she realized she could create anything and yet not be attached to the creation. Her passion was group energy and its efficacy in the transformational process, so it made sense to put it to use in some way that could help humanity build the new in a new way. Like the gardener she is, she could sow seeds, and even if they were not received in her physical lifetime, she had no agenda; she had no need for recognition.

There was no more leading or teaching or preaching or trying to rescue or save others from themselves, but to simply give them a model of how to Be. To fully live her truth rather than preach it. To share herself rather than teach it. To move away from trying to fix the outer world when she knew beyond all doubt suffering and pain is all within.

How else could she demonstrate this to you, dear reader?

As she moved through life, It had become clearer and clearer to her that many still do not understand the true nature of reality and the truth about energy and consciousness and are still trying to 'fix' the external picture rather than dealing with the true source of all their own and earth's problems.

She had seen the great power of the group in all her own personal process work during her many years of practice, which led her to develop ways to help others accelerate their own inner /external transformation. She has witnessed over the years how the transformation process is even further accelerated by using the great transformative power of the cosmic energies now available to all due to the earth's current position in the time and space of this universal hologram.

It had only recently dawned on Athena that her own journey is that of the earth itself. And has been one of overcoming abuse, becoming truly abundant in a holistic way that encompasses all aspects of life, not only the material; challenging a corrupted, patriarchal hierarchy of power, and developing a more balanced, energetic approach to existence inspired by the deep feminine principles of Being that encompasses trust, courage, surrender, allowance, non-judgment, love, compassion, nurturance, acceptance and includes full responsibility for self and all her creations as the approach to her life experience. She has actually lived and experienced these solutions. They became part of her Beingness.

"I am not the body

I am not the mind

I am responsible for everything

My ability to respond is limitless

I am mother to the world

This moment is the only moment there is."

Commentary

Athena is now seventy-two years in this incarnation. Her soul contract has been one of the most severe soul contracts in the life experience. Her main purpose was and is global empowerment through alchemy, otherwise known as transmutation, transcendence, and transfiguration. It has involved work with the deepest and darkest parts of the multi-dimensions of matter. As you can see from the life story, it has meant incarnating into severely traumatized lineages with high levels of persecution and intense levels of injustice.

Her energy field became ultra-magnetic in order to draw to itself the darkest layers of reality and transmute them, and it is one of the few fields that can hold space for this level of darkness. This ability magnetized experiences that have involved cruelty, projections from others, dark inner forces, and unconscious patterns that are all triggered by the light. She does not justify or excuse darkness but has the ability to connect with it in order to offer an opportunity for it to transmute, integrate, and then reconfigure the human template through harmonic resonance, as her energy template holds the Divine Human Angelic Blueprint. This does not mean she takes on another's karma but has the ability to awaken whatever is not in alignment or integrity within the energy field and psyche and bring to the surface the unconscious wounds of those with whom she comes into contact. This ability can, therefore, be experienced as antagonistic to the matrix and those who are heavily programmed and, therefore, must be tempered with patience and great love. Her presence can cause a level of denial of the individual and collective shadow as it gets triggered. She does not have to do anything but simply emanate what is within her to the environment and the established status quo of the third dimension. However, her ability to transmute and the ways in which this has been accomplished has often times not been known to the recipient or often even to herself. Some would still consider her unholy, dark, and demonic, even by spiritual gurus and teachers who do not have this ability, and even now, she can be condemned as a witch or malevolent Lilith because she sees through the absurdities and untruths of the new age movements and their unconscious egoic wounds not yet healed. This is her job! It happens effortlessly and brings up fear of exposure.

She is able to transmute the darkness in the majority of humans, but this gift is often feared because the human realizes this means great life change, and most do not wish for their lives to be uprooted until they have received a 'cosmic slap' or unless they are desperate. Therefore, she moves in this world, often unseen, misunderstood, or ignored. The memory of persecution in ancient times has run deep within her template and why there has been such a commitment on her part to integrate all her shadow so that it does not close her down or deactivate her gift of vision. She is here not only to transmute ancestral lineages but also the archetypes of the collective psyche. Her lifelong relationship with the field of Christ/Unity Consciousness enables her to help raise the frequency of the earth through intrinsic wisdom and knowing and to restore the balance to the awareness of Christ Consciousness by healing and empowering the distorted masculine and feminine energy in the collective. This means empowerment of all genders has nothing to do with sex and everything to do with energy (electro male), and consciousness (magnetism female). Neither does this mean we move back into a matriarchy. There are many on planet Earth now who have Self-Realized from all gender categories.

Her journey has been nothing less than the one the collective and the planet itself must also take in order to end its suffering and pain.

And it has been a wild, wild ride of travel, adventure, trust and willingness to dive deep into the unknown. No one could say she has not lived life to its fullness and will continue to do so, for there is so much more to create.

Now is the time for the full return of the Divine Feminine Principle to planet Earth in order for her to ascend and stabilize into the next vibrational frequency. We are living in unprecedented times, and as the light rises, so will the dark to counteract it. You have witnessed how this occurs frequently on Athena's journey. Each time she raises her frequency, she is challenged in another, even more insidious way. Time after time, it is a matter of choice; however, there are no real mistakes, only new ways to develop mastery and expand into even more wisdom.

Vigilance is required, but not fear. Self- responsibility is required but not self-judgement. As for the perceived 'enemy at the door,' one can only witness its choice for its own demise and wave goodbye as it dissolves into light.

Finally, Home

66When I discard all I AM not, I go even deeper in until no-thing is left. Only then I begin to be my true Self, for liberation is not *of* the person but *from* the person. I AM simply a point of awareness existent within time and space and also beyond both.

I do not judge, do not separate, do not compare, do not compete. If I slip into the negative, I rise and rise again like the Phoenix and simply Love whatever and whomever comes my way.

Every existence, consciousness, joy, sorrow, world, universe, multiverse is my own. I AM the all of it. As well as beyond it all. I AM the Supreme Reality.

I go through life without resistance; I move in allowance, just watching new possibilities arriving on the next wave, for they always do.

I AM detached, with no expectations, I face my tasks with thoroughness and care, with goodwill. I give without asking and allow whatever is my destiny to fulfill itself without pushing or goal setting. I trust Life wholeheartedly to deliver me to the shore.

I AM not gripped by fear or desires, and I know the Self as the source of all Reality and this is beyond form and beyond consciousness.

It is the nature of creative imagination to identify itself with its creations, and I can switch this off at any moment by simply drawing my attention away from it.

I do not move from place to place but allow the dream to just flow in front of me like a movie, and I observe it." Sri Nisgardatta Maharaj – I AM THAT

To find home, she did not need to take a single step for home was always there within her. It is here, everywhere, all at once. However, if she had never taken a step, she would have missed a most phenomenal life.

This book has been written as a testament to Life. A testament to what is real and what is false. It has been written in such detail to clearly demonstrate to the reader how erroneous and low-frequency thoughtforms embed into our memory, recycle over and over, eon after eon passed down through the generations, and built out from the DNA. Those thought forms cause pain and suffering and create monsters, devils, demons, aliens, abductions, earth wars, galactic wars, and whole races of parasitic beings that cannot sustain without our energy and require our energy to feed from in order to exist. There is no them and us. It is all us. We have created it all. It is all part of the One. All manifested form is either our memory or imagination held in a holographic field emerging from the Quantum Field. This is how the creator experiences all of itself, from archangels to devils, through us, the human Being. We now have the opportunity to populate the multiverse with our brilliance and Divinity. The human race is, right now, in the process of transformation, transcendence, and transfiguration as we become the Divine Angelic Human. All is resolved with Love, Forgiveness, and Compassion. This is the way, the truth, and the life.

Without the presence of darkness, one cannot know or even experience the light, for this Universe is constructed in such a way as to bring us ample opportunity to use our free will choice for both. It is showing us clearly how the Universe reveals itself through Unconditional Love, Will, and Intelligence.

Perhaps you will notice in this story that running throughout the narrative, there has been an ongoing thread of guidance and support that has never left this storyteller without recourse, even when sometimes she was unaware of its presence.

Her story has been written to demonstrate the Eternal and Infinite Love in which all is held so the reader may observe truth and redemption in action and how this Universe truly works for the benefit of all, in all ways, and that even the dark ultimately serves the Light. It is showing us clearly how the Supreme Reality reveals itself through Wisdom, Love, and Light.

And, so it is.

We live in exciting, if chaotic, times, and there is so much more for us to BE and DO but the key is to remember we are making it all up in order to evolve! It is all just a story, and none of it is the true Supreme Reality. It is my privilege and honor to walk alongside you, and I bow to the Divine within you.

ATHENA MELCHIZEDEK SANANDA

Epilogue

Now the reader can bear witness to the truth that Athena's life has been an adventure of Self- discovery with many different rhythms and scenarios that knit together in one grand design. Once she had learned about the power of her intention, her only intention was to reach the highest potential possible, in human form, this incarnation with no other specific goal or direction in her mind. She simply surrendered her life over and over again to the higher power running her show. From the beginning she was committed to living every moment to its fullest capacity, even if it meant descending into the depths of darkness, and her part was to make the decisions and take action, usually just one step at a time. These were only made when clarity arrived, without emotion and with a full body knowing and full presence, but most often, not with any understanding of her human mind, particularly in those early years.

So far, her outer life has been about working with group dynamics, family, business, and teams. Embedded within her coding is an instinctive understanding of the mechanics of hierarchies and relationships and the concept of synarchy, which is a gift that draws her into the right place at the right time. It matters not to her whether she is considered a leader; what matters most is to work with others so her skills can be useful and she and they can flourish.

There is absolute honesty and integrity in all her dealings. She perceives with clarity. Through her intuition, she is always able to discover the light that is inherent as potential in all darkness, having had deep personal experiences of the wounds shared by all humanity. She uses this to draw out this great potential in those who are attracted to her. She can very quickly comprehend another's weaknesses, but by concentrating on their strengths, she empowers both the individual and the group as a whole.

Her only requirement is to be with people whom she feels are ready and willing to jump off the cliff into the arms of Love. Her ability to bring harmony to any group she is associated with, whether it is family, friends, a business, or a whole planet, means she loves to work with others so they can find a unified bond, and this may be in an official capacity, but most often than not is hidden. Through her Being and Doing, she is taking her world into a new future where all humankind will one day recognize its inherent oneness, and this vital aspect of vision and integration is deeply embedded within her form.

Her ability to be open and honest about her intentions means people find they can immediately trust her and she can pull any group together. She has a natural understanding of relational dynamics, and by offering others her gift of trustworthiness, remarkable things can and do happen around her.

Her readiness to dive deep into the emotional realms, without any reservation, has supported the transcendence of the emotional nature through her willingness to engage in many different types of human relationships. She has challenged everything her human mind ever held sacred, even God. It was necessary for her to pass through this entire human experience once more in order to lower then raise her frequency once again at this pivotal moment of the transition of the earth and humankind into its next evolution.

Her challenge in her later years has been to balance the deep understanding of others with her own preference for space and silence. Her insights can frequently be startling and can be ignored or smothered by a group agenda, not in alignment with the highest truths. Therefore, she has to ensure she doesn't get pulled into other people's dramas.

She has noticed the speed with which the earth structures are changing and what can be considered acceptable today can rapidly change into a much broader perspective tomorrow. She knows physical life is built on shifting sand, and this she accepts, remaining open to this mutability, and welcoming in the next adventure with open arms.

She knows she is here to express her own unique essence, and by doing so, she naturally attracts others who are ready to fly. What results is a natural radiance that emerges from wisdom and a sense of hidden depths, punctuated by a lightness of being that takes none of it too seriously and allows for a sense of humor and true laughter concerning the whole human condition. By moving away from self-judgment and having no expectations, she is able to emanate a sense of real inner security and a deep sense of fulfillment that attracts others. Retreat and rest are essential for her, as well as time spent alone.

By now she has given up caring what her purpose is because she knows it is all about empowerment of self and others. She knows she and all others have an astounding power deep within that emerges without thinking or even knowing.

She has no agenda for saving the world but simply works in the direction of her passion in each moment. Empowerment of another may simply be an outcome, and it feels very, very good. This is the source of her deepest power, so she just does what she loves to do and be in life. Everything else follows from there.

Her life is an archetype of the transformation taking place at a global level. She is here now to focus on key practical issues and, therefore, realizes her own needs are already met in order to assist those who are not so fortunate. Her prosperity is unlocked by her visionary and intuitive capacities and through the gift of her own transformation and transcendence. For many, she is like a mountain standing firm in trust, just like Mother Earth.

Her true purpose is always here and now in whatever she is feeling and whatever she is doing. This is what it is to live in the present moment. Sometimes, her purpose is simply a feeling and being that. Other times, she will feel the surge of the creative potential inherent in each moment of life, and this is expressed through her own creative endeavors.

Her life belongs to the earth, the music of nature, the stars, the tides, the winds of change, and the space from which she emerges momentarily. She is an artist, and life is her easel. She is a poet, and her life is her poem. She is merely a form that life plays through without her judging or controlling the music, and she loves it wholeheartedly and breathes it in every waking moment. Her highest heart expression is liberation, devotion, and communion.

She is You. She is Love. She is Grace. She is Life and she invites you to fall in Love with yourself and with all that is.

A Final Prayer

At this time of great change on Earth as the global power structures on our planet are in the process of dissolving and transforming ....

MAY ALL BE BLESSED WITH GRACE

May the Light that is the Intelligence of Source
pour forth into the mind of all Humanity
May the ground of all BEING that is the Love of Source
stream through the heart of all Humanity
May the emanation of the Will of Source be chosen freely as
Humanity bows and surrenders to its precision
As Triune, may these glorious energies open the doors of all
ignorance and transmute, transform and transfigure all lower
frequency energies not aligned with Unconditional Love and
render them balanced, harmonized and unified as an
expression of Source upon this planet and within the
universe.

With All Gratitude and Appreciation
It is done.

Athena Melchizedek Sananda

References

Page 74" **"No More 'I Love You's"** is a song written by British musicians David Freeman and Joseph Hughes and recorded by them as the Lover Speaks. It was released in June 1986 as the lead single from their self-titled debut album. The song was covered by the Scottish singer Annie Lennox and became a commercial success for her in 1995, reaching number two on the UK Singles Chart.

Page 86. **Hands of Light: A Guide to Healing Through the Human Energy Field Paperback – May 1, 1988**

by Barbara Brennan (Author), Jos. A. Smith (Illustrator)

Light Emerging: The Journey of Personal Healing Paperback – November 1, 1993

by Barbara Ann Brennan (Author)

Page 114 from **The Poem Love after Love by Derek Walcott 13 January 2003**

Page 159 **Hands of Light: A Guide to Healing Through the Human Energy Field Paperback – May 1, 1988**

by Barbara Brennan (Author), Jos. A. Smith (Illustrator)

PAGE 165 **The Quantum Keys: Unlock Your Energetic Intelligence Paperback**

by Athena Melchizedek | 29 Jun 2017

Page 183 *https://www.ayahuascafoundation.org/shipibo-tradition/*

Page 209 **Voyagers; The Sleeping Abductees; Volume 1 of the Emerald Covenant CTD plate translations- Ashayana Deane**

Publication date: 01/05 2001 UFO, ET <u>opensource</u>

Voyagers. Volume II of the Emerald Covenant CDT plate translations: The Secrets Of Amenti Ashayana Deane

Publication date: 01/05 2001 UFO, ET <u>opensource</u>

<u>https://ascensionglossary.com/index.php/Universal_Melchizedek_Lineages#Spiritual_Betrayal_of_Blue_Flame_Melchizedeks</u>

Lisa Renee, Ascension Glossary.

Page 212 **Lisa Renee, Ascension Glossary**

https://ascensionglossary.com/index.php/Planetary_Stargate_System

Page 222 *"THE EYE OF THE I" Dr David Hawkins M.D. PhD 1927-2012*

Page 226 **Muscle Testing. Dr David Hawkins M.D. PhD** <u>https://veritaspub.com</u>

Page 228 **Power vs. Force Paperback – by Dr** <u>David R. Hawkins M.D. Ph.D</u> **January 30, 2014**

Page 281 PKOLS, The Hill of Cedars

https://www.saanich.ca/EN/main/parks-recreation-community/parks/parks-trails-amenities/signature-parks/mount-douglas-park.html

Page 290 The Residential Schools of Canada

The Guardian

https://www.theguardian.com/world/ng-interactive/2021/sep/06/canada-residential-schools-indigenous-children-cultural-genocide-

Page 297 The Trail of Tears

https://www.nps.gov/articles/trailoftears.htm#:~:text=Guided%20by%20policies%20favored%20by,Southeast%20in%20the%20early%201800s.

Page 324 **Gene Keys: Embracing Your Higher Purpose (New Edition) Paperback – Illustrated, 15 May 2015**

by Richard Rudd (Author)

Page 328 Agnes of Rome

https://en.wikipedia.org/wiki/Agnes_of_Rome

Page 330 Agnes of Bohemia.

https://en.wikipedia.org/wiki/Agnes_of_Bohemia

Page 342 I AM THAT Sri Nisgardatta Maharaj (originally published in 1973)

Republished 5 Dec 1999 Chetana Private Ltd